1:500

3°

4/2/01 - 28/2/01

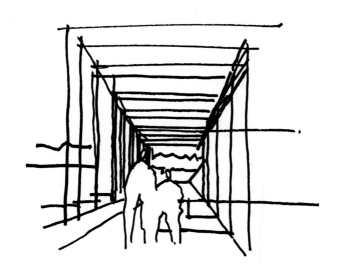

ECO STRUCTURES

WHITE STAR PUBLISHERS

ECO STRUCTURES

FORMS OF SUSTAINABLE ARCHITECTURE

edited by
gianpaola spirito

introduction
antonino terranova

text
sabrina leone
gianpaola spirito
leone spita

editorial project
valeria manferto de fabianis

editorial staff
federica romagnoli

graphic design
maria cucchi

---

1 *Sketch by Sean Godsell Architects for the Woodleigh School Science Building.*

2-3 *Madrid Barajas Airport by Rogers Stirk Harbour + Partners.*

4-5 *The 2008 Expo Zaragoza Pabellón de España by Francisco José Mangado Beloqui.*

6-7 *The Institute for Forestry and Nature Research in Wageningen (The Netherlands) by Behnisch Architekten.*

9 *The sun blind in the dome designed by Foster + Partners for the Reichstag in Berlin.*

CONTENTS

11 Residence Antilia in Mumbai designed by SITE.

Color range

INTRODUCTION

Almost without realizing it, our houses and cities have changed drastically in the last one hundred years. For centuries the old frames and facades with load-bearing walls, narrow openings and windows and pitched roofs served as rational solutions for the management of weather conditions. Rainwater flowed from the ridge-tiles to the roof-gutters, and from the cornices to the sills provided with drip grooves, and then dropped to the ground, where the French drain insulated the ground floor from the humid earth around it. However, these structures proved to be rather rudimentary regarding the layout and organization of the various services and apparatuses. Until the arrival of water inflow and outflow systems; electric lighting and appliance systems and those for heating (as replacements for stoves and chimneys); and then air-conditioning, they were also inadequate for the management of the microclimate. Le Corbusier's "machine for living in" was only the beginning of a modern process that placed a growing number of mechanical, electric and electronic machines within the new framework of beams and pillars in order to carry out those functions that had been lacking in pre-industrial society or that had been performed naturally by the buildings themselves by dint of their very configuration.

The modern solutions – which were adopted in very different conditions, even with respect to urban settings, with our cities becoming increasingly large, dense and congested – marked the beginning of a form of innovation, and in certain respects are still valid, while in others they have triggered new problems, including the latest one: the question of the environment. Thus, sustainable architecture grew gradually out of the conflicting combination of the development of modern positive technology and the anti-modern criticism of its negative effects. Among these consequences, there is the combination of the system of consumer objects that governs production, excessive mobility as best expressed by the use of private cars, and exaggerated consumption and waste of energy and irreplaceable resources.

Sustainable architecture, which has reached its first mature stage, stemmed from the more subtle and rational developments of technology in order to solve the problems caused by the gross, overpowering domination of modern Western technology – an expression of Man's dominion of the Earth – and should be viewed within the context of an overall consideration of city architecture.

The question of the environment is one of the main reasons why modern architecture – which began with the heroic and aggressive 20th century avant-garde movements – could not but evolve into the more comprehensive and articulated discipline that could be called "Contemporary Modern". What with the unsustainable population explosion, the massive growth of our cities, global pollution and the absolutely insane waste of energy and resources, the environment problem is certainly one of the main factors in the passage from Modern to Post-Modern to Contemporary Modern. The slow progression of Modernism from its triumph to its ideological crisis can be summed up by a series of events, including movies, which began in 1908. Strangely enough, the date of all these events ends with the number 8, as if this were a symbol.

1908 – The Model-T Ford became the token of both private and mass mobility and at the same time of mass production. In short, it was the emblem of the modern world in the fields of mechanics and technology, a sort of metal and rubber Frankenstein.

1948 – *Mr. Blandings Builds His Dream House*, an American movie directed by Henry C. Potter, was the first representation in the United States of the abandonment of large cities by middle-class families. Here the protagonists ask their suave architect friend to rebuild an old-style country house for them.

1958 – Another film, *My Uncle*, directed by Jacques Tati, which was followed by *Playtime* (1967) and *Traffic* (1971), contains excoriating criticism of the excesses of modernization and its dehumanizing ideology.

1968 – The films *2001: Space Odyssey* and *Planet of the Apes* are the emblems of the time of the first voyages into space by "superhuman" astronauts, and they also express doubts that are truly cosmic. For example, what is the fate of the newborn child who floats in space in the finale of Kubrick's film, after the appearance of the monolith that marks the progress of humankind over nature, and after the streak of madness and jealously on the part of the computer Hal, which rebels against the crew?

An even more explicitly catastrophic end is in store for the astronauts in *Planet of the Apes*. After landing on a planet ruled by apes, which have enslaved the primitive human civilization, they discover the head and torch of the Statue of Liberty buried in the sand, almost as if these belonged to an earlier stage of development, a stage that may have been destroyed by its self-transformation into a destructive entity.

1968 – The Club of Rome was founded, and in 1972 published its first report, *The Limits to Growth*, initiating the militant green movement phase, which first flanked and then incorporated the commitment to conservationism, which until then had basically concerned the preservation of artworks and monuments. Mention should also be made of the anti-urban movement and the Prague Spring.

1988 – The motion picture *Powaqqatsi*, directed by Godfrey Reggio, deals with the same themes discussed six years earlier in his pessimistic *Koyaanisqatsi* (a word that means "life out of balance" in the language of the Hopi Indians of America). In this film the prediction of a future apocalypse becomes a paradoxical aesthetic approach to Man's being on Earth in order to destroy it.

2008 – The Aula Paolo VI or Sala Nervi (Paul VI Hall or Nervi Hall), designed in the 1960s by Pier Luigi Nervi in the Vatican City, is covered with 2,400 photovoltaic panels that make it self-sufficient energy-wise. The panels were offered by a firm based in Bonn, Germany. The "Green Vatican" trend, as it was fondly nicknamed, had already manifested itself with the so-called Popemobile: the Pope's car driven by solar cells.

A structure that produces energy instead of consuming it, as is partly the case with the Sala Nervi, may very well be the new thematic myth of sustainable architecture. Or, more simply, the mature phase of sustainable architecture may on the other hand exclude all sectorial – and always slightly sectarian – mythography, and impose on all urban architecture the new construction materials, systems and equipment which by themselves will revolutionize our architecture, neighborhoods and cities. A mere list of these elements is quite impressive: the ecological treatment of open spaces; panels and grilles and multiple skins; loggias and large central vertical atriums serving as ventilation ducts; different facades for different orientations; marquees like bubbles providing space that is both in the open and covered; vertical gardens and espaliers; multi-use urban parks and public green areas; appropriate experimented building density instead of a priori low-density standards; systems that not only eliminate refuse but also produce energy from it; the dislocation of car parking areas in cities; a great increase in public transportation vehicles and routes; alternative ecological itineraries in interstitial areas; bicycle lanes and wind turbines. The impulse this list provides to contemporary modern and anti-classical modes of architectural composition is impactful: asymmetry rather than symmetry, assembly and stacking rather than dogmatic seriality. But, at times, there are also returns to a targeted regressive vernacular style as far as genres and niches are concerned, with a psychology of the resident that varies according to whether the construction is a shopping center, an office building or a tourist village.

Certainly, sustainable architecture can also present itself as one of the many architectural genres, such as "residential domestic", and in any case it is more inclined to certain types rather than others. But the most interesting aspect is something else that concerns the architecture of the entire city: the development and configuration of buildings, quarters and cities in a period of pervasive hybridization of the natural-artificial into a third entity that can be noted from satellites, with a reversal between urbanized, illuminated and polluted territories, on the one hand, and territories that are neither urbanized nor illuminated (rural, wild, wooded or pastoral and re-desertified) on the other.

I believe that sustainable architecture should mean new forms of the diversity that has always characterized urban landscapes, rather than a homogeneous landscape consisting of dull, neatly balanced, similar stylistic canons, something which, paradoxically, would take them back to the most utopian and standardized modernism. And this diversity must be constantly renewed and not merely preserved. A.T.

14-15 The expansion of the Nelson-Atkins Museum in Kansas City by Steven Holl.

16-17 The Tjibaou Cultural Center built in Noumea (New Caledonia) – a project by Renzo Piano.

herzog + partner *(hall 26)* - m

illuminazione headquarter) - rogers sti

barajas airport) - baumschlager & e

nouvel *(torre agbar)* - behnisch a

architects *(eden project)* - bill dunst

architects *(little tesseract)* - renzo pia

expansion of the morgan library) - unstu

predock architect pc *(academy sch*

mangado beloqui *(pabellón de esp*

eco tech:
advanced technology
becomes ecological

ario cucinella architects (iguzzini

k harbour + partners (law courts -

erle (öko-hauptschule) - ateliers jean

hitekten (thermal spa) - grimshaw

r architects (bedzed) - steven holl

o building workshop (renovation and

dio (mercedes-benz museum) - antoine

ol discovery canyon) - francisco josé

) - atkins (bahrain world trade center)

eco tech:
advanced technology becomes ecological

Climate change, increasing desertification and global warming, together with the growing awareness that some energy resources are by no means unlimited, have put environmental problems in the limelight and have also led to many international meetings such as the Kyoto summit in 1996 and the 2000 conference at The Hague. These meetings established protocols by which many nations have committed themselves to promulgating laws aimed at reducing energy consumption, promoting the search for alternative energy sources, and reducing the emission of harmful gases. These laws promote different procedures regarding production, transportation and construction, which are among the main causes of environmental degradation and the production of various kinds of refuse.

Various specialized agencies have studied the theme of sustainability and the tools needed to reduce and optimize energy consumption, and proposed two types of solutions. On the one hand, it is necessary to revive the indigenous building traditions and

to utilize locally sourced natural material which can also be recycled. On the other hand, artificial construction materials and technology must be used to create architectural elements and systems for the bioclimatic management of the building in question. The second hypothesis is the one adopted by eco tech presented in this section. Among the systems proposed by the eco tech architects, a predominant role is played by the features of the shell or framework, which has always been the element that characterizes the relationship between the building and its context, which separates the interior and outer spaces and which defines the climatic, illumination and ventilation aspects of the spaces. Among these, interactive facade structures are becoming widespread. These are like skin or membranes that change according to the exterior environmental conditions and are able to transform these natural resources into elements that can be used for heating and cooling the interior. They are modifying the traditional separation between the building and its facilities into an integrated system in

which the facades, which consist of more than one layer or wall separated by spaces in which air circulates, guarantee the environmental quality of the interior in a natural way, without consuming energy, while the systems are used only when absolutely necessary.

This type of framework structure was used by Baumschlager & Eberle in the Öko-Hauptschule (Eco Secondary School) in Mäder, Austria, where an outer layer of unconnected panels allows air to enter the building and an internal operable layer insulates the interior. Jean Nouvel also used this solution to define his architectural aesthetic. In Barcelona, in the Torre Agbar, which he designed, there are three layers: the innermost one is a structural, supporting element made of reinforced concrete; the intermediate layer is made up of colored panels; and the outer one is a sunshade system consisting of operable metal louvers that ensure comfort during the hot summer.

The iGuzzini Illuminazione Headquarter, designed by Mario Cucinella, feature a continuous brise-soleil that overhangs toward the south, screening the facade from the sun, while its louvers tilt automatically, depending on the weather. In other architectural works regulation of the environmental climate is achieved through the use of windows with different degrees of opacity, transparency and color that are effective in different ways. Cucinella, for example, used "selective" windows (glazed, transparent, or a combination of both) to reduce the need for air conditioning in the Borgognone 53 office building in Milan, while Renzo Piano selected thermal resistant glass for the headquarters of the newspaper Il Sole 24 Ore also in Milan.

In other cases glass is replaced by plastic material. An example of this is the Eden Project designed by Nicholas Grimshaw, which consists of a series of buildings including four domes whose tropical, humid and temperate interior "climate" is created by ETFE (Ethylene Tetrafluoroethylene). This plastic is lighter than glass which makes it possible to build with thinner supporting elements and to obtain better climatic and acoustic conditions. ETFE is also used for the bubbles cladding the National Aquatics Center designed by Chris Bosse of PTW Architects for the Beijing Olympic Games. It absorbs sunlight, which in turn heats and illuminates the interior.

Some architects, however, search for forms that generate air flow to regulate the temperature and humidity levels in the interior, as is the case with the Bordeaux Law Courts complex designed by Rogers Stirk Harbour + Partners, in which the courtrooms taper upward, thus triggering a duct effect. Again, in Behnisch's project for the spa complex at Bad Aibling, the pool and treatment areas, which have a great deal of humidity, are enclosed in eight domes which define the interior space and whose form facilitates the outflow of air and humidity through the top of each dome.

The Mercedes-Benz Museum in Stuttgart designed by UNStudio combines the interactive frame, constituted by glass elements and aluminum panels that regulate heat exchange, with the configuration of the entire building, with its large central atrium that serves as a ventilation duct.

Other buildings use energy producing apparatus. Besides the traditional solar panels, these include windmills placed on the roof, and wind turbines (e.g. the Bahrain World Trade Center built by Atkins).

The passage from construction to town planning entails greater complexity, not only concerning the technological means used, but also the ecological policies that strive to renew vast polluted and degraded areas. This is achieved through environment-friendly and sustainable action that embraces the optimum use of land and energy consumption, the reutilization of rainwater, and the ecological disposal of refuse. Many eco-districts are based on the above aims, including the BedZED near London designed by Bill Dunster Architects, one of the first examples of a zero emission quarter: a self-sufficient neighborhood that produces all the energy it needs by means of renewable sources and technology and systems that reduce consumption. Another example is the new ecologically sustainable Bo01 area in Malmö, Sweden, which uses energy produced on-site by windmills and bio-gas obtained from recycled refuse. G.S.

Hall 26

Hall 26 is a vast exhibition space that measures 722 feet long, 377 feet wide and with a maximum height of 95 feet. It lies in the middle of the Hanover Fair complex, whose master plan was also designed by the firm of Herzog + Partner.

Flexibility – a basic requisite for such a large exhibition area – is ensured by a structural system consisting of three 230-foot curved, wide-span bays with service areas at either end, easy access, and rest and refreshment spaces.

The roof, modeled after the typical profile of tensile structures, is the element that best expresses the formal and technical features of this building. It rests on a catenary network that connects four rows of A-shaped steel pylons.

It is made of wood panels, the inner part of which has an insulator layer, an interspace of partial steam and a layer of gravel; a combination that increases the deflection of the structure.

The suspended shading elements make for a sharp contrast with the six rectangular concrete service areas that bind the structure and contain the refreshment areas, the technical rooms and the restroom facilities. The walls are glass curtain walls.

The large A-pylons, which, as mentioned, are arranged in four parallel rows with six elements each, consolidate the structure both longitudinally and transversally. The rows of A frames are both the maximum and minimum points of the three groups of catenary networks. These ferrous elements form three large and openly laid-out volumes that define a structure which from the standpoint of circulation and accommodation can be developed virtually without limits and restrictions. They are also able to provide the necessary natural ascending ventilation.

22-23 The picture shows the sharp contrast between the suspended roofs drawing on the standard profile of tensile structures and the wood-faced, rectangular-shaped service nuclei.

22 bottom Flexibility, which is a fundamental requisite for an

exhibit pavilion, was obtained with a structural system that was not overly restricting in terms of distribution.

23 The structure includes large trestle pillars in four parallel rows, each with six elements. They consolidate the structure both longitudinally and transversally.

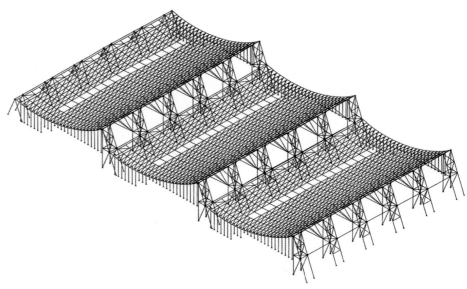

24-25 The A-frame rows are both the maximum and minimum points of the three groups of catenaries forming three large volumes with open layouts defining a structure that is not restricting in terms of distribution.

In order to solve the problem of air conditioning in such a vast space (a volume of around 14.5 million cubic feet) Herzog + Partner adopted a ventilation mechanism that makes the best use of the normal physical laws of air circulation and down flow so as to reduce to a minimum the use of artificial, mechanical elements. In the summer the cool air, which penetrates the building via openings placed at a height of +15 feet, crosses the entire pavilion, flowing down onto the heat sources (consisting mainly of people and machinery) on ground level. Once it has finished its course, the cool air ascends once again toward the roof and flows out of the pavilion through special adjustable flaps. As we have seen, the natural ascending flow of air is favored by the profile of the structure and provides almost 50% of the ventilation needed for the entire hall, which means a drastic reduction in air conditioning costs.

Artificial ventilation, on the other hand, is achieved by means of large internal ducts that make it possible to distribute and channel the air through directional diffusers. This duct area is made of large sheets of glass, thus affording a panoramic view of the entire building.

Natural illumination is provided by means of large openings to the north, external louvers, and triple glazing with light grilles on the concave surface of the modular roof on a level with the lowest points of the suspended bays. Artificial lighting

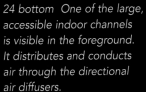

24 bottom One of the large, accessible indoor channels is visible in the foreground. It distributes and conducts air through the directional air diffusers.

25 The roof membrane is made of wooden panels. From a static perspective, this surface area takes the push from the wind

iGuzzini Illuminazione Headquarter

RECANATI, ITALY

This building is an enlargement of the existing iGuzzini Illuminazione Headquarter and was commissioned to house its administrative functions. Its linear composition makes it an ideal and avant-garde management structure for the firm, especially considering its bioclimatic features.

The building is rectangular, its long sides facing south and north, and its vertical development is in the form of a simple parallelepiped whose framework is made of concrete. On its long sides are glazed, vertical louvered windows that are transparent and can be partially opened, while the short sides have opaque glazing. The "fifth side", that is, the roof, is distinguished for its continuous *brise-soleil* that bends toward the south side, protruding for a few feet, thus constituting the principle screening element of the facade which it shields from the sun. Made of a metal frame, it has louvers that can be oriented according to the varying seasonal direction of the sun's rays. This additional cover, which makes the project both uniform and recognizable, has an opening in the central part of the roof on a level with an inner atrium – a reduction of volume effected on the building for its entire height – surmounted by 12 skylights. These have a two-fold function: they regulate and increase natural illumination in the innermost section of the building, thus preventing bothersome glare, and they facilitate natural ventilation as the atrium serves as a vent through the stack effect. The atrium walls are glazed surfaces that face the administrative and commercial offices of the first three floors as well as all the administrative and management activities areas on the top floor and the vertical connection space located to the north.

The outer walls of the long sides of the edifice are located at some distance from the structure, which leaves room for any air conditioning units that might be placed in this perimetric space, for inside Venetian blinds that prevent glare in the work areas, and for the light shelves: horizontal elements that convey natural light toward the ceiling and guarantee greater and more uniform light diffusion.

The objective of Cucinella's project was to ensure high levels of comfort, not by resorting to particularly sophisticated technology, but by striving to maximize the benefits of the passive operation of the building, which amounts to self-sufficient operation for at least half of the energy needs while the building is being used.

This result was achieved thanks to a study made on the relationship with the natural surroundings, which manifested itself partly through the use of two horizontal gardens, one placed on the roof of the parking area opposite the facade exposed to the south, and the other placed in the atrium. S.L.

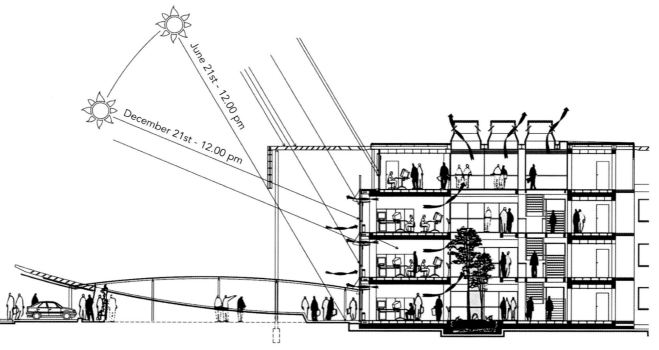

26 top The building has vertical glass enclosures on the side and the walls on the short sides are made from a transparent material.

26 bottom The cutaway view indicates the role played by the sun blind facing south and the structure's natural ventilation mechanism.

27 The indoor atrium is home to a green area, and acts as a ventilation stack and light well.

Law Courts

BORDEAUX, FRANCE

The Bordeaux Law Courts building is situated in the heart of the city, a few steps away from the cathedral. It replaced an old fortress which over the years had been used for many different purposes, the last of which was as a jail. The fortress, the only remains of which is the keep, gave way to the glass parallelepiped that contains offices, a large atrium and six courtrooms. The seventh courtroom is located outside the glazed building, at the beginning of the large external stairway that runs over a pool and connects the new complex with the rest of the city. All seven courtrooms lie under an undulating copper-covered roof.

Normally a law court is an enclosed and protected place that arouses awe in the local citizens. However, English architects studio Rogers Stirk Harbour + Partners opted, on the contrary, for a transparent building open to the public and the city, as if to inspire a positive perception of the French judiciary system through the transparency and accessibility of its structure.

The shape of the seven courtrooms reminds one of a Boeing motor, and in fact the technology utilized in their construction derived precisely from the aeronautical industry.

They have a round floor plan and a tapering upper section, whose light aluminum structure is clad with diagonally oriented wood planks.

The law courts are three-dimensional, vertical volumes which, although supported by struts that fasten them securely, seem to be floating and soaring under their glazed roofs. The upper section of the courtrooms, which, as previously mentioned, tapers upward, protrudes from the roof to facilitate ventilation. The solar heat above the law courts increases the chimney effect and generates air currents. The outside pool cools and humidifies the air before it enters the interior. Moreover, the shape of the rooms favors efficient natural ventilation, which means less energy consumption, since the need for air conditioning is reduced to a minimum and energy requirements are nearly halved compared to a normal building of the same size.

The Salle des Pas Perdus (Hall of the Subsiding Footsteps) is a large public area that gives access to the courtrooms. The judges enter via suspended catwalks that traverse the central space: an atrium that separates the public area of the complex from the five-story wing containing the offices of the judges, magistrates and personnel.

28 The seven courtrooms are located under a corrugated copper roof and are parallel to the block of administration offices, so movement by the public and the magistrates is separate.

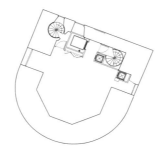

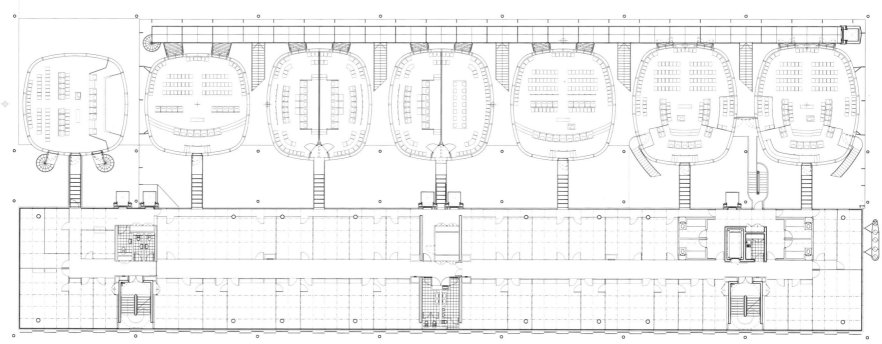

28-29 The law courts are located in Bordeaux's city center. The building replaces an old fortress whose only remaining ruins are the tower to the left.

29 bottom The planimetry highlights the layout of the public area in front of the complex with the expanse of water and the large outdoor stairway projecting towards the medieval city.

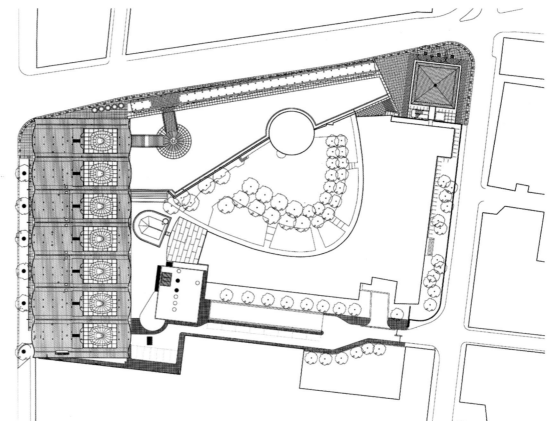

The glazed section is flooded with light, while the seven courtrooms are illuminated by a small skylight at the top.

The decision to provide such a clear-cut formal solution in the construction of the courtrooms is the principal characterizing feature of this work, and also marks Richard Rogers' break with the plethoric geometric forms he had utilized earlier and his new interest in and receptiveness to more organic forms which now interact much more with the natural surroundings. As he himself stated, "Once you get away from the very heavy machinery we use, which is based on carbon fuel, you can start to move with the breeze, with natural ventilation, and that means that the building must also be susceptible, much more changeable, much more lightweight to respond, more like flowers or trees or animals, like the chameleon that changes color and form. So you channel the wind or collect the sun, the rain or the cool of the earth and that means it is much more dynamic, much more fragile in a positive way, fragile in relation to the beat of the earth." L.S.

30-31 The courtrooms are diagonally faced with cedar strips. Their aluminum structure is lightened and they are supported by struts connecting them to the ground. The suspended walkways reserved for the judges connect the courtrooms with a 4-story

building housing the offices of the magistrates and personnel.

31 The cutaway view shows the upper part of the courtrooms as they taper off upwards and emerge from the roof to favor ventilation.

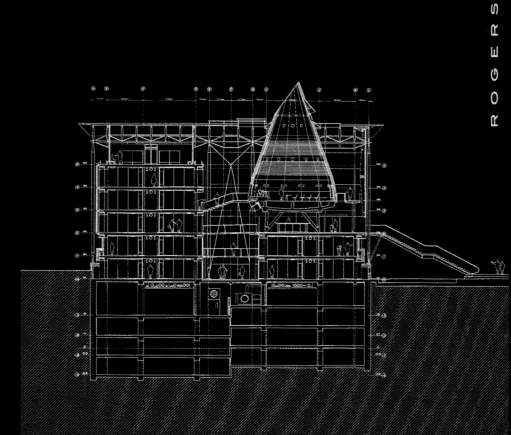

32 left The section tapering off upwards is the strategy implemented by Richard Rogers to control climatic comfort inside the seven courtrooms.

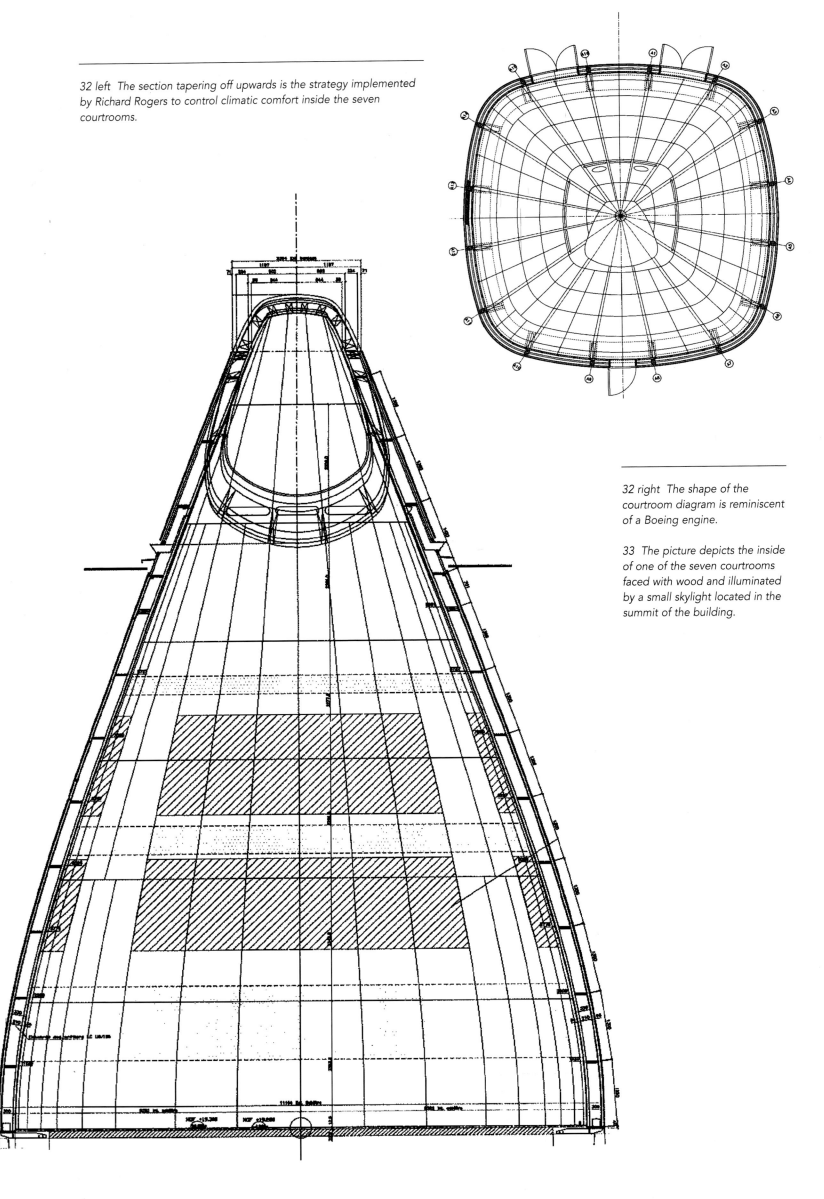

32 right The shape of the courtroom diagram is reminiscent of a Boeing engine.

33 The picture depicts the inside of one of the seven courtrooms faced with wood and illuminated by a small skylight located in the summit of the building.

Öko-Hauptschule

MÄDER, AUSTRIA

A parallelepiped totally clad in glass and situated in the middle of Mäder, a small Austrian village situated a few miles from the Swiss border, has become famous for its high eco-friendly quality that resulted from a town plan. This plan entailed a complex of public spaces linked by a network of streets, most of them pedestrian-only, extending throughout the area. The town center is enhanced by a series of rigorously ecological public buildings, most of which were designed by Baumschlager & Eberle, who built both the City Hall and the secondary school and its gymnasium annex. These architects based their work on the use of contemporary technology with the aim of achieving good spatial composition and comfort with the least expense possible.

The school complex in Mäder consists of two buildings: the school proper and the gymnasium, which are staggered and set against the edge of the property so as to create two public spaces. Both buildings are simple and compact in order to reduce energy consumption, and are made of materials and have systems that were chosen for this very purpose.

The school is a four-story construction with a square floor plan of 92 feet per side, and its structure is prefabricated and modular, with a double facade made of wood and glass.

All four floors are arranged in the same manner around a central space which on the ground floor is an atrium that affords access to the laboratories, the facilities rooms and circulation elements in the northwest corner. On the other floors this space is for recreation and is surrounded by the classrooms. All the rooms are extremely bright thanks to the natural light which penetrates through a large light well situated over the central zone. Two-thirds of the facades are transparent, and glass panels crown the partition walls. In order to prevent waste the artificial illumination is controlled by a computerized system that shows how many people are actually inside the rooms.

The double facade all around the simple block also constitutes one of the main bioclimatic instruments in the school building. The outer facade, made of unconnected scaled glass panels, is separated from the inner one, two-thirds of which is also made of glass, thus creating an interspace of 21 inches in which air circulates. A system of moveable curtains protects the building from the sun in the summer, while in wintertime the facade absorbs sunlight. This outer layer or facade also protects the inner one, one-third of which consists of larch-veneered plywood panels, thus making chemical treatment unnecessary. The use of eco-friendly, non-toxic materials reflects the project requirements. The floors are made of linoleum, the paint, paneling and casing contain no chemical solvents, the water pipes are made of polyurethane instead of PVC, and the walls and ceilings are made of walnut-veneered plywood clad with a layer of sheep's wool that serves as an acoustic insulator.

Rock wool covers the panels of the inner facade in order to improve their thermal properties, and other energy conservation is achieved through an earth collector system that heats the outside air naturally before it is conveyed into the classrooms. The rest of the energy needed to make the edifice operable is produced by 301 square feet of solar panels placed on the roof – which produce 50% of the hot water needed – and 969 square feet of photovoltaic modules that cover the gymnasium roof.   G.S.

34 The school building overlooks the plaza area with its simple, compact shape and its transparent facade revealing the activities performed inside.

34-35 The facade is defined by two layers: the external layer formed of glass sheets that are not joined together to allow air to penetrate, and the internal layer, which is in part made with glass and in part with plywood panels wrapped in larch.

35 bottom One-third of the two-story area in the gyms is underground so it could be connected to the school through an underground tunnel.

Torre Agbar

BARCELONA, SPAIN

This bullet-shaped tower represents a new development in the urban landscape of Barcelona due to its absolutely singular vertical movement, in a prevalently horizontal and typically European context. Among the many architectural projects realized in recent years in the Catalonian city, this one designed by Nouvel is distinctive because it attracts such attention, not only because of its dizzying height (474 feet) but also due to the effect its seductive exterior produces, so much so that it has already become a city landmark. This "skin" lends a sort of two-fold identity to the building, depending on the time of day and the intensity of the sunlight. Under natural light it has a rather ambiguous surface, in which colors and casing material merge, much like the many pixels on a screen, imparting a unified, bright appearance with unclear, shaded outlines. This is the desired effect, perfectly in keeping with the spirit of Nouvel's project, which expresses the idea of water that gushes out of the earth when under pressure. An effect that is in sync with the Agbar water company, locally known as Aigües de Barcelona (Waters of Barcelona), which occupies the building and is identified with it. At night the skin loses its evanescent appearance and takes on more intense coloration with changing hues, favored by the artificial LED luminous devices, which most certainly animate it.

Again, depending on the distance from which it is observed, one's perception of the shell also varies. It seems more compact the further away you are, while as you approach, its colored pixels become more visible.

The Torre Agbar has an irregular central plan that is neither circular nor elliptic. There is an inner ring or cylinder made of concrete – a core that houses the systems of vertical circulation such as stairwells and elevators, machinery rooms, and service areas – and an outer bearing structure made of reinforced concrete (for 25 stories) and steel (the upper, crowning section). The plan layout clearly shows that the core is slightly off-center, and every floor – with the exception of this core cylinder – can be utilized for various purposes since there are no supporting structures. The facade or shell is the principal feature of the building. It consists of two walls, one inside, which encloses the tower, and another made of glass on the exterior, with an intermediate empty space between them that favors the natural circulation of air and ventilation.

36 The tower stands out for its apparently casual shell, which combines colored facing elements and alternating solid areas and voids. The perception of the shell varies and changes based on the distance from which it is observed and the time of day.

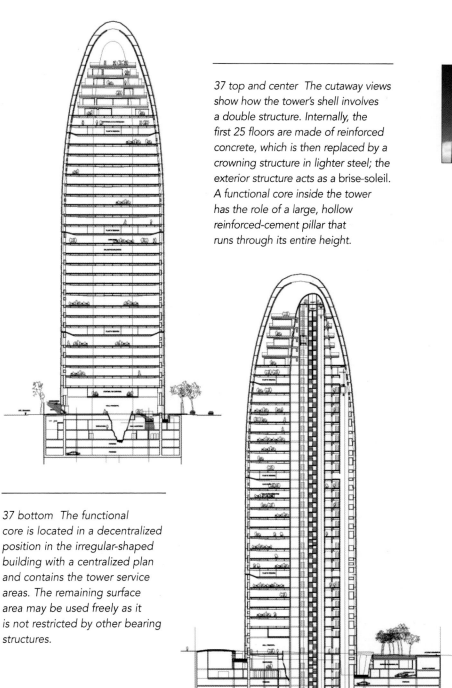

37 top and center The cutaway views show how the tower's shell involves a double structure. Internally, the first 25 floors are made of reinforced concrete, which is then replaced by a crowning structure in lighter steel; the exterior structure acts as a brise-soleil. A functional core inside the tower has the role of a large, hollow reinforced-cement pillar that runs through its entire height.

37 bottom The functional core is located in a decentralized position in the irregular-shaped building with a centralized plan and contains the tower service areas. The remaining surface area may be used freely as it is not restricted by other bearing structures.

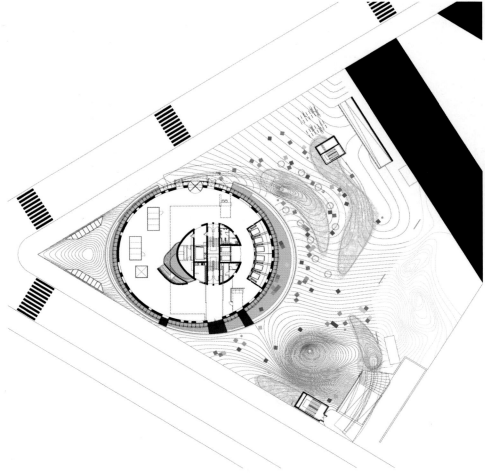

ATELIERS JEAN NOUVEL

38-39 The picture depicts the steel dome constituting the tower's transparent, lightweight crowning. The top level is closed off by this structure, which provides a charming 360° view over the city of Barcelona.

39 The crowning of the functional core is seen in the foreground. It is located in the center of the tower and contains the connecting systems and the building's main service areas.

The outer section serves as a sunshade. It has an iron framework on which there are glass plates with louvers that tilt differently – depending on the angle of the sun, on their position, and also on the presence or absence of openings – with the purpose of deflecting the sun's rays.

Furthermore, in order to help save energy, the outer concrete shell has more openings facing north and fewer facing south. The distribution of these openings and of the colored panels is basically square and conforms to a specific principle of composition. The panels, made of curved and corrugated aluminum, have a gamut of hues ranging from the bright red of the base to the light blue of the crowning section of the building.

The seemingly random combination of the colored elements and the alternation of full and empty spaces create the pixel effect on the surface of the tower.

The edifice is crowned by a completely transparent steel and glass dome, which makes it a unique and fascinating belvedere affording spectacular panoramas of the city.   S.L.

40 top The stairs stand out for their stone facing. They lead visitors from the entrance level to the underground level, which is home to a conference room and several exhibit areas.

40 bottom White finishing elements characterize the 25th floor. The area in the picture is an open space that can be closed and transformed into a more reserved meeting place.

41 The holing is clearly visible in the foreground as it starts and develops from a single square module and cuts into the perimetric reinforced-cement bearing structure.

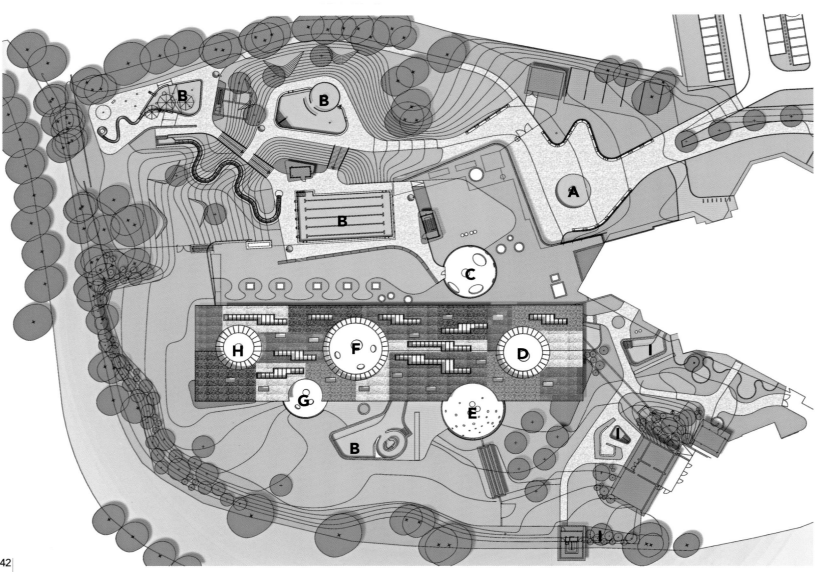

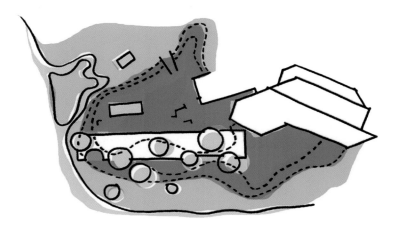

Thermal Spa

BAD AIBLING, GERMANY

Eight domes inserted into an architectural volume made of glass and steel constitute the enlargement and addition of the thermal spa at Bad Aibling, a small village southeast of Munich, which as long ago as 1838 boasted a complex specialized in mud baths. The Behnisch Architekten studio was commissioned to enlarge the existing structures and convert them into a thermal park. The Bad Aibling Spa is situated in an extraordinary setting at the edge of the village in an area of greenery delimited by the Trifbach River whose high position offers exceptional views of the Bavarian Alps. The project aimed at enhancing this location by remodeling the height of the land so that the outdoor swimming pool would be on a level with the spa roof, from which one could have a commanding view of the panorama, which is also visible from inside the new glass building. Conceived as a winter garden, it houses the entrance and relaxation areas, but also plays the fundamental role of connecting the domes, the other architectural and spatial element that characterizes the Bad Aibling Spa. The interaction between these two elements creates a rich and articulated spatial configuration. The glass is marked out by a single area whose floor is multilevel, with slight differences in height that correspond to the various materials used to differentiate the relaxation zones from the circulation spaces and the access to the domes. These zones are an archetypal form of the thermal spaces that usually define a large area, a semi-public place used for gatherings or meetings. In the Behnisch project they are smaller in order to create more intimate zones that are repeated eight times in the winter garden to create a variety of atmospheres. Each one differs from the other in size, function, the incidence of the light, and the quality and temperature of the water.

KEY

A Entrance Area
B Outdoor Swimming Pool
C Beauty Dome
D Moor Dome
E Sensual Dome
F Experiental Dome
G Thermal Dome
H Relaxation Dome
I Sauna

42-43 The picture shows the main facade of the hot springs as seen from the river. It is defined by the white domes rising up from the glass foundation.

42 bottom The diagram of the roofs of the entire complex shows how it includes the main center for wellbeing, the outdoor swimming pools located in the surrounding green area and the wood buildings home to the saunas next to the river.

43 top The planimetric sketch shows the new hot springs building complex in relation to the pre-existing building and the surrounding natural scenery defined by the orography of the ground and the river.

43 bottom The roof on the new complex seen from the pre-existing building is shared by the domes it contains, which have alternating opaque and glass sections that make the indoor area extremely bright.

Six domes are made of insulated concrete clad, an opaque acoustic material that insulates and encloses the inner space. One is made of translucent Plexiglas which creates a relationship between the interior and exterior, and another is clad in gold, inspired by the Byzantine baths.

Instead of laying out a unitary space, the decision was made to separate the winter garden area from the interior of the domes in order to define diversified and more intimate zones and also to obtain a 40% reduction in energy consumption. One of the most serious climatic problems in a spa is the humidity produced by water evaporation which in single halls leads to the consumption of large amounts of energy used both to dehumidify the air and to recover the heat lost in the evaporation process. The Behnisch architects placed the swimming pools in insulated rooms covered with domes so that in winter, the passive heat absorbed by the main body – through its south facing glass facade – would heat both the rooms inside and, by means of small holes, the spaces inside the domes. The heat evaporates the water and creates the humidity that is extracted through the top of the domes without passing through the winter garden. Furthermore, the winter garden pavement is passively heated by a mechanical room under the edifice.

Conversely, in the summer the projecting roof protects the south facade from the sun's rays, whose numerous openings, as well as those on the roof and domes, make for natural ventilation. This prevents overheating in the inner chambers which enjoy natural light all year round thanks to the glass facade and the skylights on the roof. G.S.

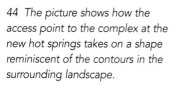

44 *The picture shows how the access point to the complex at the new hot springs takes on a shape reminiscent of the contours in the surrounding landscape.*

44-45 top *The picture shows a detail of the main facade and the portion in which the dome becomes a part of the glass building in the winter garden.*

44-45 bottom *The longitudinal cutaway view shows the elements making up the building, that is the building with the winter garden and the domes: (from left) the Relaxation Dome, the Experiential Dome and the Moor Dome, the only dome exceeding one story.*

BEHNISCH ARCHITEKTEN

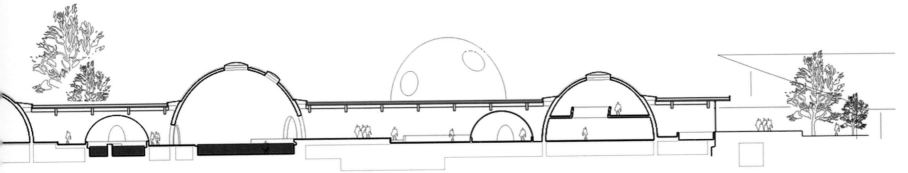

46 top The area surrounding the main building is a winter garden that constantly relates to the external landscape - an area where relations can be developed and that provides access to the different domes. It is defined both by small differences in height, the material used for the flooring

defining the different ambiences and the zenith light from the skylights on the roof, thanks to which it is quite bright.

46-47 The Moor Dome (seen here from the outside) is the only dome with two levels and large windows overlooking the scenery.

47 top The picture shows the entrance to the Experiential Dome as seen from the winter garden. The Hot-Cold Dome can be seen in the background. It is the only transparent Plexiglas dome perforated with a series of small openings.

47 bottom The area inside the Experiential Dome is defined by the blue dome with small holes allowing light to penetrate it. It provides a unique experience in which the protagonists are the movement by water and the roaring noise it produces.

Eden Project

CORNWALL, UK

48 The intervention's general plan portrays (above left) two biomes connected by a central entranceway (the building called The Core) and (below) the extended body of the Visitor Center, which is the entrance to the building.

49 The Eden Project is located in the damaged area of a former quarry that has been recuperated for the purpose. The structure combines entertainment and culture, is an exemplary realization of the application of sustainability strategies and sensitizes visitors on the matter of ecology.

The Eden Project is an ambitious display of global biodiversity and is one of the most innovative and high-profile of the Millennium Projects. Consisting of different parts which interact to restore quality to a degraded area – an abandoned clay pit on which it was constructed – the Eden Project is now a top exhibition center that attracts a great number of visitors every year. It has created job opportunities and guarantees a good return. Above all, it offers the opportunity to experiment with planning, concerning sustainability and aiming at awakening its public to the overall question of ecology.

Realized in four successive phases, the complex comprises a series of structures that offer a diversified experience to visitors, somewhere between entertainment, education and culture. The first structure, the Visitors' Centre (finished in 2000), was followed by one that includes two greenhouses or biomes (2001), which immediately provided visibility to the project, an attraction that ensured its success. Later additions were the Eden Foundation (2003) and the building known as The Core (2005). Given the positive response of the general public, a third biome dedicated to dry tropical climate is being built.

The Visitors' Centre, as its name suggests, contains facilities and services as well as shops and education galleries. It also affords access to the complex, situated in the vicinity of the parking areas and the main entrance. As an introduction to the visit – thanks to its position – it offers an overall view of the clay pit area and of the structures therein.

The biomes are two sinuously arranged sequences of four impressive domes of different sizes that intersect and interact, creating the conditions of humid tropical and warm temperate climate. These structures are connected by a building that is almost entirely underground, and which serves as an entrance. From the standpoint of layout, the structures are a development of the geodetic domes of Richard Buckminster Fuller, and make a major contribution to the culture of greenhouse design. Indeed, in the field of technological and ecologically sustainable research and experimentation, they are exemplary from many points of view. They are a model of efficiency due to the interaction between the active and passive systems and for the materials used in their construction. For example, the outer cladding is made of hexagonal modules of geodetic icosahedral ETFE film (Ethylene Tetrafluoroethylene), an innovative material that is much lighter than glass, has excellent insulating properties and can be recycled. Some of these modules can be opened to provide natural ventilation, and lie on a tubular galvanized steel frame that is easy to transport. Furthermore, ETFE does not impact the ozone layer and is not subject to any of the restrictions stipulated in the Montreal Protocol, the US Clean Air Act Amendments (1993) or the European Union regulations. Each thermoplastic ETFE hexagon consists of a triple layer of this film, inside which air is pumped and kept pressurized in order to increase its heat retention capacity and maintain a constant temperature.

Again, being transparent, this film provides excellent lighting for the greenhouse plants.

The Foundation Building, which contains offices and a library, and The Core, which houses exhibition and educational areas, are fine examples of how it is possible to achieve exemplary spatial and functional quality through low-cost, sustainable planning. The Core, in particular, not only uses photovoltaic panels but also recycled paper material.

As a whole, Grimshaw's project is a unique creation which from the outset carried out an ecological operation by reclaiming the degraded cave pit area.   S.L.

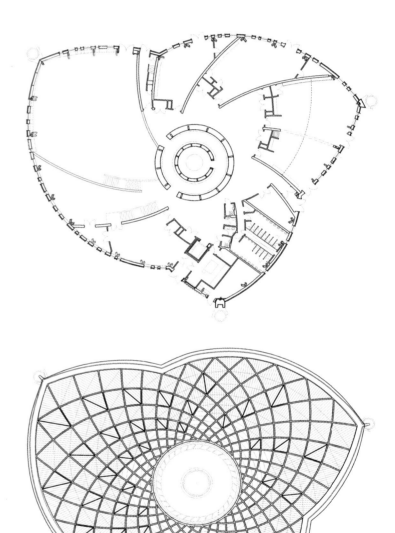

50 top left The accessible portion of the roof on The Core (a building with areas intended for exhibits and socializing) provides a privileged view overlooking the indoor central area of the building, which is home to a work of art by sculptor Peter Randall-Page.

50 bottom left The roof reaches the entrance level in three distinct points; it terminates on the ground in these points through a concrete element that acts as a counterfort and also partially as a draining point for the rainwater merging there from the roof.

50 right The diagrams show the geometric complexity of the building and the related indoor division of the areas. The functions in The Core aim to develop knowledge and include exhibit areas, workshops, classrooms and a coffee shop.

51 The roof has a series of pyramid-shaped elements (some of which are glass windows that can be opened) to provide light and natural ventilation to the indoor areas. Photovoltaic panels are located near the center. They generate most of the energy required to operate the building.

52 top and 52-53 The roof is the focus point of The Core project, which allows the building to stand out from the outside and characterizes it on the inside. The pictures show the exhibit areas and their double height.

52 bottom The triangular surface areas composing the pyramids on the roof of The Core are reminiscent of and re-used to configure analogous elements, which help improve the quality of the building's indoor lighting.

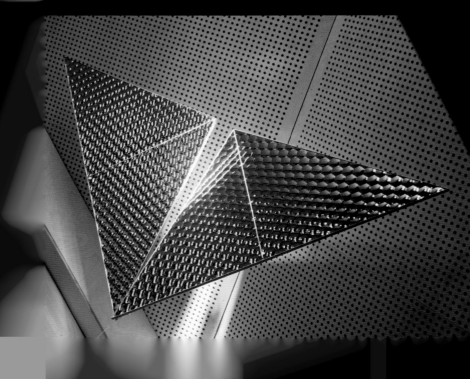

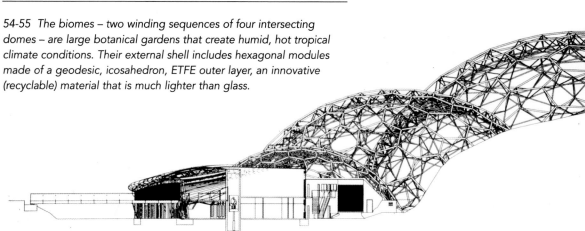

54-55 The biomes – two winding sequences of four intersecting domes – are large botanical gardens that create humid, hot tropical climate conditions. Their external shell includes hexagonal modules made of a geodesic, icosahedron, ETFE outer layer, an innovative (recyclable) material that is much lighter than glass.

55 top The cutaway view shows how the biome domes (whose radii are between 59-213 feet) intersect to produce a detailed composition that conceptually constitutes the evolution of the geodesic domes by Richard Buckminster Fuller.

55 bottom and 56-57 The structure is made of an internal steel mesh braced by an internal reticular structure with hexagonal and triangular links. This system rests on a circular, reinforced-cement foundation. The steel bearing structure is relatively lightweight and is easy to transport, thanks to the use of ETFE.

BedZED

LONDON, UK

The Beddington Zero Energy Development project was an emblematic undertaking, among one of the first realized in the United Kingdom on an urban scale. It grew out of the desire to create urban housing with reduced carbon emissions and at the same time develop enough energy to satisfy the needs of the housing development, that is, to be entirely energy self-sufficient.

Besides serving as housing, the complex includes a medical center, a nursery school, areas designed to house other community and work activities, and services that tend to integrate these functions with the social fabric, guarantee self-sufficiency and offer transport-friendly facilities partly to minimize movement. The project applied environmentally friendly and bioclimatic rules, and utilized state-of-the-art technological systems, materials and devices aiming at sustainable development to guarantee energy efficiency and conservation. On the one hand, cogenerators produce electricity and heat for the hot water and heating systems, whilst on the other hand, the study of the structure, configuration and dislocation of the architectural volumes took into consideration the natural illumination of sunlight. At the same time, this created a density development layout comparable to that of the urban surroundings, while guaranteeing an available green area that in proportion is considerably larger.

Furthermore, the difference in the homes offered in this complex goes hand in hand with the differentiation of the exterior of the housing units, which vary in height from one to three stories, and with a profile that ends at the highest part in a curved line, crowned by colored cowls. The care taken over the color selection, the choice of materials, the desire to create green areas – also for the exclusive use of those living in the complex – and, last but not least, the pursuit of variation in the design of the complex, all contributed to raising the quality of the project, from both a compositional and formal standpoint.

The chimneys, which make the housing development so recognizable, serve to provide natural ventilation in the interior, thus affording comfort that is eco-friendly.

One of the top priorities of Dunster's project was the use of thermal-efficient materials, excellent insulation on the masonry walls and loft roofs, triple-glazed window openings, and the use of photovoltaic panels. All this is aimed at heat retention and maximizing the storage of passive solar heat, partly thanks to the positioning of the units. For the most part, the building materials used are natural and when possible recycled, produced and sourced from the urban surroundings. Rainwater is also collected here and reused, which reduces the consumption of drinking water.

The operation of the low-energy consumption strategy is considered the concrete and decisive aspect of the project. It was studied so as to minimize the need for energy thanks to the use of low-consumption electric equipment.

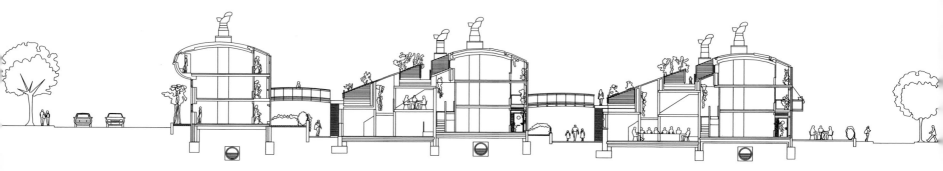

58-59 The complex's density is comparable with that of urban suburb surroundings and provides an unoccupied surface section intended for a green area far superior to average ones. The planning followed bioclimatic rules and implemented technological systems, materials and leading devices to ensure efficiency and energy saving.

58 bottom The cutaway view shows the variation of height (from one to three floors) and a profile culminating with a curved line in which the stacks are inserted.

59 bottom The thermal inertia of the buildings is increased due to the green roofs: most of the dwellings have a terraced garden and a greenhouse.

Additionally, every housing unit has differentiated garbage collection.

It would thus seem that the architects left no stone unturned in their effort to make the most of the potential in the field of technology and to curb waste and consumption, including the possibility of reducing private transportation as much as possible. The Beddington Energy Zero Development project has proved to be quite significant as it seems to address the problem of the environment while at the same time pursuing the architectural quality of the complex.   S.L.

60 top Materials with a high thermal capacity were used. The walls and attics were well insulated and triple-paned windows and photovoltaic panels were also installed. The project aimed to contain heat dispersion or thermal exchange and to favor solar captation, thanks to the exposure selected. Materials used were, for the most part, natural or recycled and produced in the surrounding area.

60 bottom BedZed has implemented a system to collect rainwater and store it in underground tanks so it can be used later for irrigation and domestic use.

60-61 Cogeneration systems were used in addition to photovoltaic panels to generate power and to heat the dwellings and produce hot water.

61 bottom The colored ventilation stacks characterize the settlement. The project pursued architectural quality through a composition including varied volumetric configurations and care in the selection of the materials used and the colored appearance.

Little Tesseract

RHINEBECK, USA

A cube made of wood, enveloped by an L-shaped volume made of steel and glass, form the addition to a small stone house situated in a luxuriant natural setting near Rhinebeck, a few miles north of New York City.

When the older house became too small for his needs, the owner decided to add two new blocks rather than demolish the original and replace it with a larger one. This choice governed the spatial and environmental quality of the three elements that comprise the house. Holl had already coped with the relationship between old and new (two fine examples of which are the offices he designed on the Sarphatistraat in Amsterdam and the reconstruction of Higgins Hall at the Pratt Institute, New York). He solved this problem by creating a new spatial reality whose complexity derived from the contrast between old and new and from the impact made by light, which played an increasingly fundamental role. The same occurs at Rhinebeck, where spaces were designed in sequence so as to highlight the different features. One enters the house via the original U-shaped part – which is characterized by the opaque quality of the stone wall and the few small apertures that this building system allows – by means of a ramp in the L-shaped addition: a one-level space that is extremely bright thanks to its transparent exoskeletal framework. Already from this point one can perceive the diagonal overlapping of the inner space of the cube, which is produced by a deformation of its top through which the zenithal light penetrates. This is the reason why the house is called "Little Tesseract". A tesseract is a mathematical formula indicating the four dimensions of a cube, a hypercube, whose principal property is the superposition of a series of inner perspectives. This became the concept of this project, and of the one the American architect was drawing up in the same period for the Department of Architecture at Cornell University. In both cases the cube is deformed in order to capture light, which floods the entire space and expands and casts it in different directions.

The spatial and phenomenic qualities thus obtained in the Little Tesseract house are closely linked to the environment, and Holl has dealt with this question in many of his recent projects, but without affecting the complexity and articulation of the bodies and the spatiality that have characterized his architectural research for years.

The intermediate body, which features a glass wall – part of which can be opened – is a continuation of the outer passageway, which can be illuminated and ventilated by natural means. Furthermore, the glass wall facing south creates a temperate zone: in winter it absorbs and retains the heat of the sun, while in summer it can be completely opened and thus allow air to circulate freely and lower the temperature in a few minutes without resorting to air conditioning.

Most of the cube is clad in wood, except for the southwest wall, which consists of glass panels that form a stack wall. In the summer the air circulates inside, cooling the rooms, and in winter the wall takes in the sunlight and gradually diffuses it throughout the structure, heating it. What is more, an artificial pool next to the house allows for the recycling of rainwater. A green roof was created over the new structure to keep it cool in the summer, and photovoltaic panels were placed on the roof of the original house to produce its own energy. G.S.

62 The north-west corner of the cube is empty and the volume is replaced by two small terraces, one on the ground level and the other on the upper level. The west side is faced with glass panels in which air circulates to form a wall-stack.

63 The new home, built to meet a need for increased space, includes two structures: a vertical parallelepiped faced with wood and a 100% glass L-shaped body on a single level wrapped around two of its sides.

64 top The L-shaped area is home to the living-room, a space whose 100% glass shell gives uninterrupted continuity to the outdoor, extremely bright landscape. The south-facing glass wall also captures and maintains heat from the sun in the winter.

64 bottom left The diagrams of the two levels of the home show the connection with the pre-existing building, which is accessed from a ramp. From this spot, the entire vertical area can be seen and the top opposite the wooden mass is distorted to allow zenith light to enter.

64 bottom right Stairs connect the living-room with the study located on the upper level. Space expands vertically here and the entire height of the building is perceived as it projects into the sky through the opening in the roof.

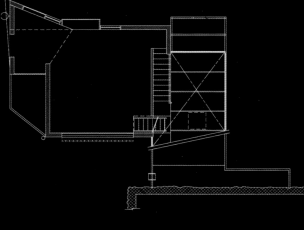

65 The north side is for the most part faced with wood, with the exception of the two large, square windows. The top of it opens up to capture zenith light.

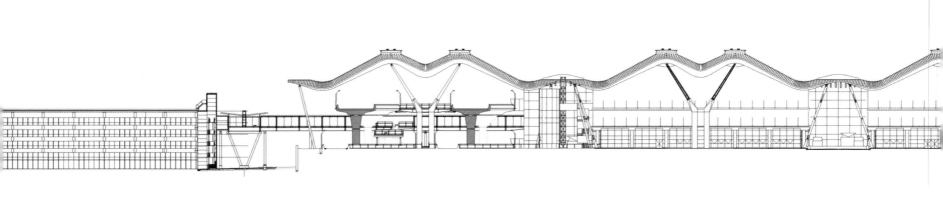

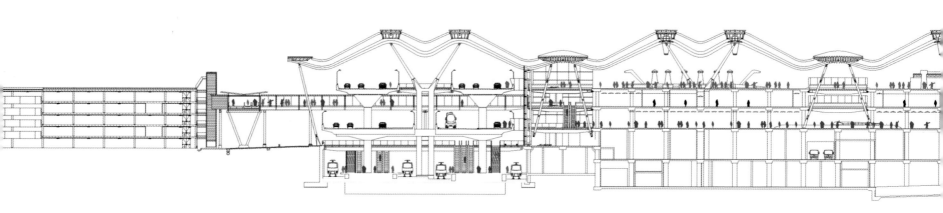

66-67 top The new terminal at Madrid Barajas Airport is a sequence
of archways sustained by tree-like columns reminiscent of the
morphology of the region surrounding Madrid.

Barajas Airport
MADRID, SPAIN

Inaugurated in 2006, the new terminal at Madrid Barajas Airport is one of the largest buildings in Europe. It is the result of a collaboration between Rogers Stirk Harbour & Partners, Estudio Lamela and TPS and Initec engineering firms. With a surface area of 13 million square feet, this complex consists of the new terminal of about 5 million square feet, the satellite (3.4 million square feet) with the boarding areas, and a garage (with a green roof that requires very little maintenance), measuring 3.6 million square feet, that can house 9,000 cars, and competes with the largest airports in Europe.

The new structure is in constant dialog with its surroundings: the series of arcades supported by wooden pillars – somewhat like a sequence of butterfly wings beating – echoes the topography of the area around Madrid, while the skylight domes dotting the large roof, between one arch and another, are like eyes that illuminate the interior and allow for efficient control of the natural light in the upper level of the terminal. In this connection, the choice of targeted rather than diffused lighting not only provides more assistance to passengers by helping them to orient themselves inside the structure, but also saves much more energy.

The relationship with the natural environment is furthered by the surrounding green areas, which are irrigated by a rainwater cistern plant.

Rogers' interest, which has always been aimed more at the city and urban context than at the architecture, and the notable size of the edifice are two major aspects that have contributed to the functional definition of a construction conceived as a small city animated by passengers in transit who move around along the repeated linear units which are covered by prefabricated steel wings. Passengers follow different types of circuits, along which it is almost impossible to get lost because there are so many visual signs helping them along the way. Furthermore, this huge complex is divided into a series of areas that impart a human scale to the terminal.

Thus the result is an inviting, attractive atmosphere whose materials, colors, finishing touches and details create a feeling of serenity.

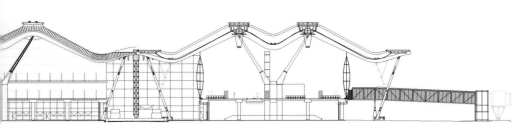

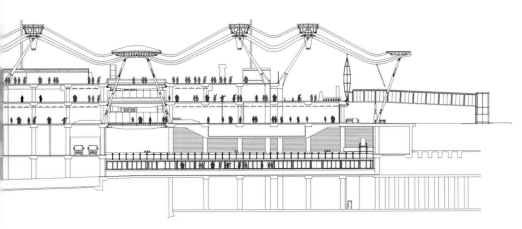

66-67 center and bottom The south-facing elevation and cutaway view of the terminal buildings (and the parking lot to the left) show the three areas of the airport under the corrugated roof and separated by the canyons.

The ceiling is made of thin strips of bamboo that form a smooth, jointless surface. By contrast, the pillars produce an infinite perspective with various nuances of color.

The lower levels of the airport complex offer a fascinating contrast with the light transparent passenger areas on the upper level, in which "canyons" invaded by the light separate the parallel levels with the passengers' "routes": from the arrival area to the check-in and security control areas and on to the boarding waiting rooms.

Like most buildings created by the Rogers Stirk Harbour & Partners studio, the Madrid Barajas terminal aims at a drastic reduction of energy consumption. In this case the saving is obtained by a system of stratified conditioning in which the ventilation mechanisms are situated in the pillars, and the air conditioning is integrated in all those areas with high passenger density.

What is more, the total shading of the facades and skylights means a strong decrease in reflection and overheating, while at the same time optimizing the conditions of natural lighting.

Lastly, the choice of a modular system for the overall floor plan will allow for enlargement in the future.   L.S.

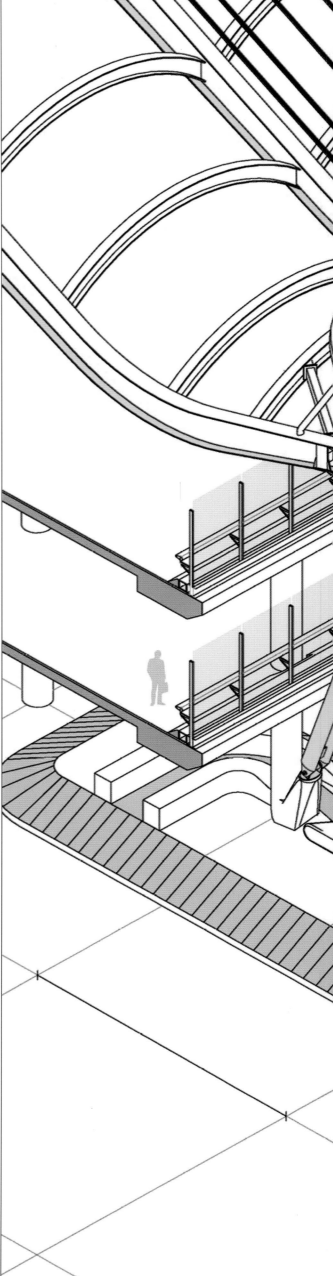

68 The check-in areas are located on the upper level in Terminal 4 while arrivals and the subway station are located on the lower level. The color strongly characterizes the area and is used as a reference element to guide passengers.

68-69 The axonometric section of the terminal shows the obvious, large eyes-skylights illuminating the areas and the isolated air-conditioning units providing ventilation in areas where passenger concentration is the heaviest.

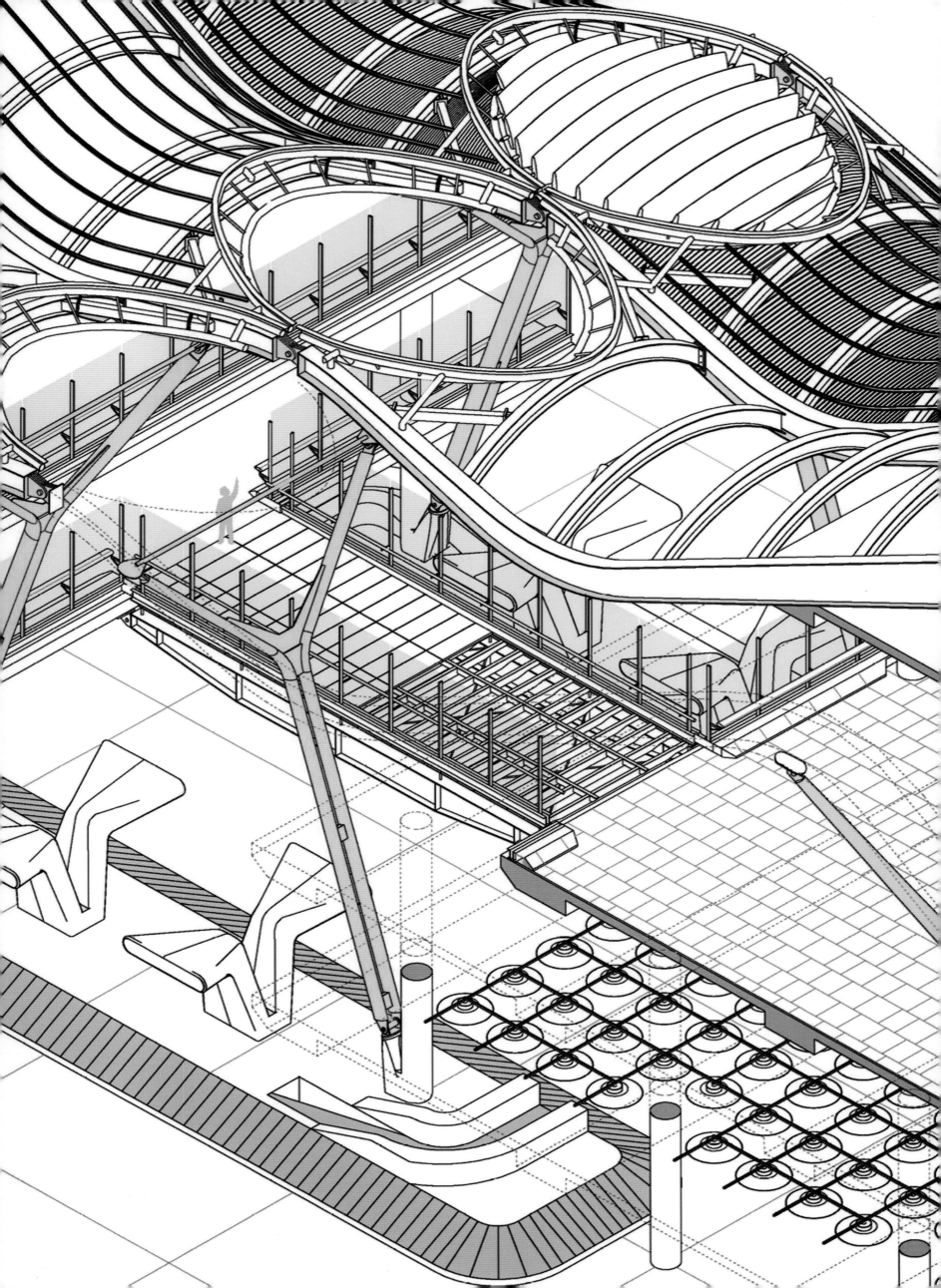

70 The view of the boarding area on the northern side highlights the sequence of pillars reproducing the colors of the rainbow.

71 Thin strips obtained from pressed bamboo blocks face the corrugated roof; subtle changes in color and the characteristic knots in the bamboo are visible.

Renovation and Expansion of the Morgan Library

NEW YORK, USA

This project involves the last enlargement phase of a building that houses an extremely interesting collection of medieval and Renaissance works. Before Renzo Piano's project was carried out, the Morgan Library consisted of three structures dating from different periods. The first one was a classical construction built in 1906 by MacKim Mead & White and commissioned by J.P. Morgan, the owner of the valuable collection. This structure was enlarged in 1928 with the addition of another building, the Annex, which was commissioned by J.P. Morgan Junior after his father's death, when it was decided to turn the collection into an institution open to the public. The third structure was added in the 1980s, utilizing the Morgan House as an integral part of the complex.

Piano's design represents the most recent enlargement phase, which confronted the two-fold challenge of creating space in an area that was almost completely utilized and of adding an innovative feature that also included environmental sustainability and amenities.

This project can therefore be regarded as an operation of urban ecology in that new spaces were created without using other areas in the city. This was achieved by occupying the available areas on the edge of the property and by creating three new structures below street level which also meet the institution's needs for security. These additions house the library's new functions: an exhibition space and reading room, areas for a permanent exhibition of part of Morgan's prestigious collections, and an auditorium and offices.

The central part of the project is a roofed urban space that is a "square" and which serves as the main entrance to the new structures and the older buildings. It is also the component of the project which affords the most compelling image of the rejuvenated foundation, which now operates as a complex system of complementary functions that are near at hand.

The limited invasiveness of the project within its context, the respect shown for the older structures, and the attention paid to environmental quality – which profited from the experience Renzo Piano's studio has with state-of-the-art knowledge of illumination technology and comfort – all impart to the new complex the great consideration of environmental sustainability typical of each work designed by the Genoese architect.

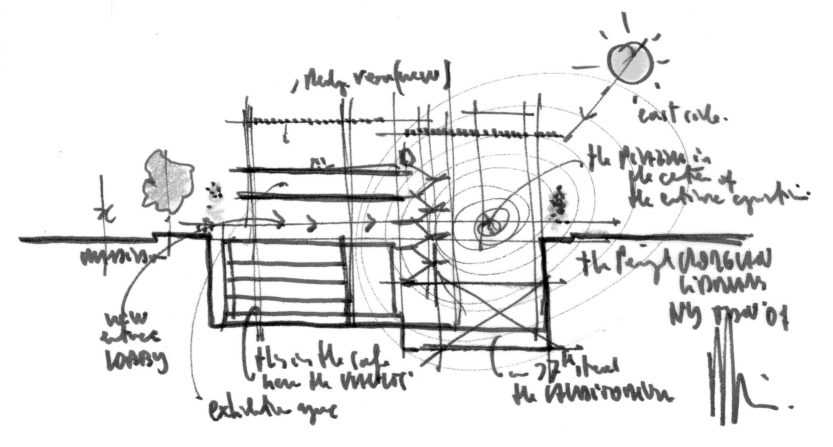

72 The expansion of the Morgan Library makes way to an area that is already densely occupied by existing buildings, which for the most part include underground structures. The project aims to ensure the public areas located above and below the street level as much natural lighting as possible, air exchange and environmental comfort.

73 The entrance to the renovated complex and the older buildings is the largest part of the intervention above ground. It provides access to every corner of the library. This structure simultaneously functions as an indoor plaza and makes use of the surrounding public areas.

74 The entrance occupies all the available
space and ends next to the existing
buildings. The formal choices, technology

74-75 In addition to the effects from the natural
lighting, the indoor quality of the entrance is also
based on an interplay of volume dividing the large

Furthermore, there is the eminently European feature of the never-ending work of stratification in a district in the heart of an urban fabric, in this case Manhattan, which is tantamount to ongoing dialog with the past, a value that has always been one of the major aims of this institution. In fact, while the project tends to implode in the available space, the parts that are visible above street level contain all those contemporary features of a building and architectural plan that is only slightly invasive, and yet pays due consideration to the possibilities of adding more significance to pre-existing structures. S.J.

Mercedes-Benz Museum

STUTTGART, GERMANY

Constructed in the outskirts of Stuttgart, the Mercedes-Benz Museum lies in the vicinity of the elevated expressway, in an area that was once identified with the football stadium, a gasometer and a factory, with rolling hills in the background.

The project meets the needs of the Mercedes-Benz firm for a showcase. It is adapted to a suburban context that is both natural and man-made and to the functional requirements of such a special exposition structure – an "automobile gallery" – and also reflects the most characteristic architectural research of UNStudio, both in terms of technology and aesthetic expression.

The museum relates principally to the infrastructure of the neighboring Daimler factory, opening out to it with its very large glass surface, thus creating a relationship between interior and exterior, between the automobiles on exhibit inside and those in circulation, while at the same time referring to the hilly landscape. The theme of mobility or movement is incorporated into the exhibition structure, which visitors can traverse freely by means of the various ramps that form a loop and that allow them to move between the two display areas – devoted to "collections" and "myths" – that relate the history and production of the Mercedes firm.

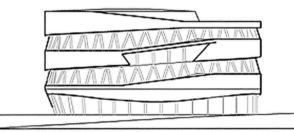

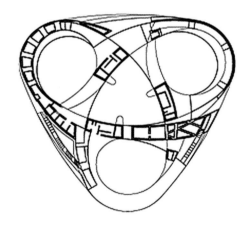

77 center The theme of fluidity and continuity between the spaces can be seen in the elevation and design details. UNStudio used this project to re-propose the concept of the Möbius strip (already used in another project), which led to imagining continuous areas where the boundary between the functional areas vanishes and simultaneously, the net differentiation between sections disappears.

77 bottom The perspective section through the exhibit and distribution area. This drawing succinctly describes the natural exchange of air: the central space in the entrance hall serves as a large ventilation stack.

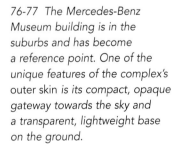

76-77 The Mercedes-Benz Museum building is in the suburbs and has become a reference point. One of the unique features of the complex's outer skin is its compact, opaque gateway towards the sky and a transparent, lightweight base on the ground.

77 top The museum's offices are housed externally in a space constituting an ample amphitheater.

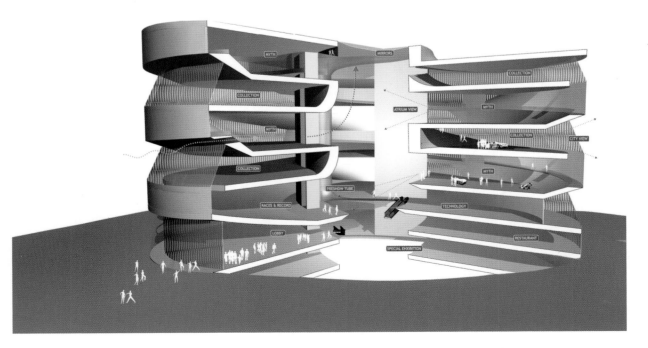

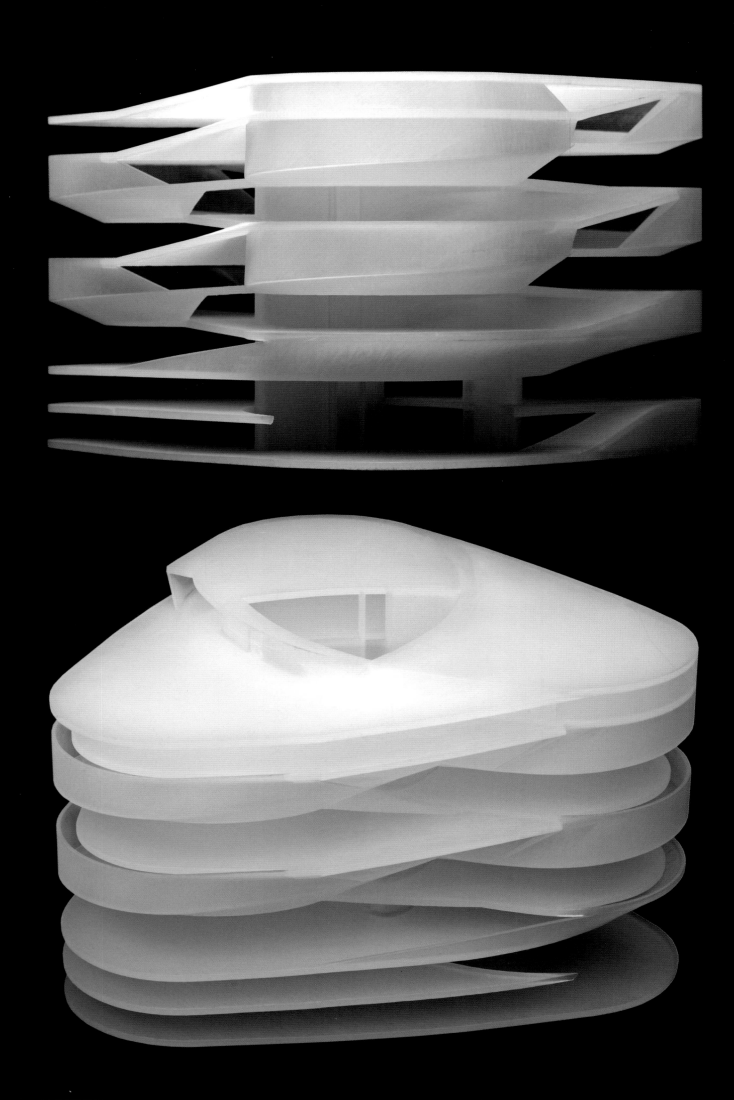

78 The plastic model (seen from the side and from above) only indicates the opaque parts of the project and completely leaves out the transparent surface areas to clarify the continuity between the exhibit and distribution areas wrapped around the central entrance hall. This hollow space is identified by three vertical elements similar to large pillars, which house the elevators and service areas.

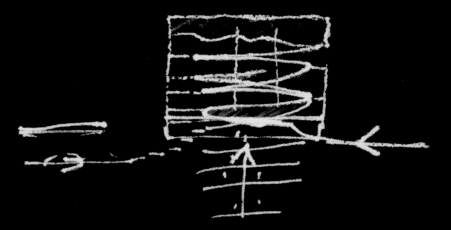

The architects planned the route of the visit to be a descending one, proceeding from top to bottom, and just past the entrance there are elevators that take visitors to the top floor, where the visit begins. The very concept of the project was based on the Möbius strip – already utilized by this team of architects – which suggests the continuous movement of spaces in which the exhibition functions follow one another and the confines separating the various sections are vague. In this sense the museum creates a feeling of disorientation, a state of confusion, that you may experience along the visitors' route, while at the same time being fully aware that you cannot possibly get lost, since by following the ramps you inevitably arrive at the lowest section of the museum, which marks the end of the visit. Furthermore, this spiral route leads one to consider the questions of the "pedestal" and of how one observes the exhibition; questions that are an integral part of museology problems. The route follows ramps situated along the outer perimeter of the exhibition spaces and not only favors thoughtful observation, such as can be had by being in the same exhibition rooms, but also dynamic and multiple viewing, with a 360° variation of the vantage points that oscillate from above to below. At the same time the UNStudio architects wanted to contradict the idea of a museum as a work of architecture being more important than what it contains. They therefore designed a building that rests on the ground in the guise of a glass "shell". In other words, the conception of the museum is the very negation of a pedestal, as it does not entail any sort of "solid" contact with the ground, thus creating the "non-celebration" of the architectural work.

In keeping with this approach the project did not neglect the ethical aspect and therefore took the bioclimatic factor into consideration. The floor plan of the museum is a spiraling shell with three "vertexes" – a reference to the Mercedes trademark – and there is an empty space in the interior that functions as a ventilation duct. Moreover, the opaque parts of the building envelope present an external casing that is a ventilated wall.

This aspect rounds off the idea of a new type of museum that also betrays the influence of other famous architectural works: the National Gallery in Berlin, designed by Ludwig Mies van der Rohe (the flexibility and continuity of the exhibition spaces); Frank Lloyd Wright's Guggenheim Museum in New York (the use of ramps as the visitors' itinerary); and the Centre Georges Pompidou in Paris designed by Rogers and Piano (the position of the visitors' routes, which animates the interior and is an open invitation to experience the museum to the full). S.L.

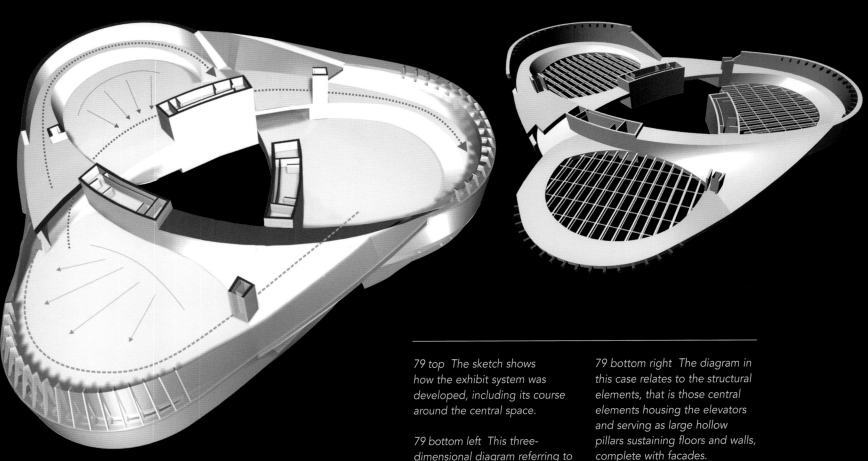

79 top The sketch shows how the exhibit system was developed, including its course around the central space.

79 bottom left This three-dimensional diagram referring to a part of the museum shows the internal distribution system of the exhibit areas, galleries and stairs.

79 bottom right The diagram in this case relates to the structural elements, that is those central elements housing the elevators and serving as large hollow pillars sustaining floors and walls, complete with facades.

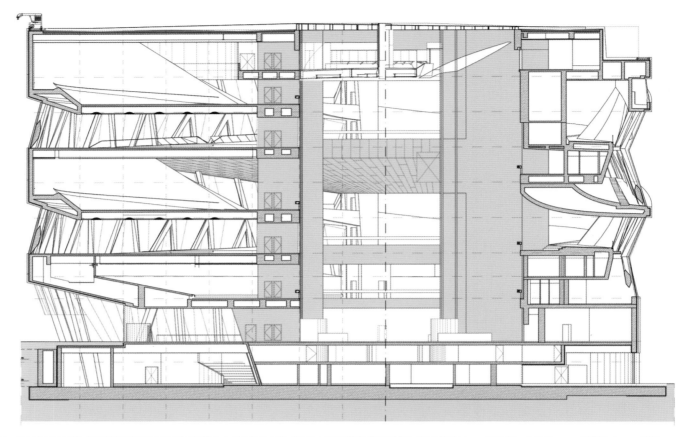

80 top The cutaway view shows how alternating spaces-solid portions characterizing the elevation are perceived from the inside. On the outside, transparent walls reveal the movement by individuals on the stairs, while internal walls connect the building with the urban surroundings and infrastructures.

80 center The sought-after relationship with the surrounding infrastructures aims to relate the cars on display with those on the road. The theme of mobility and/or movement is introjected in the exhibit area where the visitor is an itinerant observer who freely moves along the area's routes and stairs.

80 bottom The detail describes the facade: alternating glass and opaque portions penetrate the air and contribute to its natural exchange through the entrance hall.

81 The building's closing, opaque surface areas are externally faced with aluminum panels.

UNSTUDIO

82 The picture is an upwards shot of the large space in the central entrance hall overlooked by the exhibit areas and routes. The space is characterized by three vertical elements with elevators that transport visitors to the beginning of the route. The top ceiling is equipped with a system to shield and diffuse natural light.

82-83 The museum was conceived to study a new exhibit system able to display a unique product such as automobiles. In addition to identifying a system to visit the areas and their sequence, the matter of the pedestal and possible exhibit methods were also dealt with to ensure the exhibit was as diversified as possible.

84 and 85 bottom The sequence of interior photographs describes several exhibit possibilities offered by the museum. To ensure the cars displayed are completely experienced by the visitors, they can be seen both in the standard fashion (standing in the rooms and contemplating the objects) or in a more dynamic manner from several perspectives (from the stairs and the areas overlooking the exhibit areas through the entrance hall) up to 360° oscillating from top to bottom.

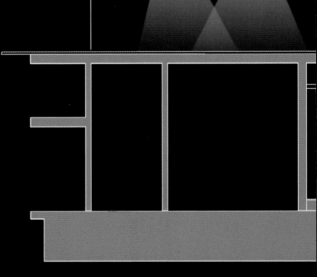

84-85 The building's various lighting systems resolve all of the museum's needs by integrating and varying the most diffused light in several areas to sensational lighting in others.

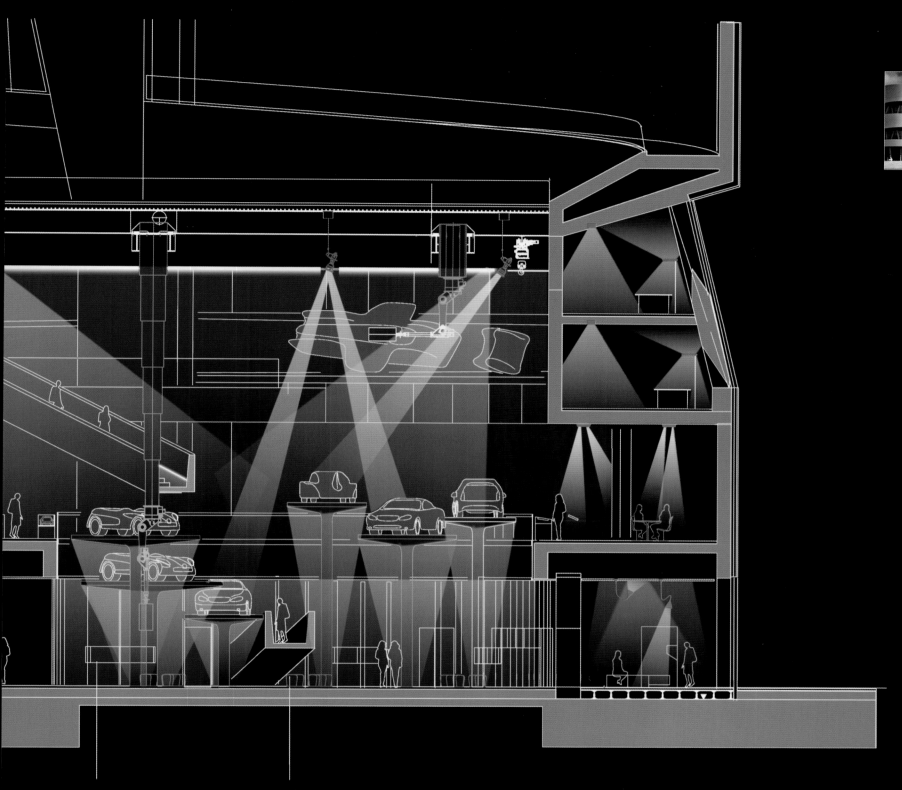

Academy School Discovery Canyon
COLORADO, USA

The Academy School Discovery Canyon is a center for meetings and communication among the students, the school and visitors; in other words, a place for learning. While the various scholastic levels are usually separated into elementary, middle and high schools, here all 12 public school grades are united.

The person who conceived this complex is the American architect Antoine Predock, whose poetic vision interprets the empty spaces of the desert landscape through a network of relationships with natural elements. The project called for classrooms that project outwards toward terraces and courts used for playing and educational purposes, making optimum use of natural light for the rooms and spaces in the interior.

This didactic complex comprises a continuous series of spaces; a flexible structure that interacts with the seasonal changes of the Colorado Springs environment.

The east-west orientation of the complex and the treatment of the framework of the school's architectural volumes, with a marked preference for horizontality, help to mitigate the effect of the harsh winters and the cold west wind.

The objects and volumes scattered over the terrain create an abstract landscape whose masonry color was carefully selected in order to blend with the site. The surface of the terrain is enhanced with a rich variety of plants and grasses typical of this area of the Rocky Mountains of Colorado.

The areas used for sports, gardens, the amphitheater, the pool and the riparian habitat all form an integral part of the school by merging with it. The theater, gymnasium and administration offices are on the south side of the canyon, which ends with a pool laid out close to the elementary school.

86 The pictures respectively depict a view of the building from the school and the campus entrance with the Colorado Rocky Mountains in the background.

86-87 top This view of the Spiral Plaza, which is one of the Academy
School Discovery Canyon's outdoor areas, shows a section of slate
wall hangings.

86-87 bottom The rooms in the 12 public schools on the Academy
School Discovery Canyon overlook courtyards and terraces home
to games and teaching.

ANTOINE PREDOCK ARCHITECT PC

88 The axonometric exploded diagram illustrates the complexity of the facility: the sequence of areas defines an abstract landscape, an observatory and a participatory area.

The pool contains life forms and serves as an educational tool, teaching the value of preserving and safeguarding the various living species.

The views of Pikes Peak – one of the tallest in the Rocky Mountains and a popular attraction throughout the United States – were one of the priorities of Predock's project.

The building functions as an observation and participatory space on various levels and the basic principles of scientific thought are closely linked to the school and the site.

The gravity tests carried out on the science terraces, the observation of the sun and the study of the systems of solar thermal control, both active and passive, reveal its movement and course. The courts that open out among the constructions echo the alternation of the seasons by means of the broad-leaved deciduous trees and the planting strategies based on ethical permaculture.

The towers and bridges relate to the topography of the canyon and at the same time identify one of the programmatic elements of the project: the fusion of different schools, ages and groups.

In the intelligent play of volumes and three-dimensional figures that are spaced out and staggered, placed together and separated, and partly hidden, Predock realizes his metaphor for the canyon.   L.S.

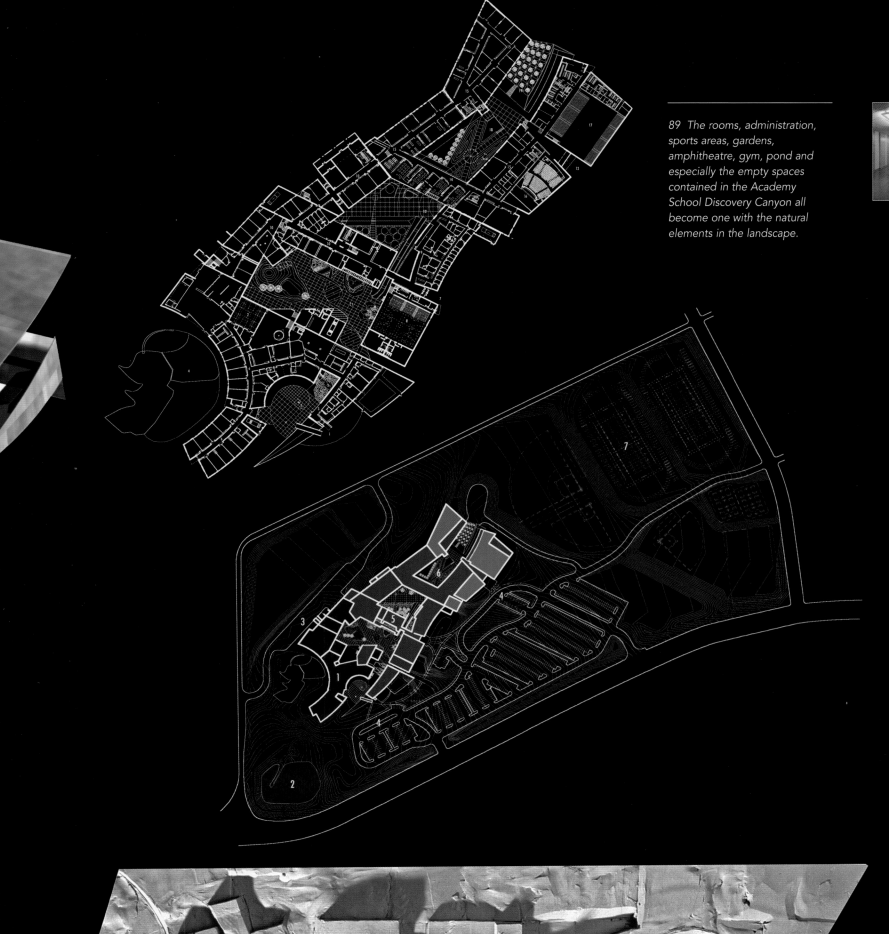

ANTOINE PREDOCK ARCHITECT PC

89 The rooms, administration, sports areas, gardens, amphitheatre, gym, pond and especially the empty spaces contained in the Academy School Discovery Canyon all become one with the natural elements in the landscape.

90-91 The school's squares contain areas for circulation and recreation while offering true didactic opportunities: the places on the campus demonstrate specific scientific principles.

90 bottom The elementary-school rooms can be identified by the colors belonging to the so-called visible spectrum in the electromagnetic spectrum.

91 bottom Majestic Pikes Peak, one of the highest in the Rocky Mountains, is visible behind the regular buildings in the Academy School Discovery Canyon whose focus was on horizontality.

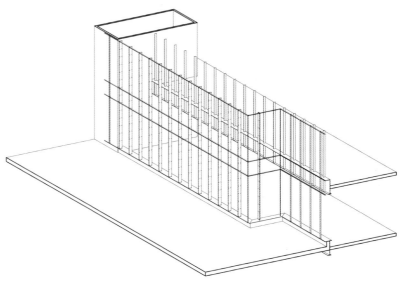

Pabellón de España

ZARAGOZA, SPAIN

This building lies in the broad context of the 2008 Zaragoza Expo, which was dedicated to water and sustainable development. Since this city is washed by three rivers (the Ebro, Gallego and Huerva), it was only natural that it should choose water and sustainable development as the themes of this major exposition. Indeed, the theme of water continued to live on even after the closure of the Expo: the end of the event was marked by the signing of the so-called Zaragoza Charter for the defense of water resources, by which the capital of Aragon will become the UN water conservation headquarters as well as one of the world centers of research on climatic change. Among the buildings featured at the Expo (which covered a surface area of 25 hectares, an area that will be converted into a pole for the development of business, cultural and public administration), one of the most highly acclaimed was the Pabellón de España (Spanish Pavilion), which covers an area of 114,000 square feet. The pavilion was designed by the Spanish architect Francisco José (Patxi) Mangado Beloqui (in collaboration with the Centro Nacional de Energías Renovables de Pamplona, or National Center for Renewable Energy of Pamplona), who won the competition for the design. The recurrent metaphor used to describe this structure is a forest: a forest of poplars, a bamboo forest, and a forest of terracotta columns. Certainly, the tall ceramic columns are quite important, because they make a major contribution to the rhythm of the glass facade, which produces an intermediate space between the interior and exterior, and because these columns are able to collect and preserve water at a constant temperature and then vaporize it into air currents toward the low area of the portico, which cools the interior and also creates a microclimate around the entire structure. The 750 columns (39 and 52 feet high), whose placement seems to be random, consist of a metal core covered with layers of insulating terra cotta that are equal and superposed and can easily absorb water. But if we leave aside for a moment the nature metaphor, it might be more apt, as the Italian architect

Enrico Molteni suggests, to refer to a classical temple, whose columned area (peristyle) in ancient Greece and Rome surrounded the area (*cella* or *naos*) housing the statue of the god to whom the temple was dedicated. The large roof, which rests on the profiled columns, covers the entire surface of the pavilion and is made up of panels of wood shavings. The thickness of the roof (10 feet) allows for the placement of solar heat and rainwater collectors, the former to produce energy and the latter to collect water that is then used in the pavilion's cooling system. The pavilion is made of such classic building materials as wood, cork, galvanized steel and crystal, as well as the above-mentioned terra cotta and water.

The exhibition areas inside the pavilion, which occupy a space of 86,000 square feet distributed on three levels, were built with hardboard planks and recycled resin and are divided into five halls enveloped by the rows of columns. The glass panels, which are adequately insulated, can be utilized as mobile partitions, resulting in a high level of flexibility – an indispensable feature in the use of the pavilion as an exhibition space. The panels also provide the total visual and acoustical insulation needed for the future use of the pavilion as a cinema center. The other buildings, which housed the exhibition spaces of the other countries that participated in the exposition, were designed to become offices in the future. When the Expo ended on 14 September 2008, it was admitted that the outcome did not meet expectations, and not all the structures and pavilions built expressly for this event were sold. However, as was stated above and as had been planned, the organizers and the local administrations hope to succeed in converting the complex into a large park for scientific-industrial development.   L.S.

92 top The layout of the columns and rear position of the glass buildings in the pavilion create an in-between area, a passageway and mediation place between the indoor and outdoor areas.

92 bottom The overview of the building shows how it is characterized by a series of dense, high ceramic columns

that contribute to the measured articulation of the glass facade behind the portico.

93 This section shows ceramic shafts in the foreground positioned in an apparently casual manner. They gave rise to the recurring metaphor of bamboo and poplar forests in the descriptions of this building.

FRANCISCO JOSÉ MANGADO BELOQUI

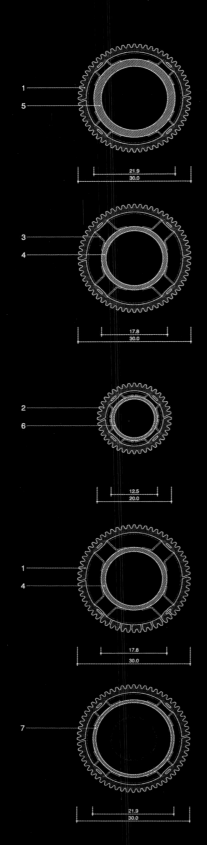

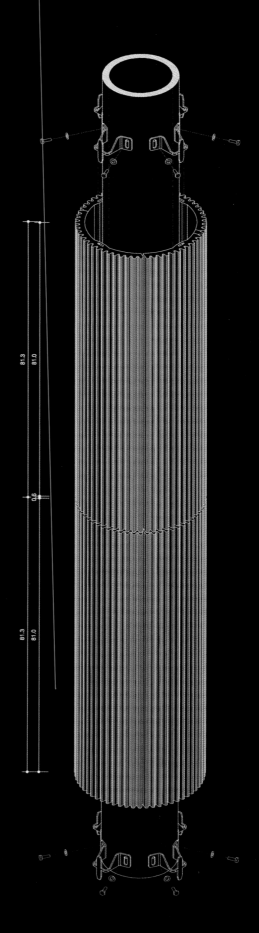

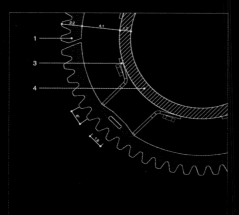

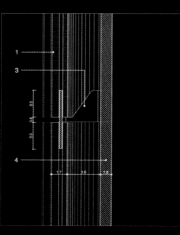

94 The pillar (whose construction detail is shown here) consists of an iron pipe with a diameter of 0.5in., 0.7in. and 0.9in. and whose thickness ranges from 0.3-0.8in. and a ceramic facing with semi-circular sections 0.6in. thick. The special ceramic piece is fastened with aluminum supports screwed onto the iron pipe.

95 This view over the paths on the water among the ceramic bamboo shows the ability of the Spanish architect to reconstruct and evoke the verticality and depth of a forest.

96 The black cork facing the ceiling shown in this picture shows the designer's interest in natural or recycled Spanish materials, such as the wood and ceramic used in the building.

97 The significant presence of 750 thin pillars like many overlapping layers reminiscent of the colonnades in traditional temples (peristasis) also indicates the pathways through the exhibits.

98 and 99 The exhibit areas in the pavilion cover 86,000 square feet and are separated in five halls. These rooms were built with particle board planks and recycled resin and were designed to meet the need of flexibility required by exhibits and to complete the visual and acoustic insulation in the event the building was reutilized as a cinematographic center.

100-101 The evening view of one of the building's facades emphasizes the presence of the diaphanous mass appearing in the voids left by the column forest.

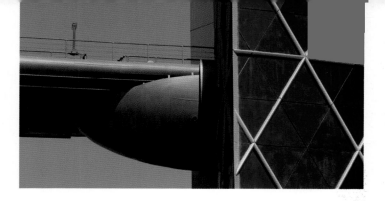

Bahrain World Trade Center

MANAMA, BAHRAIN

The Bahrain World Trade Center (BWTC), one of the more than 300 centers that make up the World Trade Center Association, is one of the tallest buildings in Bahrain. Situated in Manama, this edifice has been called "a wind skyscraper" because of its three 95 ft-diameter wind turbines which are supported by three horizontal bridges. These bridges weigh about 68 tons each and connect two identical 50-story towers that are 787 feet high and shaped like sails. The project was the work of the Atkins studio in collaboration with Norwin, a firm which specializes in wind turbines. The BWTC is the first architectural work in the world to incorporate generators of this scale into its design. The elliptical shape of the two towers will help to funnel and accelerate the flow of air between the edifices, thus improving the efficiency of the wind turbines, which face north, from where the winds in the Persian Gulf mostly blow. The projected energy yield from the turbines amounts to between 1,100 and 1,300 MWh per year which is approximately 11% to 15% of the office tower's electrical energy consumption. This is the equivalent to lighting more than 250 homes for more than a year. In carbon emission terms this equates to an average of 55,000 kgC (UK electricity basis). These figures are conservative, since this is a world first, and as wind turbines have never before been placed 525 feet above ground level and between buildings, the yield may even be higher. Glass and steel are the materials used in the construction of this building and the frame of the panoramic sails that house offices, banks, as well as fine dining restaurants and cafés, a fitness centre, shops and a prestigious 5-star hotel. Notably, one of the features of this iconic and innovative development is MODA Mall which is located on the ground floor of the BWTC. It is a high-end boutique shopping mall, with tenants comprising a veritable who's who of the global fashion community. The tenant portfolio is hand-picked to offer MODA Mall's clientele a truly exclusive shopping experience, and sees many international luxury designer brands opening their own dedicated outlets for the first time in Bahrain. The foundation of these tapered architectural structures facing King Faisal Highway has a large central-plan courtyard illuminated by a skylight that is shaded by a network of large triangular screens which reduce the sunlight in the hottest part of the day. Furthermore, there is parking space for 1,700 cars. The shape of the BWTC – with its twin towers that taper increasingly as they move upward, its turbines and three bridges – was created to make the best use of the wind energy of the Gulf and at the same time is a successful attempt at making an energy-producing mechanism beautiful. This work has become one of the landmarks of the city. After months of wind tunnel tests, analysis and optimization procedures, in April 2008 the wind turbines became officially operational and began to rotate simultaneously. Shaun Killa, the Atkins chief architect, stated that the BWTC represents a significant project that testifies to a special technology destined to become a fundamental element in future sustainable design. L.S.

---

102 The gigantic wind blades (95 feet in diameter) are located in the center of the two large skyscrapers in the World Trade Center Association in Manama (Bahrain).

103 top The picture depicts the detail of one of the three walkways-bridges connecting the two twin towers.

103 bottom The two glass and steel towers similar to large sails are united by three pillars equipped with three wind blades. The building appears as an aeolian skyscraper due to the three wind turbines that generate part of the power required by the center.

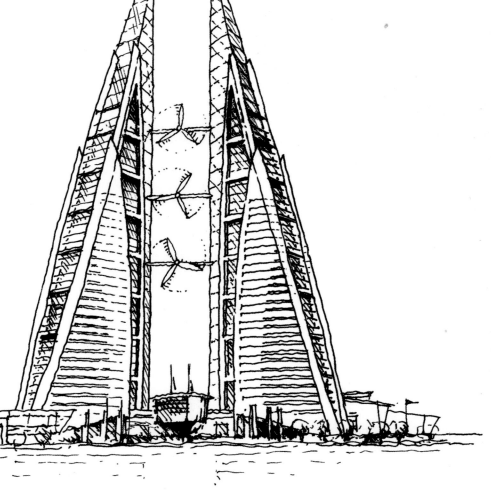

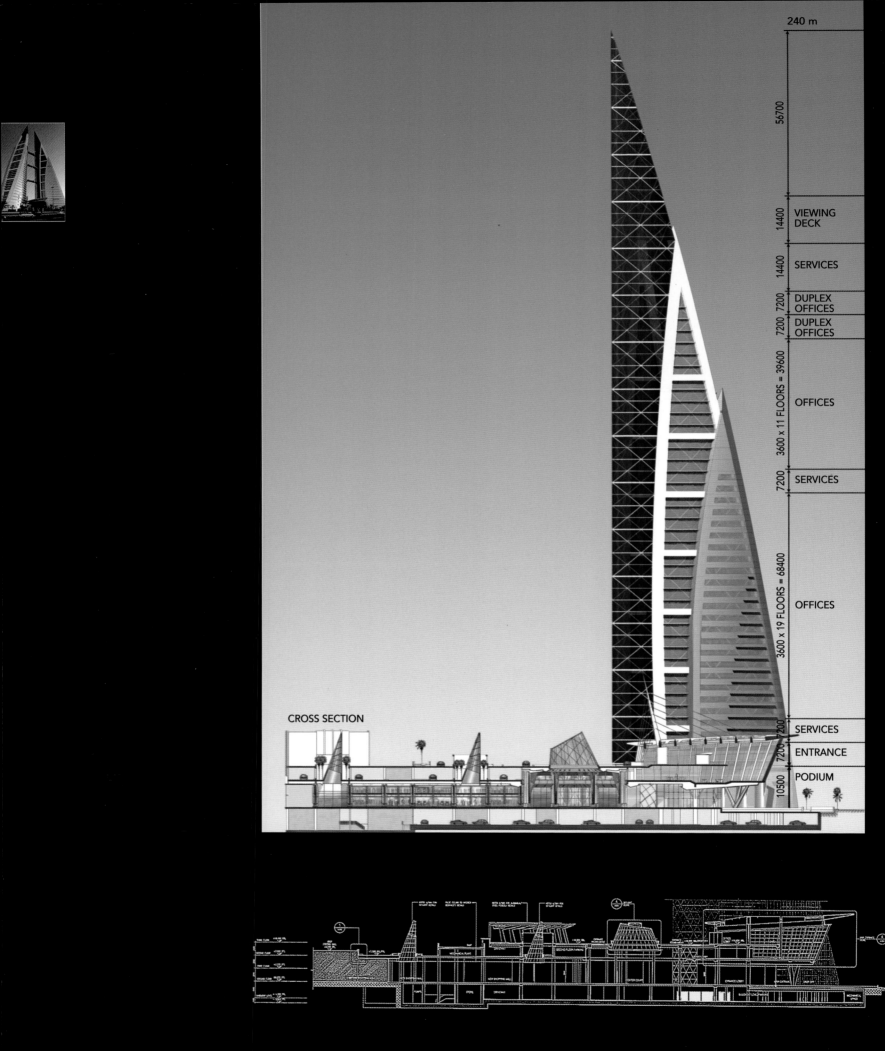

240 m

56700

VIEWING DECK — 14400

SERVICES — 14400

DUPLEX OFFICES — 7200

DUPLEX OFFICES — 7200

OFFICES — 3600 x 11 FLOORS = 39600

SERVICES — 7200

OFFICES — 3600 x 19 FLOORS = 68400

SERVICES — 7200

ENTRANCE — 7200

PODIUM — 10500

CROSS SECTION

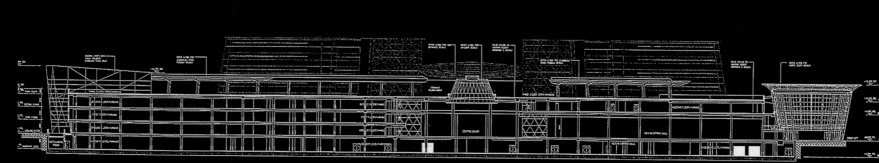

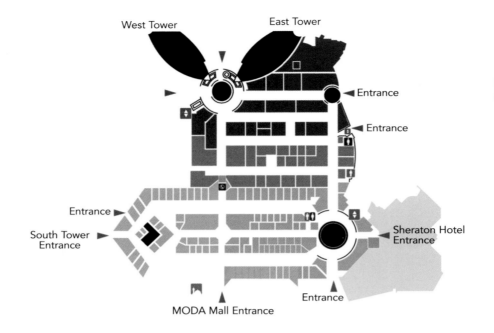

West Tower

East Tower

◀ Entrance

◀ Entrance

Entrance ▶

South Tower
Entrance ▶

Sheraton Hotel
Entrance ◀

Entrance ▶

MODA Mall Entrance

106 top The distribution layout
of the ground level shows the
location of the entrances to the
MODA Mall and the hotel. The
two towers are decentralized
with respect to the planimetric
development of the square.

106 bottom The image was
taken inside one of the two
towers, officially opened in
mid-2008: in the foreground
a view of the structural
window with point-fastened
glass spider fittings.

107 The picture of the foyer
shows the large brushed-steel,
spiral stairway, the flooring and
the support-column facing for
the stairway in precious marble,
and the structural glass wall with
spiders to point fasten the sheets.

paolo soleri *(arcosanti)* - renzo pi

tjibaou cultural center) - glenn murcu

sean godsell architects *(woodleigh*

deboer architects *(pabellón zeri)* - s

kuma and associates *(great ba*

aravena *(quinta monroy)*

low tech:
local natural materials for
sustainable architecture

no building workshop *(jean marie*

(arthur & yvonne boyd education center) -

:chool science building) - simón vélez-

geru ban *(japanese pavilion) -* kengo

boo wall) - elemental-alejandro

low tech:
local natural materials for sustainable architecture

In the 1970s, great concern over the first oil crisis led to an awareness of the need for ecological architecture, but only rarely did architects adopt an approach which resulted in low tech solutions.

However, in recent years there has been a widespread, endemic interest in architecture whose objective is to live in harmony with the Earth and that often coincides with the use of natural materials, which are at times "poor" but are utilized intelligently and in new ways: architecture dominated by modesty and decency, sensitive ecology.

The prevailing values of the "smooth and polished" espoused by modernism (understood as the aesthetic sensitivity that dominated industrialized society on an international level roughly from the 1950s to the end of the 20th century) is discarded in favor of what the Japanese call wabi-sabi: the cult of the imperfect and rough, of the beauty of temporary, unfinished, humble and even unusual things.

In this case the primary sources of inspiration are simplicity, naturalness, and the acceptance of reality, as exemplified in the work of the Rural Studio, a project workshop in the poverty-stricken countryside of Alabama connected to Auburn University, that conceives architecture prevalently as a social commitment. Building for the poor in this area allows the students of architecture in the university to deal firsthand with the difficulties of on-site construction and to learn the ABC of architecture through personal, hands-on experience. Most of the buildings constructed in the past 15 years are intended for the public at large: houses for low-income families, meeting places, children's playgrounds, markets for local farm products and service structures for the nature reserves. Here the projects are drawn up together with the locals for whom they are intended, in a sort of wide-ranging participatory, shared planning which, based on the mystical inspiration of its founder, Samuel Mockbee (who died in 2001), produces a type of architecture solidly and concretely rooted in the reality of the area.

In the low tech approach to architecture it is the observation of nature that leads to truth. Neglected or seemingly insignificant details take on importance, and become the distinguishing features. A case in point is the architecture of the Australian Richard Leplastrier, who creates simple, comfortable, relaxing spaces for those who live or work in the structures he builds. They can suddenly open out and become new spaces with new confines, qualities and contents, which are equally simple and complete in themselves, and which then open out once again, forming a third or an infinite number of spaces, all with the same qualities. This is a question of equilibrium, reciprocity and respect for nature, and the rights of the site and its context.

A moral principle that aims at doing away with everything superfluous and at concentrating on the essential aspects whilst ignoring the normal "hierarchy" of building materials lies at the basis of Colombian architect Simón Vélez's criticism of those compatriots who still build with reinforced concrete or bricks. In Vélez's opinion, utilizing these materials for construction in a country that abounds in bamboo is nothing more nor less than the abusive use of technology, given that Guadua angustifolia, a species of bamboo that is particularly well adapted for building, produces oxygen and makes it possible to erect structures which cost only 10% the amount normally spent on concrete buildings.

He proposes buildings made of bamboo – whether they are the luxury homes of rich Colombians, low-cost houses, bridges, or the bus stops in Bogotá – as a means of adapting and responding to the country's climate. Because of his famous buildings with their large roofs that almost look like the hats of mariachi band members, Vélez has been called the roof architect: an expression of a country and its climate.

Disputing the rigid, cold nature of modernist constructions, many architects, some of them internationally famous, such as Japanese Shigeru Ban, have encouraged those who will work or live in the structures to take part in their design and even in their construction. This anti-authoritarian philosophy has inspired some of his best-known works, made of recycled paper and cardboard tubes. Examples of these are the Paper Church in Kobe, which was built in five weeks by 160 volunteers after the disastrous 1995 earthquake; the 50 temporary Paper Log Houses, each of which was built in only six hours by a group of students for the homeless Vietnamese community; and the shelters for the refugees in Ruanda who fled from the ethnic war of 1994. Again made of paper tubes, this reduced the serious deforestation problem caused in Ruanda by two million refugees who wanted to fell trees to build new dwellings.

A personal dislike and rejection of wastefulness and the discovery of cardboard tubes (those normally used to roll up plastic material or cloth) led to the birth of paper architecture, which culminated in the construction of the Japanese Pavilion at the Expo 2000 in Hanover, in collaboration with German architect Frei Otto, in which all types of structural technological joints were abolished and replaced by ones made of cloth.

Evoking a natural process made up of irregularity, intimacy, modesty, coarseness, indetermination and simplicity is the strategy of the Italian architect Paolo Soleri. The major exponent of low tech, or even better, of "no tech", Soleri merged the two disciplines of architecture and ecology into "arcology" to propose a new type of city, which he called Arcosanti. This is a condensed city in which the buildings and human activities are concentrated to the utmost, quite the opposite of what occurs in our contemporary cities, in which the maximum dispersion prevails. The implosion of the megalopolises foreseen by Soleri will lead to a new, more efficient city, in which concentration and complexity will be governed by the intelligent and perspicacious use of technology, without wasting space, energy and resources.

The examples provided in this section by no means take in all aspects of low tech architecture, nor is there any attempt to set them against high tech architecture. They are merely aimed at providing an overall, albeit discontinuous, view of the singular type of global research that reveals a well governed architecture in which the use of mostly natural building material makes for less energy consumption, without risking a return to models directly inspired by traditional architectural works and "neo-regional" stereotypes, which often prove to be inadequate as regards respect of both the natural and man-made environments. On the contrary, these examples reveal a wise mixture of building material, personality and aspirations that integrate the protection of the environment with the natural ambition to be a part of one's own time.   L.S.

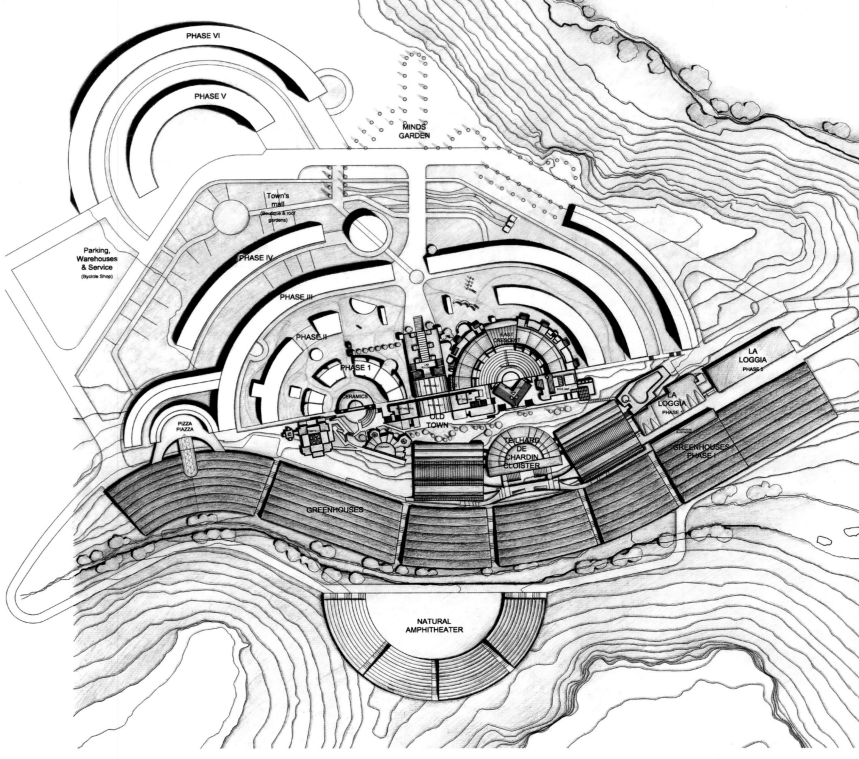

PHASE VI

PHASE V

MINDS
GARDEN

Town's
mall
(Boutique & roof
gardens)

Parking,
Warehouses
& Service
(Bycicle Shop)

PHASE IV

PHASE III

PHASE II

PHASE 1

CERAMICS

CRESCENT

OLD
TOWN

LA
LOGGIA
PHASE 2

LA
LOGGIA
PHASE 1

GREENHOUSES
PHASE I

PIZZA
PIAZZA

TEILHARD
DE
CHARDIN
CLOISTER

GREENHOUSES

NATURAL
AMPHITHEATER

112-113 top The planimetry (original design) of a section of the Arcosanti complex shows the phases of the new and future building.

112-113 bottom The overview clearly shows the Craft Three building in the center and a glimpse of the Ceramic Apse on the right.

113 Paolo Soleri gave life to this utopian project on a desert plateau in Arizona in front of a canyon in the 70s. The picture shows a phase of the work, which has been ongoing for more than 30 years, making Arcosanti a city in progress.

Arcosanti

ARIZONA, USA

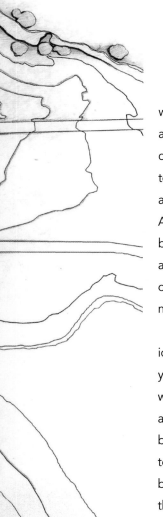

Arcosanti is an urban laboratory in which for over 30 years students, volunteers and researchers from all over the world have been experimenting with a prototype of a city intended for 5,000 inhabitants. It is an urban system whose aim is to become an alternative to the development of metropolises and their squalid outskirts in order to resolve the pressing problems of temporal and spatial relations and those related to energy consumption by minimizing waste. Arcosanti, a utopian city that has become a reality, was conceived by Paolo Soleri, an architect from Turin, who after constructing an initial series of buildings at Cosanti (a combination of *cosa* or "thing" and *anti*), decided to expand the size of the urban nucleus and purchased an even larger tract of land.

Thus, in the 1970s, on a desert plateau in Arizona, his ideal city began to take shape, extending its borders every year. Designed and realized by Soleri himself, in keeping with the principles of "Arcology", a new discipline combining architecture and ecology, the city developed horizontally, but by layers, in a complex 34-level structure. Soleri set out to concentrate the community in a limited space that would be totally self-sufficient and without any automobiles, and that would blend in harmoniously with the environment without harming it. A condensed city, as it were, in which the buildings and human activities achieved maximum concentration, just the opposite of the dispersion typical of our present-day cities.

Arcosanti is a city in progress made of earth and concrete.

The key word in Soleri's philosophy is "frugality", which in Arcosanti materializes above all in the "do more with less", that is, fewer energy resources, less pollution, and less wasted space and material.

One of the most interesting aspects of the city is the attention paid to the quality of life, both from an architectural and social standpoint. Of paramount importance in Soleri's philosophy is the construction of a human habitat that is receptive to, and in well-balanced interaction with nature, through an understanding and assimilation of the structure, connections and various relationships of the latter. The community's activities take place – at times overlapping – in the protective apses and large open spaces that remind us so much of ancient Roman basilicas and baths, as well as in the glazed-domed houses that blend in so well with the land.

Large structures in the shape of half domes whose upper floors are arranged in a semicircle, large barrel vaults, and concrete arches the color of earth that remind one of traditional Indian villages: all these architectural creations have a strong visual impact; they are structures that interact with the natural and urban surroundings and take in the irregular flow of life in the town.

The shape of the buildings is closely linked to that of the city itself, so much so that is it difficult to distinguish the one from the other. But Arcosanti is not only architecture, since the urban

laboratory also has a department for the design and construction of greenhouses for organic farming. Part of the energy needed to keep Arcosanti going comes from a wind generator and solar panels, and one of the objectives of the city is to become totally energy self-sufficient. The community of Arcosanti finances itself almost exclusively through the production and sale of the Soleri wind bells: bronze and ceramic bells whose thin metal sails make them ring solely with the force of the wind. Now, more than 30 years after the project began to take shape, the constructed area consists of barely 5% of what was originally planned.

Arcosanti is open to the public and is visited by around 50,000 people every year.   L.S.

114-115 and 115 The Craft Three (sketches also shown here) is home to the Visitor Center, a gallery, baker's shop and a coffee shop. Passageways and spatial hollows open up in the above-ground building. The drawings and sketches illustrating the concept behind this and other buildings were taken from Paolo Soleri's sketchbook. He is responsible for elaborating the new discipline of arcology, a source of inspiration behind the creation of this desert city.

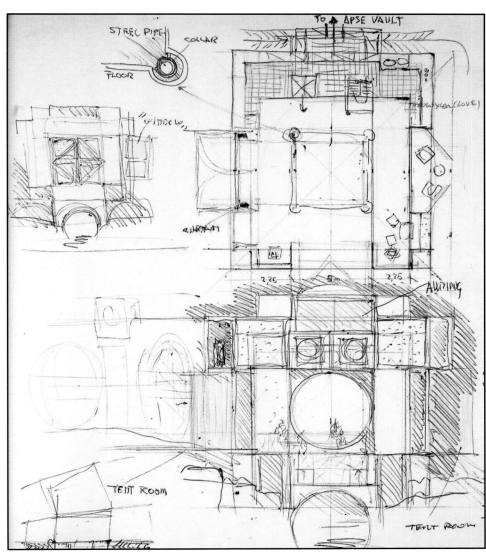

116 top The Ceramic Apse (built in 1972) is characterized by a large molding connected to the arch. The arch on the facade was first prefabricated on site and then served as a support and reference for the Foundry Apse, a near-by structure built later. Both buildings have a radius of 23 feet.

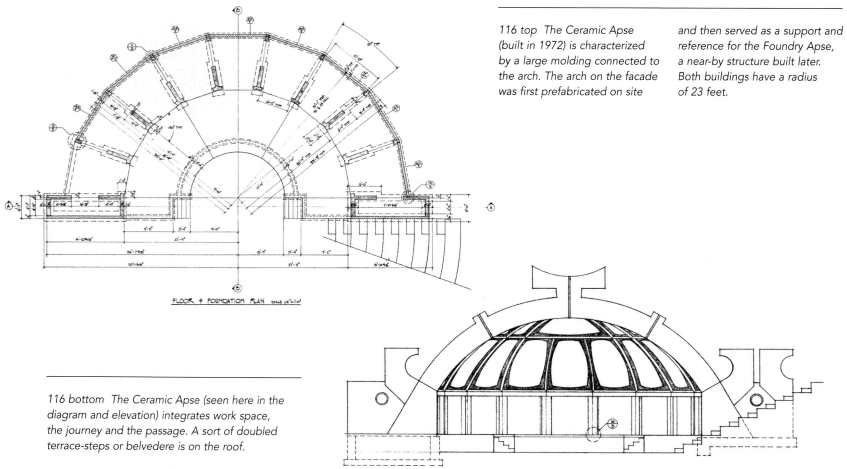

FLOOR + FOUNDATION PLAN SCALE 1/8"=1'-0"

116 bottom The Ceramic Apse (seen here in the diagram and elevation) integrates work space, the journey and the passage. A sort of doubled terrace-steps or belvedere is on the roof.

FRONT ELEVATION SCALE 1/8"=1'-0"

117 top This section of the complex shows the Foundry Apse to the left surrounded by residential cells involving symmetrical pairs of units partially underground and connected by a ring overlooking the entire apse.

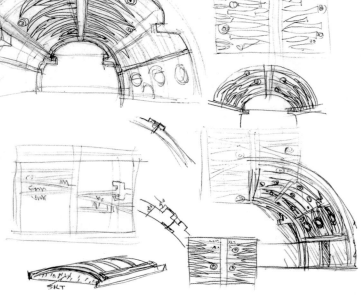

117 bottom The Lab Building home to the carpenter's shop is characterized by frescoed vaults whose sketches highlight the layout. The photograph emphasizes the integration obtained between the cavity enclosed by the building and the surrounding landscape.

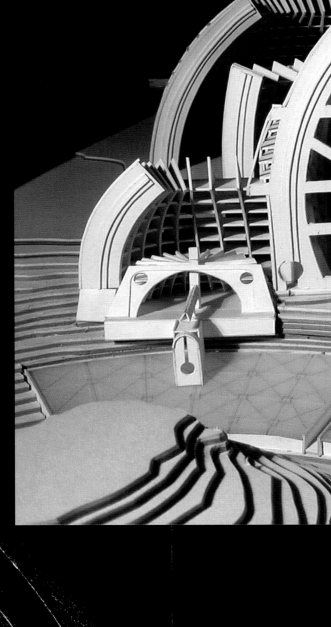

PAOLO SOLERI

118 and 119 The plastic model and drawings relate to a project called Arcosanti Arcology. The study section illustrating the four founding effects is of particular interest. The first is the Apse Effect and refers to a method to transform architecture into a passive energy machine that operates in relation to the changed position of the sun throughout the day and the seasons. The second is the Greenhouse/Horticulture Effect in virtue of which the concentration of solar heat within a specific area ensures a natural basis for agriculture and to conserve water resources, which allows intensifying the production of food and sustaining the energy system for arcology. The third is the Chimney Effect and refers to a process to produce hot air to heat the environment and for other uses by using as little energy loss as possible. The fourth and last is the Heat Sink Effect connected to the ability of stone or cement to accumulate heat when room temperature is higher than its own and to dissipate it slowly when it is lower.

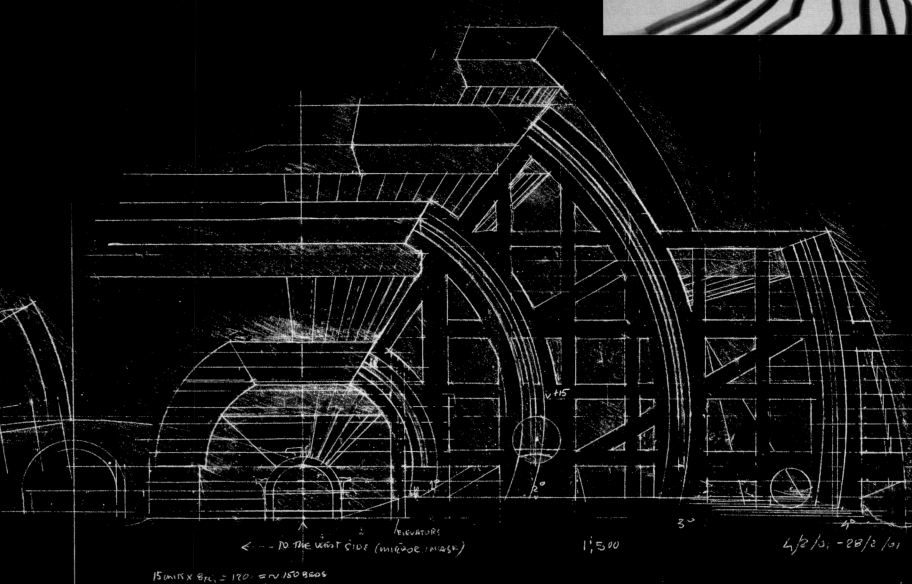

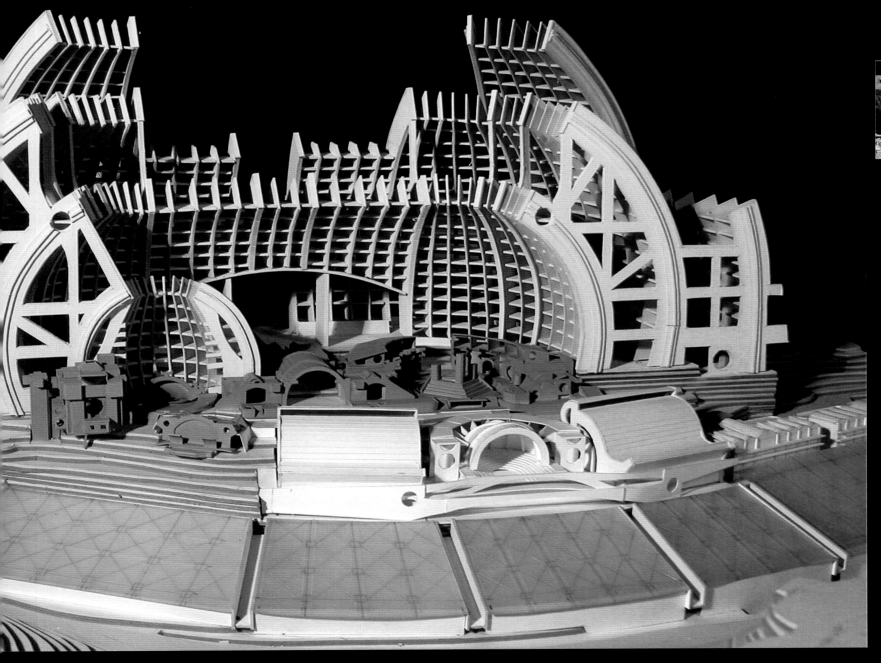

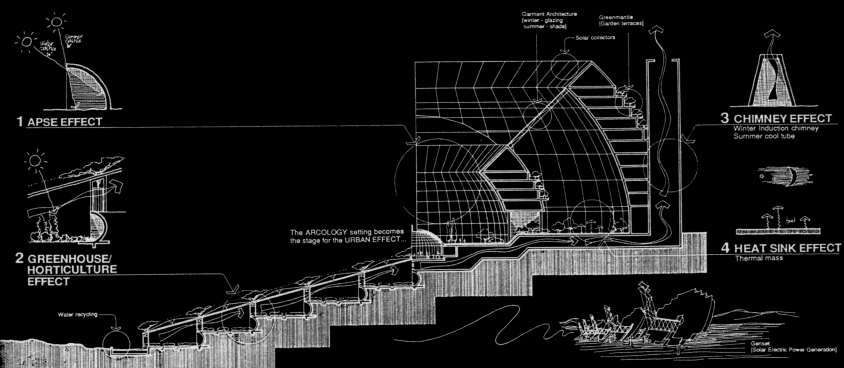

1 APSE EFFECT

2 GREENHOUSE/ HORTICULTURE EFFECT

Water recycling

Garment Architecture [winter - glazing summer - shade]

Greenmantle [Garden terraces]

Solar collectors

The ARCOLOGY setting becomes the stage for the URBAN EFFECT...

3 CHIMNEY EFFECT
Winter Induction chimney
Summer cool tube

4 HEAT SINK EFFECT
Thermal mass

Genset [Solar Electric Power Generation]

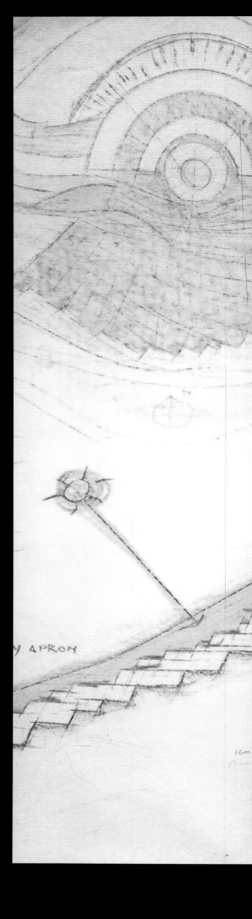

APRON

MEADOW SLOPE

BUT EVEN THERE AT SUCH PAID
STACKER OF THINGS "THE COOPERA-
TIVE" URGE PUSHES MATTER INTO
A FURIOUS QUEST FOR DE ISO-
LATION, AND THE LONG JOURNEY
TOWARD AN ESTHETO COMPASSION

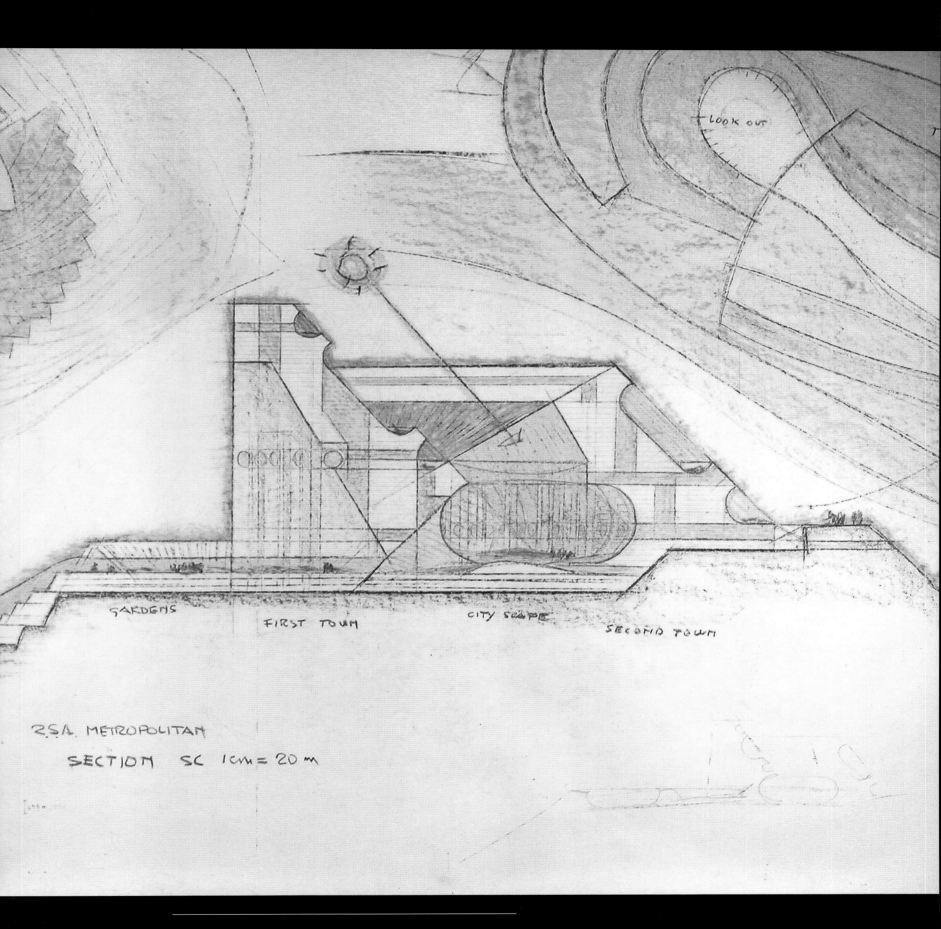

GARDENS   FIRST TOWN   CITY SCAPE   SECOND TOWN

2.S.A. METROPOLITAN

SECTION SC 1CM = 20 M

LOOK OUT

120 and 120-121 Two Sun Arcology is the title of a series of projects to realize self-sufficient structures conceived for extreme climatic conditions. In short, the key element is the city energized by the sun. All work by Paolo Soleri rotates around man-society-nature research and the principle of frugality or the Lean Alternative. The idea of more with less is at the basis of his arcology development project.

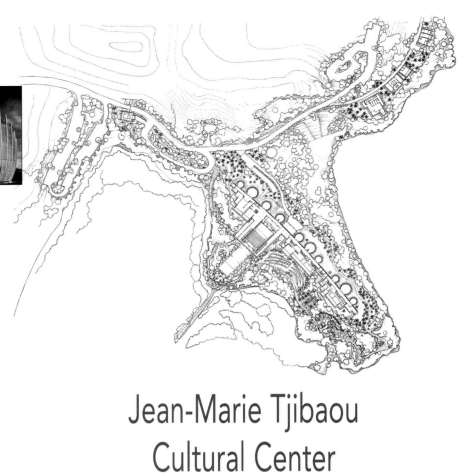

Jean-Marie Tjibaou Cultural Center

NOUMEA, NEW CALEDONIA

This cultural center drew its inspiration from the desire to commemorate the memory of Jean-Marie Tjibaou, a local politician and a leading exponent of his country's independence movement, who was assassinated in 1989. Upon the request of New Caledonia, the French government financed the construction of a complex one of whose aims is to spread knowledge of the local Kanak culture as a tribute to its leader.

Renzo Piano's project basically called for 10 pavilions equal in shape but of different sizes situated in a preserve. The pavilions wind their way in a continuous walkway that accompanies the configuration of the ocean shore and is a connecting link for the entire cultural center system. The constructions, which range in height from 66 to 92 feet, are flanked by structures that are more modest – not so much in size as in their form and placement – and that extend over the land on the same level. These buildings house part of the center's functions, particularly those activities that the pavilions themselves would find difficult to host because of their form and size.

The group of pavilions that make up the main – and certainly the most poetic – part of the complex emerges from the earth, creating a clearly recognizable Kanak identity in the surrounding vegetation, a symbol embracing the territory that integrates so well into its characteristic features.

In general the complex is articulated in three series of constructions which provide space for complementary functions. The first one houses temporary and permanent exhibitions, as well as an auditorium and an amphitheater. The second is the space for research and contains a library, a conference hall and the administrative offices. The third has spaces for artistic activities: dance, music, painting and sculpture.

Each of the pavilions is both a concrete and formal evocation of the local Kanak culture which, from a technological and structural standpoint, combines systems and material, commonly used in this area, with Western experience and methodology.

Every structure has a complex ribbed facade made up of horizontal, spaced slats of wood which on the whole remind one of the typical patterns of local handicrafts.

122 top The intervention's general plan shows how the project is included in a natural context to become an integral and characterizing element, while respecting the culture and places.

122 bottom The center includes two types of structures connected by the same path: circular pavilions and buildings with one floor above ground, which are home to all functions that can't be accommodated in the pavilions.

122-123 The Jean-Marie Tjibaou Cultural Center was realized within a natural reserve surrounded by indigenous vegetation found in New Caledonia. It follows the development of an oceanic beach while simultaneously being integrated within the surrounding landscape.

123 bottom The diagram shows the sequence of the pavilions and their relationship with the more standard structures integrating the spaces. These are structures with an open, circular plan whose configuration and functionality draw on the models of traditional huts in New Caledonia.

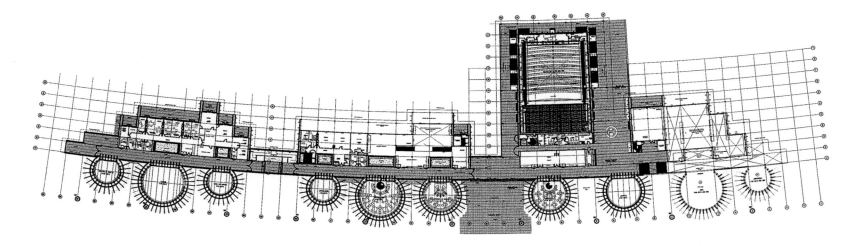

These "ribs" allow air to pass through, and when the wind blows seem to reproduce the same oscillation, or vibration, of the surrounding plants. This skin is supported by structures made of glued pieces of iroko and steel. Iroko is a wood particularly resistant to rot and insects. It can easily be glued, and is the right size for this type of structure.

The most ambitious objective of the Jean-Marie Tjibaou Cultural Center project was to respect and reflect the Kanak culture, traditions and environment without reproducing their features and forms in a banal or obvious manner, while at the same time not making the opposite mistake of introducing architectural elements wholly foreign to such a specific context, thus failing to consider and respect the needs and sensitivity of the local population. In fact Renzo Piano's study of the Kanak culture and its symbols led him to design the pavilions in such a way that they would be at once a reference to and free interpretation of the shape and texture of the huts in New Caledonia. The great success enjoyed by the Cultural Center is due not only to the formal composition and technological choices made in its creation, but above all to the fact that it relates to and blends in perfectly with its natural context, light, wind and vegetation. S.L.

125 The project combines local systems and materials with Western experience and methods. It pays homage to the well-defined Kanak culture by respecting its traditions and not proposing a trivial historic reconstruction (by simply copying a local village) or a completely foreign model. The building detail (original design) shows the relationship between the structure and its natural surroundings, the environment and man. The wind blows through the pavilion, which protects against the sun and is permeable to onlookers. The drawing shows the galvanized steel joints connecting the elevated, local wood structure to the foundation.

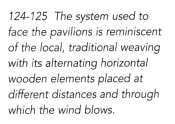

124-125 The system used to face the pavilions is reminiscent of the local, traditional weaving with its alternating horizontal wooden elements placed at different distances and through which the wind blows.

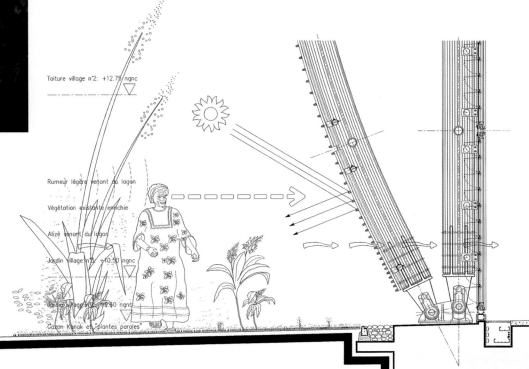

126 top There are 10 pavilions in all ranging from 65-90 feet high. They have been grouped into three types of buildings home to various functions or based on specific themes of the Kanak culture.

126 center Vegetation is introduced into certain areas within the structure as a sign of the precise desire to integrate the building system with the natural system.

126-127 bottom The cutaway view shows the transversal sequence characterizing the project: pavilions, connecting paths and buildings with a single floor above ground. The project completely relates to its surroundings. The most impressive structures – the pavilions – are located close to the highest trees, while the lowest buildings with the least impact are located on the opposite side.

126-127 top The photo shows the structural complexity of the pavilions made with iroko wood, a particularly resistant local species. The density and compactness of the elements characterizing the foundation tend to completely disappear in proximity of the crowning, and to finally vanish gradually towards the sky.

128-129 top The pavilions and their woven facing don't prevent air from entering and appear to re-propose the same oscillation or vibration of the surrounding vegetable elements when the wind blows. As mainly local materials were used, the coloring also tends to take on the shades of the surrounding landscape in its daily chromatic variations.

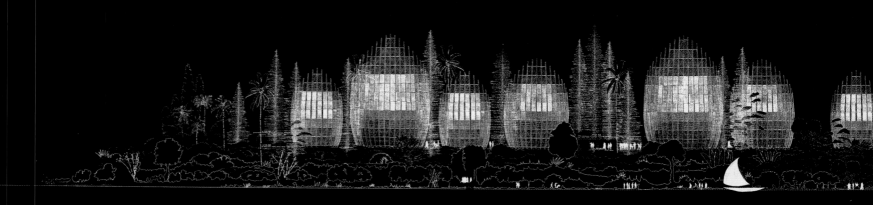

128-129 bottom The group of pavilions in the Jean-Marie Tjibaou Cultural Center is the main and certainly the most poetic part of the project. It rises from the ground in a series of repeating elements, which however contain different rhythms and sizes and constitute a clearly recognizable sequence in the surrounding landscape, a signal on a regional scale that is integrated with its distinguishing elements.

Arthur & Yvonne Boyd Education Center

RIVERSDALE, AUSTRALIA

The Riversdale Art School offers residence to artists, and also takes in 32 young students from all over the world who live and work there for brief periods. This foundation is devoted to artistic education and is run by the Bundanon Trust, an institution that administers the bequest that the painter Arthur Boyd made to the Australian state. The site, which was formerly Boyd's residence, is a vast farmstead lying on a ridge sloping down toward the Shoalhaven River, about 186 miles south of Sydney. In all the works of Glenn Murcutt (this one is really a project drawn up together with Wendy Lewin and Reg Lark, two of his former students) the natural scenery of Australia, an ecosystem that is at once delicate and strong, is the basic element that gives rise to the definition of the operative and functional program of the design.

A stay in the Boyd Education Center allows artists to gain direct, impactive experience and knowledge of the rare scenery in this part of Australia, something that will surely influence their work. The students who visit the complex do nothing more nor less than perpetuate the habit of Arthur Boyd, who conceived the stay at Riversdale as a sort of full immersion in Australian nature. And indeed, Murcutt's architecture becomes the means whereby this type of experience is accentuated and emphasized.

The complex dominates the valley. The canteen ends on a large veranda that opens out to the north and east, providing a view of the panorama: the river, woods, and the mountains in the horizon. Just behind the large hall is a nucleus consisting of the kitchen, storeroom and bathroom which bends a few degrees and marks the starting point of the long wing made of unpolished cement that houses the bedrooms. A large square that can be transformed into an amphitheater with a seating

capacity of 350 is the element that separates the new building from the older ones. Eight residential units with four beds each are situated under the thin metal roof. When necessary, each bedroom can be divided in two by means of a sliding wall contained in the brise-soleil that marks the rhythm of the residential wing overlooking the river.

The roof is one of the fundamental elements in Murcutt's architecture. In the hall, the overturned pyramid serving as the roof also acts as a rainwater drainage system and echoes the topography of the valley sloping toward the river.

The rigorous geometry of this complex, with its irregular foundation, lies softly on the level space between the cultivated and spontaneous vegetation areas.

The Education Center is made of cement, plywood and sheet metal, but above all, recycled wood. A cistern in the ground takes in the rainwater, and the garbage is treated in a small sewage purification plant. The amenities of the complex do not depend on any mechanical means but are provided solely by natural devices and systems that are created with forms that are never arbitrary and always necessary.

Murcutt belongs to that group of architects who are closely connected to, and rely upon, the very craft of their profession. Although he is internationally known – he was awarded the prestigious Prizker Prize in 2002 for his "interpretation of landscape in constructed form" – he is quite removed from the "star system". He has never designed a structure outside his country, and when asked the reason why, he replies: "I live in a country that is a continent and I can work with all types of climate."

The spaces that Murcutt designs allow one to perceive the air, the sun and the water with which he works in order to assert their presence and inscribe them in the materials he utilizes.   L.S.

130 top The sketch depicts the study of the roof of the veranda at the Arthur & Yvonne Boyd Education Center and the nucleus of services behind it.

130 bottom The complex (whose overview is shown here) is positioned in the direction of the Shoalhaven River.

130-131 top The upside-down pyramid acts as a roof and resembles the geography of the valley with a slope that slowly descends towards the river.

130-131 bottom A long row of rough cement is behind the veranda and contains the rooms housing the young students of the art school.

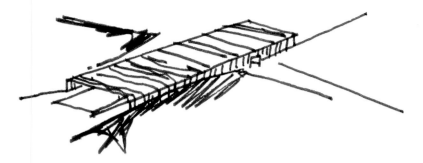

Woodleigh School Science Building

BAXTER, AUSTRALIA

This one-story building designed by Australian architect Sean Godsell and intended as a "science gallery", is a rectangular volume measuring 197 x 66 feet. The objective was to make it a transit area along which the activities carried out in the school are on view, as it were, and can be commented on. A place that stimulates an exchange of ideas and encourages interaction among those who use the center.

Oxydized steel and recycled ironbark – a particular species of eucalyptus with ash gray bark – are the materials that characterize the rhythmical movement of the east and west facades.

The almost obsessive repetition of the vertical architectural elements on these two facades enhances the configuration of the terrain, which is slightly sloping. The frame not only imparts a good deal of abstraction to the rectangular volume but also acts as an intermediate space between the interior and exterior and betrays the influence of Japanese architecture, an influence that Godsell openly acknowledges. This roofed passageway, a transition area that runs along the two sides of the building, protects the interior from excessive sunlight and also leads to the school's five classrooms.

There have been some rather forced critical interpretations that see an analogy with biology in this work: the warm and soft parts of the body (endoskeleton) are protected by the rigid "shell" (exoskeleton). The arrangement of the different widths of the interior spaces gives the impression of a bar code. An aquarium and a hothouse interrupt the rhythm of the modular space of the classrooms, while a project room marks the end of the south side of the edifice and becomes an outdoor educational area, even though it lies under the same roof as the rest of the structure.

The materials used in the construction, the circulation strategy of the spaces, and the apparatuses utilized to light the classrooms and the natural materials, are all components of Godsell's project, whose objective was to characterize the building as a place for educating the students and helping them to develop and mature. The shade that the slender pillars cast on the walls of the school

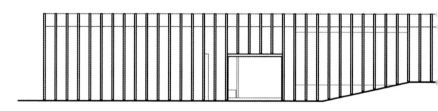

132 top The perspective sketch shows the study of the low and elongated school building resting on the ground while respecting its orography.

132-133 top This outdoor view shows how the elevation and the school's distribution system formally use the bar code as a formal reference whose vertical rhythm contrasts with and highlights the slope of the site.

shrouds the didactic areas and delicately keeps noise and distractions at a distance.

One of the recurrent themes in Godsell's architecture is his interest in applying a holistic approach to his work on the environment which considers the whole not merely as the sum of its parts but as a much more complex and interacting entity.

"I think that there is a group of architects around the world at the moment who are fundamentally shape- and form-makers," he says. "They design buildings to have shapes and don't pay enough attention to how they can make a building perform to its optimum in terms of its environment".   L.S.

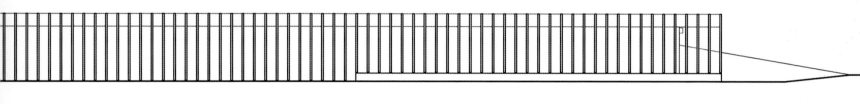

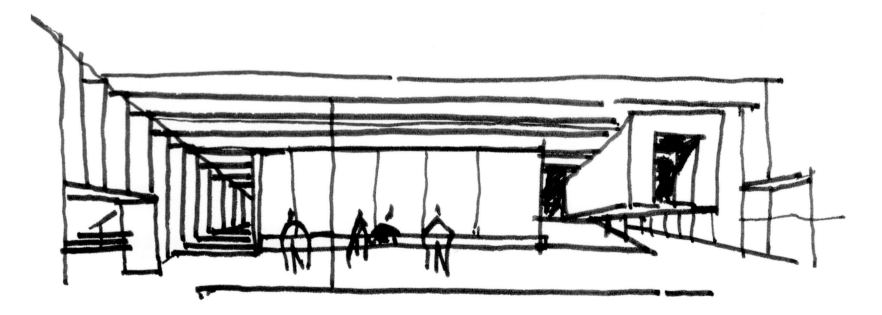

132-133 center The elevation of the building highlights the obvious asymmetry of the entrance; left of the foyer there is access to the project room and the five schoolrooms and school service areas are to its right.

133 bottom The perspective sketch of the foyer shows the two indoor galleries leading off it and occupying the long sides of the building and thus also protecting the indoor areas against the heat.

134-135 The picture depicts one of the two indoor passageways characterizing the east and west facades of the building. The rhythm of the oxidized-steel and recycled-wood pillars differentiate the school's rectangular volume.

135 top The project room (seen inside here) is at the end of the south end of the building and becomes a space for outdoor teaching.

135 bottom This section of the school entrance highlights the beginning of the indoor gallery constituting a diaphragm between the natural landscape and the school rooms.

Pabellón Zeri

MANIZALES, COLOMBIA

Colombian architect Simón Vélez (DeBoer Architects) designed the "organic" pavilion of the ZERI (*Zero Emissions Research Initiative*) Foundation at the EXPO 2000, held in Hanover, which was based on the theme of ecology. The pavilion is made of a South American bamboo (*Guadua angustifolia*) and has a total surface area of 22,000 square feet. It is a structure that has been tested positively for its tension balance and resistance to fire, as required by the European Union building codes and also by the severe fire prevention legislation in Germany, thus proving the practicability of this material even at very distant latitudes.

The importance of this pavilion lies in the fact that it has provided an admirable demonstration to the Western world of the potential and fascination of this natural material, thus refuting the notion that bamboo is a "poor" material for the poor. In fact, since it was gradually but ineluctably replaced by concrete and steel for construction, it became known as "poor people's wood". The high percentage of renewability of bamboo compared to wood, and its surprising structural capabilities, which are comparable to those of steel – so much so that it has been called "plant steel" – have made this material a major resource in construction, capable of solving the housing problem on a worldwide scale.

The potential of bamboo as a building material is still little known in the West. In Latin America, and especially in Colombia, *Guadua angustifolia* – one of the species of bamboo best adapted for construction – has made it possible for Vélez to realize bold architectural works: from splendid villas in fantastic sites to sheds and stables, and from bridges built in natural and urban settings to low-cost homes.

The Colombian architect has stated that he trusts only the masters of the past and that the present-day manifestations of modern architecture do not interest him in the least. What Vélez proposes is to utilize another species of *Guadua* bamboo, *Bambusa americana*, thus following in the steps of the colonists in his country and of certain indigenous communities. Further confirmation of the suitability of bamboo for construction is that it is both a raw material and a product, because it can be used in its natural state. It has excellent resistance to traction and compression, qualities that increase with time, and it also reacts well to seismic stress. Bamboo also has the exceptional capacity to counteract atmospheric pollution: in a year, a plantation is able to absorb up to 17 tons of carbon per hectare, which is 40 times more than the amount absorbed by a wooded area in the same extension of land. Furthermore, its roots provide excellent protection against erosion and landslides.

The illustrations show the full-scale prototype of the ZERI pavilion, which was built in Manzales, Colombia, in order to carry out some static tests. This prototype also gave the architect the opportunity to devise various types of connection elements. Unlike the case of the structure built for the Expo 2000 in Hanover, this one was not destroyed and is now being used as part of a cultural complex in a park.   L.S.

136 top and 136-137 This pavilion in Manizales, Colombia realized by Vélez, takes advantage of the potential of bamboo and has a 23ft. cantilevered roof protecting the structure against the sun and rain.

137 bottom The details of the roof show how the prototype allowed the fine-tuning of various types of unions included in the pavilion's structure.

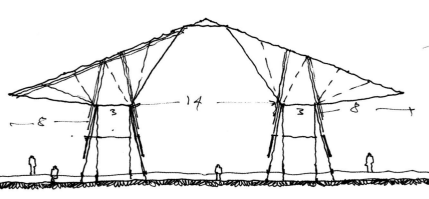

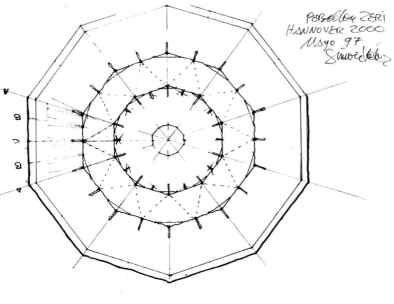

Japanese Pavilion

HANOVER, GERMANY

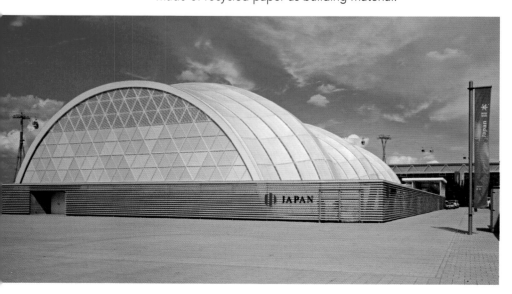

The Japanese Pavilion at the Hanover World Exhibition held in 2000 was the result of the collaboration between Japanese architect Shigeru Ban (who was chosen to represent Japan at the Hanover Expo, the theme of which was ecology) and Frei Otto, a German architect who is a pioneer in the use of lightweight structures and who analyzed natural phenomena, utilizing their organic rationality long before "ecology" became a household word. Frei Otto enthusiastically accepted the offer to work as a consultant for the construction of the Japanese Pavilion because he was very curious about the idea of using tubes made of recycled paper as building material.

The main subject of this theme park was respect for the environment, and the materials used for the pavilions, once the Expo was over, had to be easily disassembled and recycled.

The technique of paper tube architecture as a structural element had been developed in 1995 by Shigeru Ban in the Takatori Catholic Church in Kobe and the Miyake Design Studio Gallery, thanks to the support of engineer Gengo Matsui and free access to the analysis equipment provided by Waseda University. Five years later the opportunity to collaborate with Frei Otto was one of the motives behind Ban's spontaneous offer to construct the pavilion before he was selected to do so.

Frei Otto's contribution to the Japanese Pavilion project concentrated on the definition of the form of the grid structure and on the details of assembly and construction. The objective was to build a pavilion without using concrete. The structure had to last throughout the summer and be totally recyclable after the closure of the Expo.

Rather than complicated mechanical joints made of aluminum or steel, the two architects opted for low tech details. Thus, their challenge was to design the joints by using common materials.

The two worked on the development of the structural behavior of the tunnel-like cardboard tube structure, which consisted of a horizontal grid framework of tubes (connected

139 center and bottom *The horizontal grid of the paper tubes was distributed on framework whose manual telescopic system was lowered or raised to distort the pipe network and obtain the desired curvature.*

only with tape) laid out on a scaffold. By means of a hand-operated telescopic system the scaffolding was lowered or raised until it succeeded in shaping the paper tube grid into the desired curve that was to be the pavilion roof. The only advanced technology element used were the 10 antennas of the GPS satellite system, which checked and controlled the geometric configuration of the roof.

The joints of the structure were made of cloth, and therefore no concession was made to high tech or the use of heavy machinery in the construction procedure.

In order to replace the protective membrane, which is normally made of PVC – a very poor material that with time emits dioxins – the architects sought a type of paper that would be both waterproof and fireproof. A timber frame was used to support the paper shells (10 x 10 feet) and brace the paper tubes.

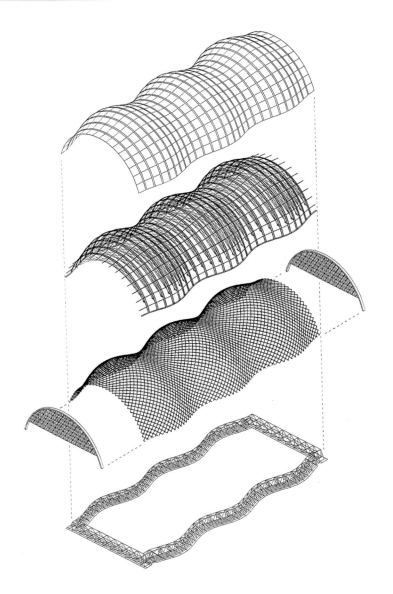

138-139 *Long cardboard pipes finished with a translucent membrane intertwine on the large shell with a double curve, which is 82 feet wide and 230 feet long.*

138 bottom *The picture shows the entrance to the Japanese Pavilion at Expo 2000 in Hanover, which proposed the development of themes tied to the sustainability of architectural structures.*

The foundations consisted of common wooden formworks filled with sand which were much more suitable for a pavilion destined to be dismantled. In fact, concrete foundations would have entailed using a great deal of material and the production of refuse that both this project and the theme of the Hanover Expo wanted to avoid. When the Expo was closed, the German industry that had supplied the paper took it back for recycling, and the foundations were easily utilized once again.

Since the destiny of the edifice was its very demolition, the objective of Ban and Otto's work was dismantling and recycling.   L.S.

140 and 140-141 The
structure was conceived
as a self-supporting fabric with
a diagonally-crossed frame and
has low-tech joints made with
fabric and metal binding.

The winding weave of the
pavilion was stiffened using
a system of reticular arches
and crossed wood beams
whose role was also to support
the roof membrane.

Great Bamboo Wall

KENGO KUMA AND ASSOCIATES

This construction is part of an initiative promoted by the Chinese Government in which 10 Asian architects were invited to build guest houses for diplomatic personnel in an area of greenery near the Great Wall of China. The choice of the name for his contribution, "Great (Bamboo) Wall" – note the use of the term "wall" instead of "house" – reveals Japanese architect Kengo Kuma's interest in that colossal monument which unfolds like an endless carpet along the crests of the immense Chinese countryside. But in this case his "wall" was not built to seal off Chinese civilization, as it were, but to unite the cultures of China and Japan.

Kuma possesses the formidable capacity to transform a project into an occasion for profound meditation on the environment and on the symbolic and formal implications of its components. His objective is to leave the features of the surrounding landscape intact and to use local building material as much as possible.

In this Great Wall project he also sought to respect the nature of the site and to incorporate, and even dissolve, the architecture into nature. But disguising the architecture with mimetic colors or covering it with vegetation was absolutely out of the question, as was the idea of producing a totally transparent Miesian-like box.

The choice of material was the starting point, and in this case the architect's passion for bamboo became the trigger for dwelling on the intrinsic nature of this Oriental plant (or in particular, its skin) and dealing with a major architectural theme: the outer surface of buildings. Therefore, Kuma's passion for bamboo concentrated on the "skin" of this material: so delicate and simple, yet at the same time expressing strong tension.

"Skin and outer surface are different," Kuma states. "Concrete has an outer surface but not skin. What is more, I don't find concrete particularly attractive, because without skin the soul never appears. Bamboo has especially beautiful skin and has a soul residing within. In Japan there is a legend that relates

how Princess Kakuyahime, the moon goddess, was born inside a bamboo cane. And people believe in this fable precisely because since bamboo has a skin, it also possesses a soul."

Depending on its density and diameter, bamboo provides a rich variety of ways to divide space and at the same time becomes a means for capturing natural phenomena.

As is known, bamboo canes are made up of segments separated by joints near which the hollow section of the cane has thick leathery areas that serve to stiffen the cane. In order to make the cane utilizable as a structural pillar, the fibrous membranes inside were removed and a steel rod inserted through the entire length of the stem. Cement was poured into the canes, turning them into formworks.

The material, which came from the area, was processed in Japan because the technical means to hollow the canes were lacking in China. The canes were bound to form constructive elements which, in correspondence with the openings, became sliding brise-soleil elements that filter the sunlight.

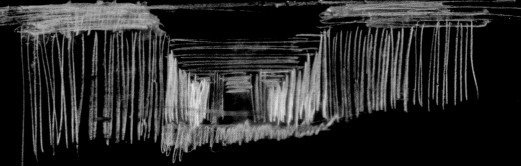

142 The building is faced for its entire height on the south-west side with crystal sheets, which are shielded by a sun blind made of bamboo reeds with a two-inch diameter.

142-143 The structure follows the ground and implements the building method used for the nearby Great Wall of China.

143 center The sketch highlights how the architect concentrated on the central part of the building right from the start and considered it the throbbing center of the home. The thickening vertical lines define the layout and elevation of the bamboo lounge separating the living and sleeping areas of the home.

143 bottom The south-west view highlights how the home was developed on two levels, one of which is partially underground

The inside walls are, on the other hand, made of rice paper, a typical material used in local architecture as well as in traditional Japanese architecture. For the floor, Kuma used slabs of dark colored local slate to mitigate the forceful geometric pattern of the bamboo membranes. The house runs around the lounge, which is the hub of the structure and where the most optimum contact is made with the natural environment. Two stone footbridges connect the lounge with the day and night zones.

The material envelops every space, and accompanies visitors along a route marked by the vertical rhythm of the juxtaposed bamboo canes. L.S.

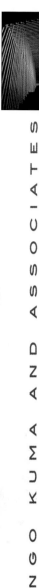

144-145 The bamboo lounge is the heart of the home and best expresses the relationship with the natural environment. Two stone walkways-bridges connect the living and sleeping areas.

145 top This view of the kitchen and the dining room highlights the floor finished with local, dark slate sheets designed to mitigate the strong geometry of the bamboo.

145 bottom Stairs lead to a partially underground level, which is home to two guest rooms, bathrooms, store-rooms and a machine room.

Quinta Monroy

IQUIQUE, CHILE

An illegally constructed "shanty town" in the middle of Iquique, a city in the Chilean desert, where 100 families had lived for 30 years, has been transformed into a functional lower-class neighborhood through a program of social sustainability. The main problem to solve here, with a subsidy of only 10,000 dollars per family, was how to buy the area without uprooting the inhabitants by moving them to the outskirts of town and destroying the economic and human relationships and bonds they had established. Furthermore, it was necessary to install infrastructures – the majority of existing shacks had no direct light or ventilation – and build small houses, since the budget allowed for a space of no more than 320 square feet for each one. Given these conditions, Alejandro Aravena, the architect who was commissioned by the Chilean government in 2003 to draw up the project, studied all the possibilities offered by the various types of architecture. He came to the conclusion that the only possible way to accommodate all 100 families, each with a house limited to 320 square feet, was to build in such a way that the structure would only be the initial nucleus which could be enlarged and extended into a house of 750 square feet by do-it-yourself construction. In order to do this, Aravena divided the Quinta Monroy area into plots of 30 x 30 feet arranged around four courtyards that would house 20 families, so that this collective and public space would be the right size to allow for the development of forms of cooperation and solidarity among these 20 families. This choice was discussed and negotiated with the inhabitants themselves, who participated in the entire planning process. In fact, it was they who decided that they preferred four collective spaces rather than a single central one. Two families occupied each plot: one in the ground floor apartment measuring 20 x 20 x 8 feet, the other on the upper floor, which measures 10 x 20 x 16 feet and is twice as high. Both apartments have a main room, bathroom and kitchen. Thus, a part of the plot, an "L" shape of 9 x 20 feet, remained empty, and could be enlarged "spontaneously", but without invading the public spaces or altering the quality of the urban facades. In this way the do-it-yourself building is eco-friendly. However, this "self-construction" must follow the guidelines of the project. Aravena built supporting frameworks that can sustain the families' additions to their houses. In order to do this, he further strengthened the reinforced concrete slabs that serve as both the roof of the ground floor apartments and the floors of the upper apartment of the duplex. The upper floor has a C-shaped configuration so that the fourth side, made of corrugated sheet iron, is a wall that can be removed easily to make room for the additions. The ground floor apartment can easily be enlarged in the space left under the slab supporting the upper floor, or partly in the courtyard behind the duplex, but in such a way that the inner spaces have natural ventilation and illumination, as well as direct access to the public courtyard. G.S.

146-147 top The view of the front of the district shows the finishing modifications by the inhabitants that divide and enliven the homogeneity of the original front section without altering its proportions and alignments.

146-147 bottom *The axonometric diagrams portray the apartments on the first and second levels, the building elements used and the areas left free in which the inhabitants can expand their home (color-highlighted in the axonometric diagram on the right).*

tr hamzah & yeang sdn bhd *(mer*

emilio ambasz & associates *(*

partners *(commerzbank)* - behnisch a

research - genzyme center headquarters buil

(hedge building) - site *(residence antilia)* -

the environment) - steven holl archi

park) - ateliers jean nouvel *(tour sign*

(energy plus building) - feilden clegg b

green arch:
nature in man-made structures

ra mesiniaga - elephant & castle eco tower) -

efectural international hall) - foster +

chitekten (institute for forestry and nature

g) - atelier kempe thill architects

auerbruch hutton (federal agency for

ects (whitney water purification facility and

) - skidmore, owings & merrill llp

adley studios (one gallions)

green arch:
nature in man-made structures

The progressive and growing attention paid to ecological problems and the safeguarding of our environment – as a reaction to the unlimited use of land and energy – has radically modified the relationship between nature and the contemporary constructed environment, as regards the scale of both the buildings and the urban setting. This has led to various stances and nuances in architectural projects: the "re-naturalization" of architecture, its imitation of natural forms, plant camouflage, and the ecological approach. These are all tendencies that consider nature one of the basic elements of architectural composition, with the intent of defining its spatial and formal features as well as climatic and environmental ones. What follows is an attempt at indicating the various procedures adopted by contemporary architects, artists and landscape architects.

In plant camouflaging the natural elements are used as an ecological maquillage to conceal the artificiality of the architecture, to integrate it into natural contexts, and to modify the image of the city by inserting nature into it. Among the first to adopt this procedure of utilizing greenery were Roche DSV & Sie.P with their 1993 "Growing Up" project in Compiègne, France,

François & Lewis's rural houses in Jupilles, built in 1997, Patrick Blanc's Vertical Gardens and two of the most famous projects: the Musée du Quai Branly in Paris designed by Jean Nouvel and the CaixaForum Madrid, the work of Herzog & de Meuron. The Prefectural International Hall in Fukuoka designed by Emilio Ambasz represents a similar approach: a building with a stepped roof is covered with a mantle of plants as a continuation of the park in this area, thus giving back to the locals that part of the land that had been removed to build the edifice. The Hedge Building designed by Atelier Kempe Thill to mark the entrance to the International Garden (IGA) Exhibition is covered with plants to symbolize the theme of the event which was agriculture.

Now while it may seem that all these proposals utilized the natural element in a rather ephemeral fashion to define their image – which, for that matter, is never an attempt at becoming wholly incorporated into nature, since the architectural volumes always have regular geometric shapes – in reality they introduce vertical gardens or garden roofs in cities and buildings to improve climatic conditions, reduce pollution, and purify the air, thus becoming ecological solutions which replace technological ones.

Instead of using greenery to decorate the

shell or roof, other architects place it in large empty spaces created inside the building itself, which revive some traditional forms of architecture such as the court, greenhouses, or the spatial features of Mediterranean cities whose buildings have full and empty or recessed spaces.

The theme of the court, which is often roofed, is a feature of many contemporary architectural creations, such as the Genzyme Center Headquarters Building in Cambridge, Massachusetts designed by Behnisch Architekten, a regular parallelepiped with an atrium throughout its entire height which illuminates all the interior, acts as a ventilation duct and, thanks to the presence of green areas, provides a temperate environment.

In some cases the court or atrium takes on more complex and articulated configurations. One example is the Federal Agency for the Environment at Dessau designed by Sauerbruch Hutton, where a rather low building 1,600 feet long is sinuously laid out so as to create an open courtyard facing the outside, which consists of a park that in fact continues in the interior with the central atrium. Another example is the Institute for Forestry and Nature Research at Wageningen, another work by the Behnisch firm, in which the comb configuration creates two courts.

In other works, architects revive the volumes consisting of empty and full areas so typical of Mediterranean cities. This feature had already been employed in a series of mega-structures designed in the late 1950s: large, "mat-like" configurations as in Le Corbusier's project for the Venice hospital, the Free University in Berlin designed by Georges Candilis, Alexis Josic e Shadrac Woods, and the Amsterdam Orphanage by Aldo Van Eyck.

Recently this type of spatiality was proposed in smaller buildings by Herzog & de Meuron in the Rehab in Basel, Mansilla + Tuñón in the MUSAC (Museo de Arte Contemporáneo de Castilla y León) in León, Spain, and by SOM who conceived the project for the Energy Plus Building in Paris, where the building is progressively emptied, so to speak, until it becomes a sort of irregular net.

In all these projects the formal solutions, together with the presence of greenery, ensure the bioclimatic functioning of the building.

Similar spatial configuration and bioclimatic operations are typical of certain skyscrapers that have a series of open spaces in their interior. These are the social and circulation areas, both public and semi-public, either natural or simply outdoors, of buildings that set out to reproduce the complexity and configuration of parts of cities. This is true of TR Hamzah & Yeang Sdn Bhd's Elephant & Castle Eco Tower in London and of Residence Antilia in Mumbai designed by SITE. Often these atriums extend to the full height of the building, in a sort of spiral that makes it possible to generate air currents that regulate the internal climate and thus save a great deal of energy. This type of configuration is to be noted in the Menara Mesiniaga in Selangor designed by Yeang and in Foster's Commerzbank.

Jean Nouvel's recent project for the Tour Signal in the Défense district of Paris, on the other hand, consists of a series of superposed cubes with large loggias that are a reinterpretation of Italian Renaissance cities.

Much like what occurs in the case of buildings, whether they be prevalently horizontal or vertical eco structures, the system of open areas or atriums for socializing and circulation, which also include greenery, is also a distinguishing feature of the urban environment. These areas have always played a fundamental social role in our cities, a role that is enhanced by the environmental, climatic and landscape qualities they offer to the city. Designing parks, green areas and gardens therefore becomes a sustainable strategy for the upgrading of city neighborhoods and districts as well as entire territories. These are places in which one can graft a process of social sustainability, renew degraded areas and improve the climatic conditions of our human habitat. Their realization on the part of architects and landscape architects means linking the environmental and vegetative features with the figurative, social and functional aspects of the architecture. This is the case with Carlos Ferrater's Botanical Garden in Barcelona, whose fractal floor plan marks out the spaces and passageways, thus reducing to a minimum the removal and movement of the terrain and whose irrigation system functions thanks to the energy produced by the photovoltaic panels. Further examples are The Whitney Water Purification Facility and Park at Hamden (New Haven) designed by Steven Holl, whose vegetation theme is linked to that of the purification of water; and Battle y Roig's creation, the Val d'en Joan Park in Barcelona, where a dumping area was converted into a park. Besides the parks, other smaller scale projects attempt to renew and upgrade the urban environment. A fine example of this is the Ecoboulevard de Vallecas in Madrid designed by Ecosistema Urbano, a boulevard dotted with "air trees" – temporary pavilions consisting of metal structures that support solar panels so as to be energy self-sufficient – and plants, so that greenery is to be found even in the most densely built-up districts of the city.   G.S.

Menara Mesiniaga

SELANGOR, MALAYSIA

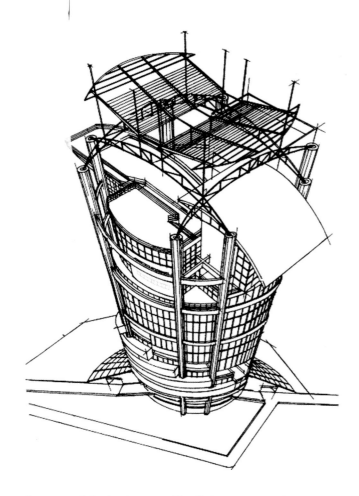

The Menara Mesiniaga building is one of the edifices symbolizing a responsible approach in architecture to environmental problems and represents a veritable catalog of bioclimatic technologies. Home of the IBM offices in Malaysia, this tower is considered the first bioclimatic skyscraper to combine a high tech aesthetic with low energy consumption which, by means of a careful study of its form, has limited the use of machines and motors, and concentrates on the extensive use of natural ventilation and lighting, and on an active, intelligent system for automated energy saving.

The plants, which are true vertical landscapes that spiral up from the ground and envelop the building facade, are the distinguishing feature of this project, as is the case with many works by Ken Yeang, the founder of the T.R. Hamzah & Yeang Sdn Bhd studio in Kuala Lumpur, and a pioneer in designing skyscrapers with low energy consumption.

The vegetation seems to be nibbling at the curved facade of the tower and penetrating the recessed terrace gardens with three different heights that create space in the upper part of the building and provide an area where office staff can relax and socialize. The plants create shade and help purify the air; the terraces allow fresh air to pass into the tower and flow through the passageways. All the floors used for offices have green areas that are separated from the working spaces by ceiling-high sliding glass panels, to control the level of the natural ventilation that cools down the elevator lobbies, the

stairways and the bathrooms. The light green windows protect the interior, insulating it completely.

The "shell" of the tower consists of a glass curtain wall that covers only the north and south facades, while to the east and west (the hottest areas) the glass surfaces have external louvers made of aluminum to reduce the heat.

The structure ends with a terrace – which is protected from the sun by a roof made up of a network of steel and aluminum bars – a swimming pool, and a gymnasium.

For years Yeang has been engaged in disproving the common belief that tall buildings are very harmful to the environment. On the contrary, he thinks skyscrapers are necessary in order to solve the problem of population growth with respect to the available land.

And to refute the conviction that in order to improve environmental comfort we must increase energy consumption, Yeang states: "An ecological building [...] can contribute positively to the environment. A green area is a productive area. So the building can generate energy instead of consuming it." L.S.

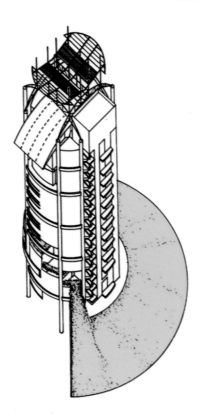
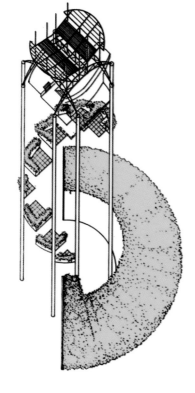

152 top The drawing shows the built shape with open courtyards and a roof with steel beams.

152 bottom Terraces at three different heights set back and covered with vegetation open up in the high part of the tower like vertical landscapes spiraling upwards.

153 Only the northern and southern facades are covered with a glass curtain wall, however the glass surfaces to the west and east have external brise-soleils to reduce the heat from the sun.

Prefectural International Hall

FUKUOKA, JAPAN

This hall occupies a huge space that was once the only square in the city of Fukuoka. Flanked by a canal, its two facades overlook one of the most prestigious streets in town to the north, and a city park, to the south.

The basic question of the architectural project was to meet the need to utilize an available area for a new structure – respecting purely economic parameters – and at the same time consider the necessity of restoring the city park whose land it was to occupy. The Prefectural International Hall is a hybrid building, with several layers and levels, containing one of the most easily recognizable features of the Argentine architect Ambasz's projects: plants used as building material.

When viewed from the park, the impressive size of the building merges with that of a new "hill" in the city, midway between the natural and the artificial. The simple geometry of the facade overlooking the green area consists of a series of landscaped terraces, a stepped area of urban dimensions colonized by a mantle of vegetation that seems to regain possession of the terrain of the park, which was hypothetically lost. This precise configuration leaves no doubt in one's mind as to the artificiality of the structure on which the natural elements lie, since the architect did not seek more organic forms in which to accommodate them, nor did he attempt to incorporate the structure in them. The series of increasingly recessed garden terraces marks out the profile of this side of the building, which moves back toward the bay in proportion to its height. Thus, the top provides a stunning view of the bay and the urban landscape of Fukuoka.

The terraced south facade of the building can be easily traversed, and provides green areas for relaxation, exercise and meditation, or simply as a means of momentarily escaping the chaos of city life. At the same time, the terraces constitute a "technological stratification" that improves the amenities in the interior. This is the element that in various ways imparts more architectural quality to the building, a quality that is also felt and echoed to quite a degree in the urban surroundings.

What is more, with the hybrid and multilayered character of this south facade, the Prefectural International Hall develops, on different levels, a multipurpose functional program that embraces a series of activities both governmental and private, added to which are others that derive from the very configuration of the project. In fact, besides the offices and administrative sections, the hall houses an auditorium-theater, large conference and convention facilities, and shops and exhibition spaces. The addition of two smaller volumes, one fully walled and the other glazed, leaves room for yet other activities. The "solid" element, which stands at the foot of the terraced side of the building, is the entrance. It has a stage for shows, and affords air exchange in the underground sections of the structure.

154 The main facade consists of a series of landscaped terraces, and has a significant sequence of ramps providing access to all levels of this public green area.

155 The building's main facade appears as the true continuation of the public area it overlooks. The ample green surfaces are urban areas that can be used by citizens.

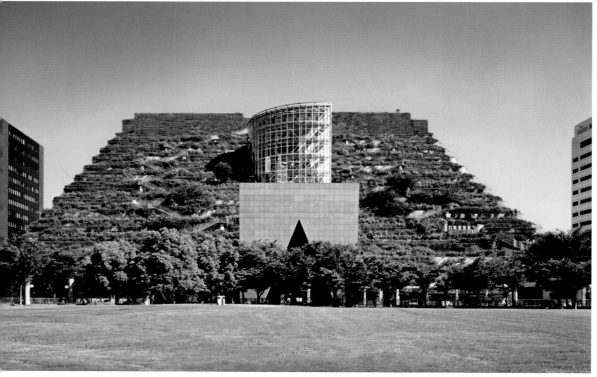

The glazed addition, which is inserted into the same facade as a protruding element – and surmounts the atrium, thus providing its core with a large amount of natural light – affords views of the city from the inside balconies, which line its entire height. These two sections, added to the south terraces, are fine belvederes, particularly during the period of the year when special festivities take place in the city.

The ecological and ethical dimension of the project is accompanied by the more poetic and aesthetic one that is such a distinguishing feature of Ambasz's works. The Prefectural International Hall in Fukuoka is one of the most significant of those works which aim at developing the theme of artificially created land and vertical gardens, an approach to architectural design that has become widespread today.   S.L.

156 top The green facade tends to withdraw towards the bay and to provide a new area (the highest part) overlooking the expanse of water and the urban panorama. The vegetation used to finish it appears as a new relief in the city and the fact it has become a public area allows the once unoccupied area to be returned to the city.

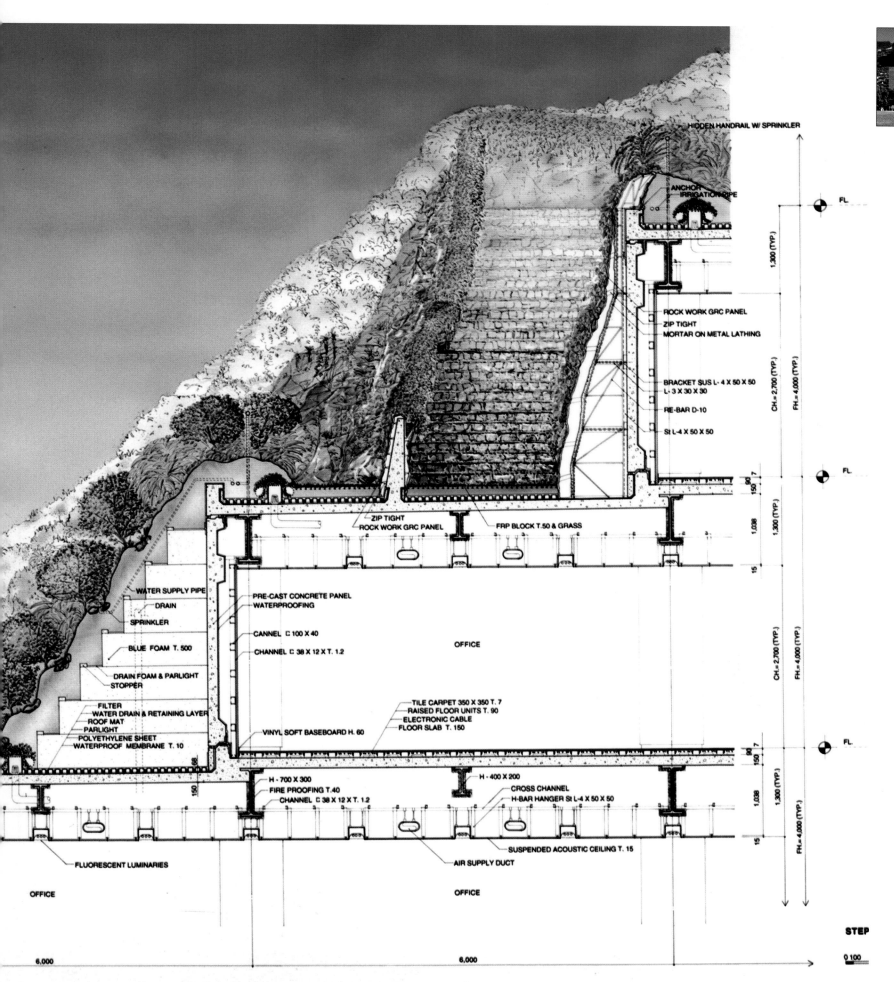

HIDDEN HANDRAIL W/ SPRINKLER

ANCHOR
IRRIGATION PIPE

ROCK WORK GRC PANEL
ZIP TIGHT
MORTAR ON METAL LATHING

BRACKET SUS L- 4 X 50 X 50
L- 3 X 30 X 30
RE-BAR D-10
St L-4 X 50 X 50

ZIP TIGHT
ROCK WORK GRC PANEL

FRP BLOCK T.50 & GRASS

WATER SUPPLY PIPE
DRAIN
SPRINKLER
BLUE FOAM T. 500
DRAIN FOAM & PARLIGHT
STOPPER
FILTER
WATER DRAIN & RETAINING LAYER
ROOF MAT
PARLIGHT
POLYETHYLENE SHEET
WATERPROOF MEMBRANE T. 10

PRE-CAST CONCRETE PANEL
WATERPROOFING

CANNEL C 100 X 40
CHANNEL C 38 X 12 X T. 1.2

OFFICE

TILE CARPET 350 X 350 T. 7
RAISED FLOOR UNITS T. 90
ELECTRONIC CABLE
FLOOR SLAB T. 150

VINYL SOFT BASEBOARD H. 60

H - 700 X 300
FIRE PROOFING T.40
CHANNEL C 38 X 12 X T. 1.2

H - 400 X 200

CROSS CHANNEL
H-BAR HANGER St L-4 X 50 X 50

FLUORESCENT LUMINARIES

AIR SUPPLY DUCT

SUSPENDED ACOUSTIC CEILING T. 15

OFFICE

OFFICE

FL

FL

FL

1,300 (TYP.)

CH.=2,700 (TYP.) FH.=4,000 (TYP.)

90 7
150
1,038
15
1,300 (TYP.)

CH.=2,700 (TYP.) FH.=4,000 (TYP.)

90 7
150
1,038
15
1,300 (TYP.)

FH.=4,000 (TYP.)

STEP
0 100

6,000

6,000

E M I L I O   A M B A S Z   &   A S S O C I A T E S

156 bottom Two elements with very precise
geometry have been added to the facade: the lower
opaque one identifies the entrance to the building.
It is home to a stage and allows air to be exchanged
with the underground areas. The higher glass element
provides an indoor observation point overlooking the
entire urban surroundings.

156-157 The construction detail (original design)
shows the complexity involved in creating the
vegetation-covered surface on the facade. This system
not only provides the project with architectural quality
which positively affects the surroundings, but is also a
technological solution that improves the indoor comfort
of the building by increasing its thermal inertia.

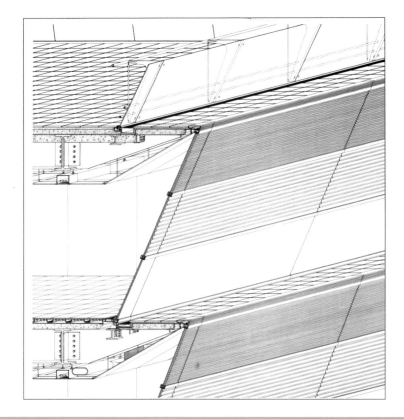

158 top This facade, overlooking one of the most important streets, is made of a series of horizontal glass strips tilted downwards reflecting the passers-by on the street level, and dematerializing the majestic bulk of the building.

158 bottom The cutaway view shows how the building is less compact than it appears in the photographs; it is repeatedly hollowed out to allow natural light to reach the first two underground levels.

159 The picture shows the balconies located in the large indoor void close to the cylinder-shaped glass mass on the main facade. In addition to overlooking the city, this space also acts as a large light well for the building.

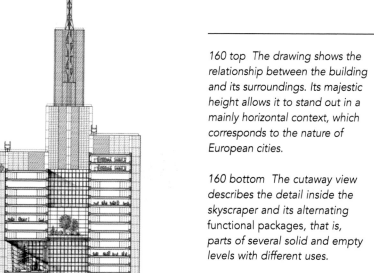

Commerzbank

FRANKFURT, GERMANY

The type of skyscraper that characterizes and symbolizes part of the skyline of many geographic areas and many cities and towns is not a typical feature of the urban areas of Europe, which predominantly tend to develop horizontally.

The headquarters of the Commerzbank, which until 2005 was the tallest high-rise in Europe, owes its popularity – on both a political and social level – to the quality of the project drawn up by Foster + Partners, which boasts another record: it was the first ecological office building based on low energy consumption levels as well as on construction efficiency and economy. In short, it is an intelligent architectural organism that totally fulfills the needs of a comfortable working environment.

With its typically European approach, Foster's project deals with the surrounding urban fabric by constructing its entrance section more or less at the same height as that of the nearby buildings, thus integrating it discreetly and lessening the impact of its huge volume. This lower level has various independent or complementary functions besides being the entrance to the Commerzbank.

In tune with these guidelines is the fact that the impressive size of the edifice is made as light as possible by a type of articulation comprising full and empty sections that balance one another and are distributed vertically in order to alternate. In particular, the recessed spaces, which house the winter gardens, follow a spiral configuration on different levels, alternating with the "full" areas containing the offices. Each of these minor "blocks" consists of 12 floors, four occupied by green areas that are four stories high, and eight utilized as working spaces.

The plan of this skyscraper is that of an equilateral triangle with rounded corners. The areas along the facades house these activities, which are the serviced areas. The corners contain the core functions of vertical circulation and the other servicing parts, as well as carrying the vertical load support of the structure, while the hollow of the central atrium formed in the interior acts as a ventilation duct and natural light shaft.

The offices along the facades have views of the outside and a ventilated wall that guarantees temperature comfort. A special feature of this wall is an inner window that can be opened, to which an outer window with an adjustable interposed sunshade is added to help regulate the lighting and protect the office from excessive heat.

160 top The drawing shows the relationship between the building and its surroundings. Its majestic height allows it to stand out in a mainly horizontal context, which corresponds to the nature of European cities.

160 bottom The cutaway view describes the detail inside the skyscraper and its alternating functional packages, that is, parts of several solid and empty levels with different uses.

161 The vertical internal division by functional package can also be recognized from the outside: the shell tends to be divided in various heights similar to the surrounding buildings. The corner parts, home to the vertical connections, increase volumetric continuity.

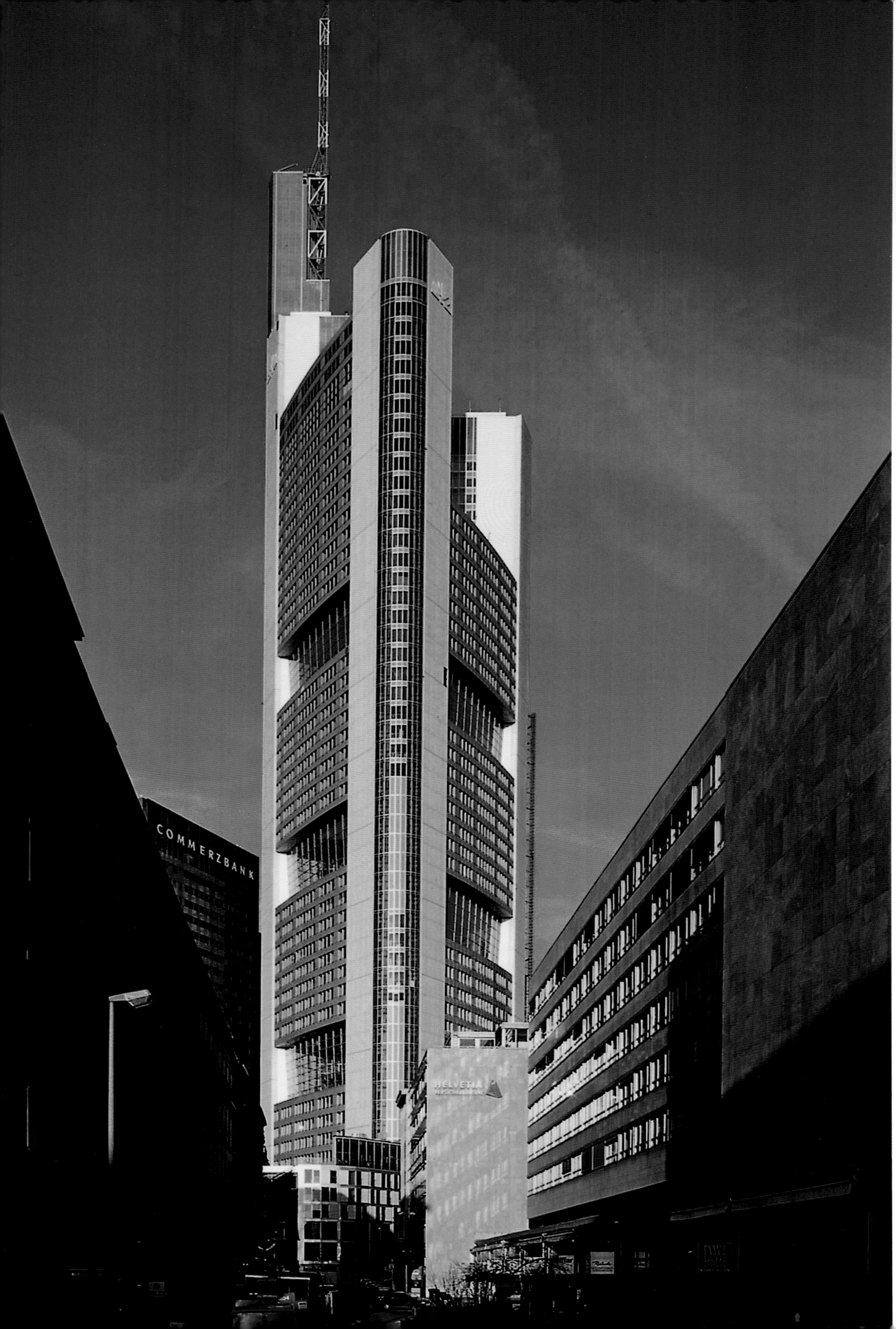

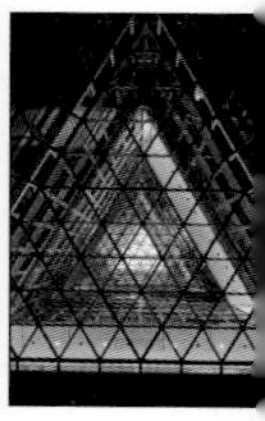

FOSTER + PARTNERS

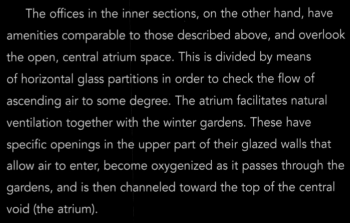

The offices in the inner sections, on the other hand, have amenities comparable to those described above, and overlook the open, central atrium space. This is divided by means of horizontal glass partitions in order to check the flow of ascending air to some degree. The atrium facilitates natural ventilation together with the winter gardens. These have specific openings in the upper part of their glazed walls that allow air to enter, become oxygenized as it passes through the gardens, and is then channeled toward the top of the central void (the atrium).

Intelligent computerized systems – which, however, leave ample room for independent regulation on the part of the office workers – control the heating and cooling, the opening of windows and shading and artificial lighting systems, thus minimizing energy consumption.

Another interesting factor in the composition of this building is the choice of plants for the winter gardens, as there are different types of vegetation depending on the orientation of the garden. This feature also provides a diversified image of the spaces, decreases the repetition of the inner distribution of volumes and differs from the typical skyscraper configuration.   S.L.

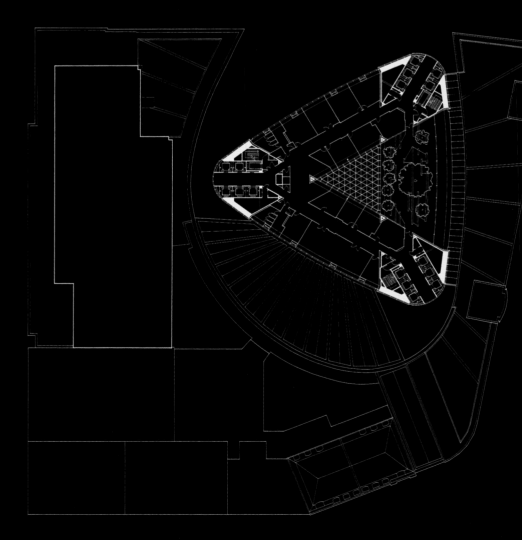

162 left The lower level has the role of mediating the building's impact with the fabric of the surrounding city. Several autonomous or complementary functions (to those already in the skyscraper) are also located in the lower level in addition to the main entrance.

162 bottom The diagram describes the internal division of the skyscraper. The serviced areas are located along the sides of the triangle while the servicing areas are in the corners and the remaining central space provides natural lighting.

162-163 The role of the winter gardens is to contribute to exchanging and therefore improving the air in the skyscraper. The moment air travels through the gardens it is oxygenated before and then conveyed upwards by the central void.

163 bottom Horizontal glass surfaces have been added around the central empty area of the Commerzbank, which acts as a light well and a natural ventilation stack.

Institute for Forestry and Nature Research

WAGENINGEN, THE NETHERLANDS

An area in the northern outskirts of Wageningen in The Netherlands, which for years was used for intensive farming to such a degree that it became dry and arid, was revitalized thanks to the construction of a building designed in keeping with criteria of sustainability that guarantee a well-balanced relationship with the environment and with those who use it – both eco- and user-friendly. These are the basic principles behind the "environmental humanism" philosophy elaborated by Günther Behnisch, who also conceived the project for the Institute for Forestry and Nature Research at Wageningen. The construction creates a new landscape, not by echoing its topographical features, but rather by gradually integrating the natural elements into the artificial ones in order to reconstruct a context in which certain ecosystems (the cycles and alternation of various climatic conditions such as wet-dry, hot-cold, sunny-shaded, etc.) that had been destroyed by intensive farming could be revived. To this end, the building was conceived as a comb-like structure: a longitudinal body facing north that contains the laboratories, on which are grafted three transverse wings housing the offices, among which are two large roofed courtyards. These constitute the core of the project both from the standpoint of the layout, since it is here that the elements of circulation and links among the various parts are concentrated, and from an environmental point of view, due to the presence of a series of opportunely diversified natural elements, between the first court space rich in luxuriant vegetation, and the second one, consisting of a network of pools that contributes to the bioclimatic functioning of the building.

The two courtyards have a glass roof and operate as agents for the passive use of solar energy. In winter the sunlight penetrates and heats the air, while in summer these spaces are cooled by the vegetation and evaporation produced by the watercourses, so that all year long they are a sort of temperate zone facing the offices, which can enjoy natural ventilation without sudden and rather drastic changes of temperature. Furthermore, the rainwater collected in the watercourses in one of the courtyards is then reused for toilet flushing, thus reducing the consumption of water, which like energy is becoming an increasingly precious resource. Consumption of both water and energy is also reduced by means of the green roofs that serve as thermal insulation for the areas below them and regulate the natural water cycle.

164 The picture shows the continuous front side of the longitudinal body that encloses the courtyard to the north and houses the laboratories. This building surrounded by lush vegetation contains the transversal bodies in which the offices are located.

164-165 Like the other external facades, the east side of the last diagonal building has fiber cement parapets, locust-tree facing and numerous double-pane, insulating glass surfaces. The materials were chosen on the basis of their impact on the environment.

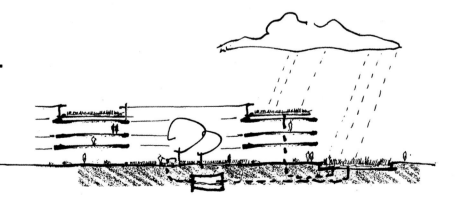

165 center The two sketches show how the large central courtyard covered by the glass surface captures sunlight in the summer. During the rainy winter season, the green roofs and landscaping regulate the natural water cycle.

165 bottom The elevation of the research institute is preceded by a row of trees that integrate the building even more within the context, and allow users working inside to enjoy views overlooking green areas.

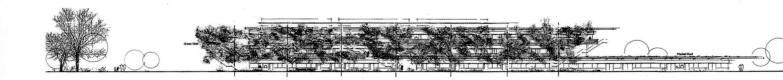

Again, certain technological devices increase the bioclimatic efficiency of the courtyards: the glass roof has a system of mobile blinds activated by light level gauges, which in summer close to shade the areas below and in winter open to collect sunlight. This device also insulates the roof to prevent heat dispersion.

A system of electrically operated valves absorbs smoke and hot air, and at night triggers air circulation to cool the room and reduce energy consumption.

The building material was also chosen on the basis of sustainability and impact on the environment. Although the structure is made of concrete, mostly for economic reasons, 40% of the inner walls, which are not subject to pollution or atmospheric conditions, are clad with short pieces of larch (a local wood that does not cost much to transport or to process), while the remaining 60% is covered with glass. In this way the offices can be illuminated most of the day with natural light. The outside walls are clad in robinia, a local wood that has a great degree of natural durability and double glazing. G.S.

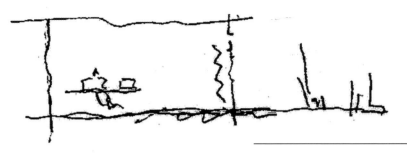

166 top and 167 top
The sketches show how each office overlooking the courtyard can be extended outwards and naturally ventilated and lit.

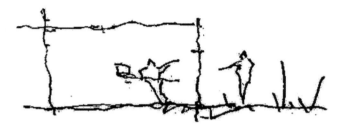

166 bottom All spaces overlooking the courtyard are defined by chosen materials based on the principles of sustainability: larch strips, a material that is easy to obtain in the area and doesn't require excessive transportation costs or installation treatments, and glass so the areas can be lit with natural light for most of the day.

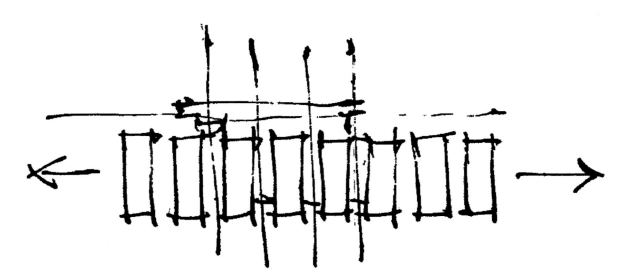

167 bottom The presence
of vegetation and water basins
in the courtyard allows water
to evaporate making the
environment fresh, even
in the summer.

168 top The picture shows how the glass roof over the courtyards and green rooftops isolate the areas below and also regulate the natural cycle of water.

168 bottom The planimetry shows the sequences of green areas forming a sort of bar code. They are located between the buildings and outdoor areas and transform the entire area into a kind of park.

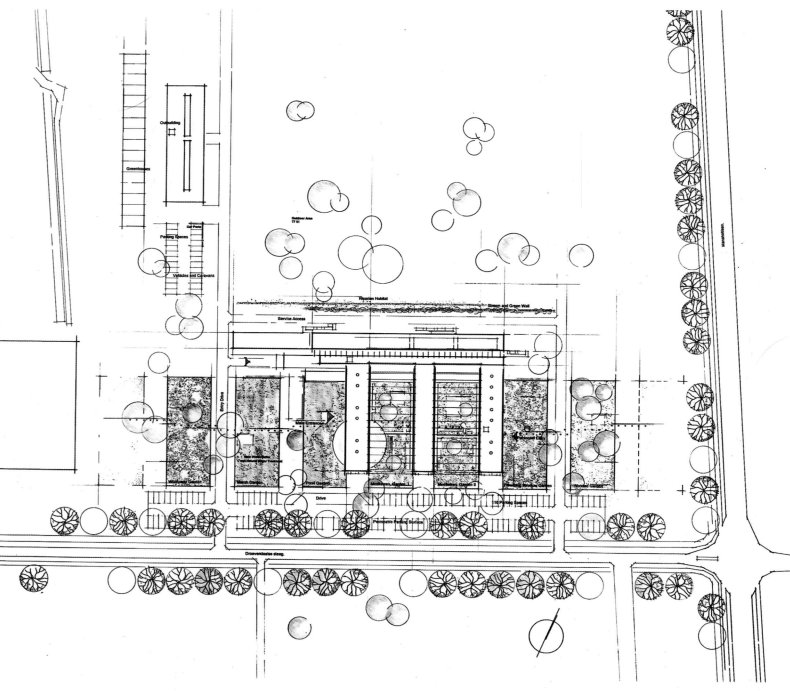

169 A mobile drape system has been added to the glass roof, which thanks to devices that detect the level of lighting, closes the drapes in the summer to provide shade to the areas below and opens them in the winter to capture the sunlight. This device also insulates the roof to prevent heat loss.

Hedge Building

ROSTOCK, GERMANY

This exhibition pavilion was designed for the 2003 International Garden (IGA) Exhibition held in Rostock, Germany. It is a temporary structure which acts as the exposition entrance, and is a combined architectural and environmental project.

The criteria of impermanency and economy that determined the choice of the building materials and systems employed in this structure also concerns the green walls, and took into consideration the ethical and environmental aspect, which was the driving force behind this 2003 exposition. Constructed with a steel framework, a plastic roof and a foundation made of cement, the pavilion can be easily disassembled and, for the most part, used again in other contexts.

Temporary events such as expositions contrast with a structure whose "shell" consists of vertical gardens. The need for a pavilion symbolizing agriculture, since it was the entrance to the show, was the basic motive for a project calling for an organism with walls made of plants that would fully express the total rationality and industrialization of German agriculture and at the same time allow for rapid assembly.

The simple and compact volume of the pavilion, arranged in the form of a parallelepiped, is articulated into four sides with horizontal bands. Each side has a steel framework housing channels of earth that are irrigated by means of a computerized system of tubes. The plant used here was an ivy hedge (hence the name of the pavilion). Arranged in sections measuring 4 x 6 feet that had been cultivated in a greenhouse and that formed "smart screens" inserted in the channels, they partly conceal the supporting structure of the pavilion, thus imparting a sense of lightness and uniformity.

Controlled irrigation and recyclable plant elements – which can be removed and placed elsewhere, or reassembled should the pavilion be placed in another location – are basic aspects of a project that truly respects the environment and is in sync with the spirit of the exposition.

Furthermore, the effect of a continuous vertical garden produced by these elements on the outside, and of a pleasant and welcoming atmosphere in the interior, is the feature that epitomizes the overall spatial and architectural quality of the project. These factors develop the poetic potential of the aspects of German agriculture that they celebrate, imparting an unexpected sensorial or, as suggested by the authors, romantic dimension. S.L.

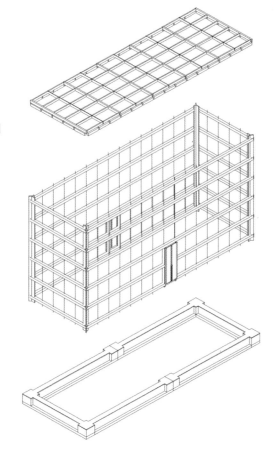

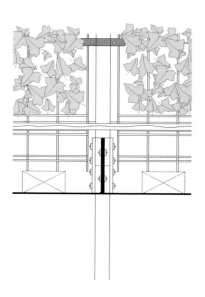

170 top The axonometric exploded diagram describes the components in the pavilion: a concrete foundation, an elevation structure framed with steel (with angular pillars) home to smart screens and a horizontal steel roof equipped with a plastic enclosing material.

170 bottom The horizontal and longitudinal cutaway views and cross-section are of the junctions between the horizontal elements equipped with smart screens and the vertical columns along the facades. A tank and planting grille are inside the horizontal steel strips along with an irrigation system and a plant element.

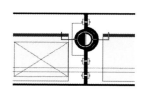
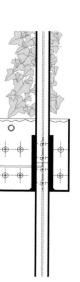
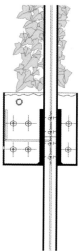

170-171 The pavilion shell is made of smart-screen walls, which produce the effect of vertical, permeable, light gardens outside and a welcoming, protected atmosphere inside, completely surrounded by natural, diffused light.

171 bottom This picture inside the outfitted pavilion shows how the walls connect the open outdoor area with the indoor exhibit area. The roof, made of plastic material, is clearly visible and contributes to softening and spreading natural light indoors.

Residence Antilia

MUMBAI, INDIA

This tower is one of the most recent experimental projects carried out by the SITE group. Situated in a particularly rich cultural context and in a difficult urban setting such as Mumbai, it meets the specific needs of the client, who wanted a building that would be well above the standards of first-rate international architectural projects.

Situated on the top of a hill, the residential tower has a vertical development with functional stratification that was conceived as a mixture of nature and architecture. The tiers of this structure are inserted into one another and supported by the three principal elements of the building: a central core (the "spine"), a large platform surmounting it, and reinforcing steel tension cables.

The concept of the project is a multi-tiered composition, an architectural landscape in sync with the ancient Hanging Gardens of Babylon. Therefore it was created as a garden that soars up toward the sky, free from the usual spatial constrictions imposed by human management of the land. The basic philosophy of this layout conforms to the Vastu principles of Hinduism, wherein the spine is regarded ass the main source of support, leading upward to "enlightenment", thus associating architecture with Man. The architects considered all aspects of this tradition, including the psychological ones, thus imparting multi-cultural references to the tower. The new and old worlds are placed together in a sort of universal architecture that is also specifically environmental and that ideally extends toward the future. The tower is a timeless structure with an ambiguous meaning that represents the possible development of architecture in the future.

For the SITE organization the combination of the above-considered elements reflects the 21st century, the age of information science and ecology. It expresses part of the team's aesthetic – which goes beyond the ecological approach in the common sense of this term and beyond the tendency to "revive" nature as part of the work. In other words, this is architecture conceived as an extension of nature. The vegetation constitutes the floor, walls and structure; the plants *are* the edifice and at the same time create it. The seven residential levels of the tower are therefore supported and articulated by the stratification of the central, supporting section – the "backbone" of the project – which together with the steel cables support five larger intermediate stories, making them look as if they are floating. These residential spaces have complementary functions and are equipped differently according to the activities they house: a variety of gardens, green terraces, verandahs, trellises for the plants, panoramic platforms, small waterfalls or pools, and recreational facilities.

Each of the floor planes that "overhang" with respect to the "spine" – a direct reference to the image of the vertebrae in the backbone – ideally plays the same role as an intermediate element in an ascending structure. This paradigm, which is in line with Vastu principles, is for the SITE group a point of reference for an infinite number of project combinations of artistic and technical features and aspects. From an aesthetic standpoint the horizontal partitioning produces the effect of stratification that is multiplied upward to the sky, thus providing natural light, the necessary shelter and a new landscape. The less extensive floor planes provide the tower with protected relaxation and recreational areas, green terraces and service spaces. This project, in keeping with the Indian Chakra centers of energy, associates in architectural terms a meaning to each of the zones of the tower, which are related to the themes of earth, water, fire, air, sound, light and information. The main residence, on the top level, gives continuity to the numerous tiers that are the principal feature of the tower. This floor, which comprises a heliport and a garden featuring the spectrum of Indian plants, is enclosed by large glass plates that offer a breathtaking panoramic view of Mumbai and its waterfront.   S.L.

WATERFALL BUILDING -
MUMBAI, INDIA 2003

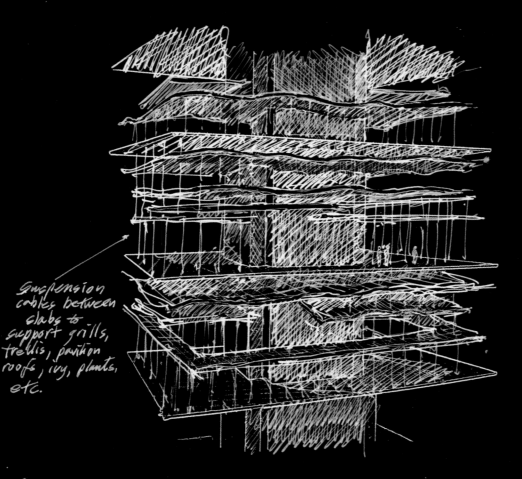

Suspension cables between slabs to support grills, trellis, pavilion roofs, ivy, plants, etc.

176 top The exploded diagram of a portion of the tower shows the idea of a building developed over subsequent levels. For designers, these overlapping layers are poetically reminiscent of a mille feuille effect on the background of the sky.

Residence Antilia -
"Mille feuille" idea of floor planes and floating trellis and other structures

176 bottom The sketch mainly describes the structural functioning of the tower. Its floors, which seem to float in mid-air, are sustained by a central support structure acting as an enormous pillar under a large platform (it also has a bearing function) from which cables descend through each floor to contribute to the system's static quality.

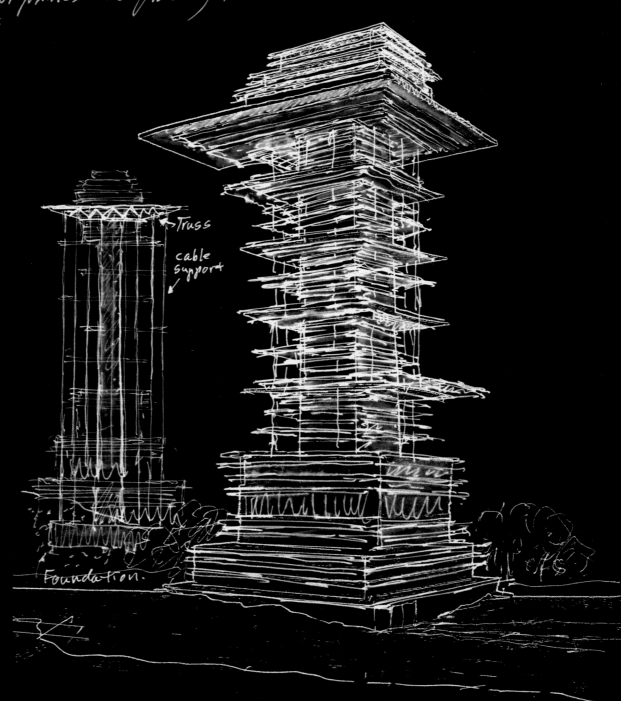

Truss

cable support

Foundation.

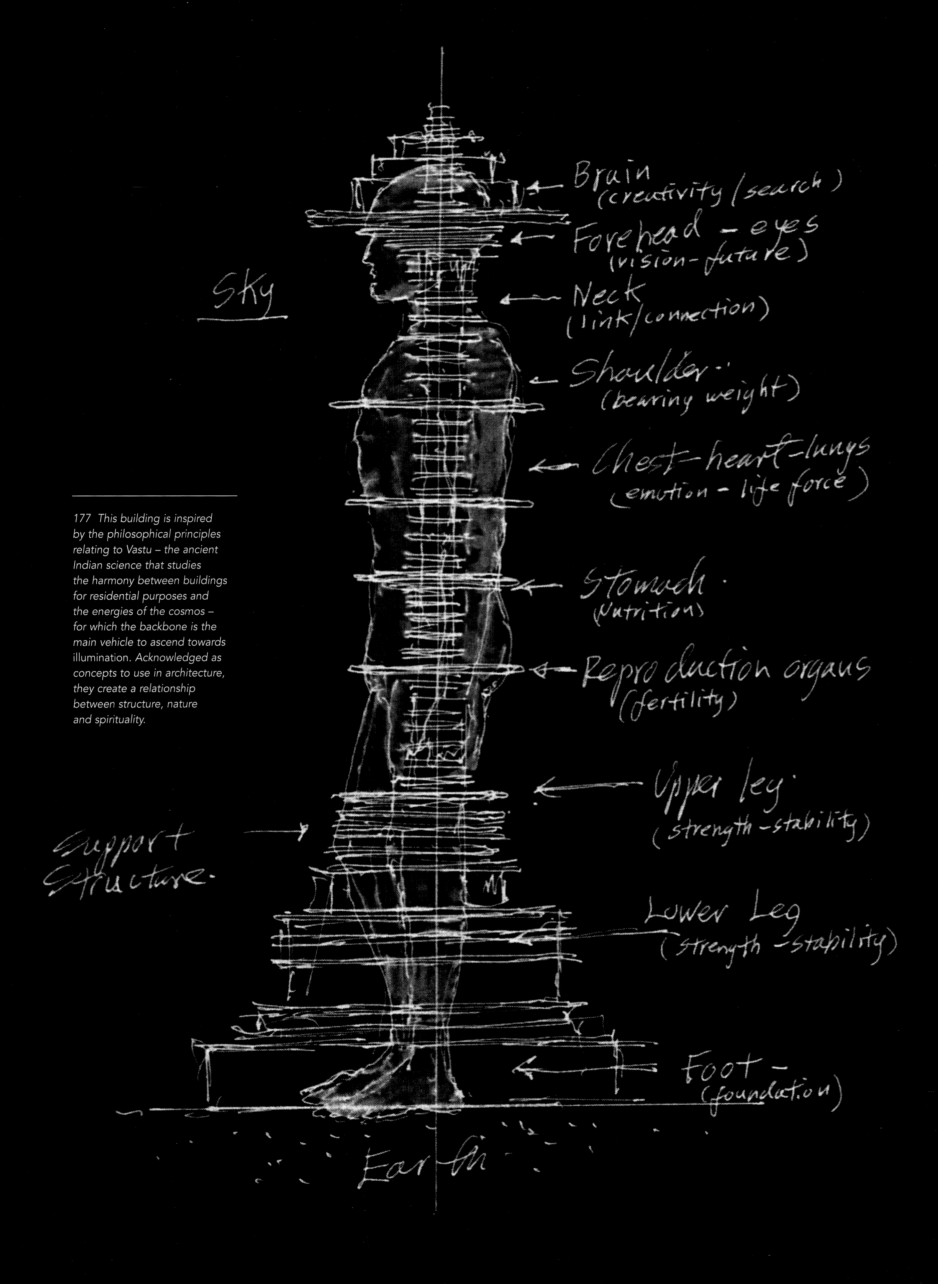

Sky

Brain
(creativity / search)

Forehead – eyes
(vision – future)

Neck
(link / connection)

Shoulder
(bearing weight)

Chest – heart – lungs
(emotion – life force)

Stomach
(Nutrition)

Reproduction organs
(fertility)

Upper leg
(strength – stability)

Support
Structure

Lower Leg
(strength – stability)

Foot –
(foundation)

Earth

177 This building is inspired
by the philosophical principles
relating to Vastu – the ancient
Indian science that studies
the harmony between buildings
for residential purposes and
the energies of the cosmos –
for which the backbone is the
main vehicle to ascend towards
illumination. Acknowledged as
concepts to use in architecture,
they create a relationship
between structure, nature
and spirituality.

178-179 The building is characterized by a transparent shell. It is located in an area home to other research institutes with opaque, compact volumetries and it stands out from the surrounding buildings – as from the projects of similar structures – for its use of strategies tied to sustainable planning.

179 The transparent shell of the Genzyme Center Headquarters, which was designed to meet local climatic conditions, is made of high efficiency glass with windows on each floor, and approximately one-third of the surface area has a ventilated double-wall system.

Genzyme Center Headquarters Building
CAMBRIDGE, USA

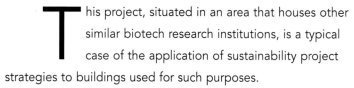

This project, situated in an area that houses other similar biotech research institutions, is a typical case of the application of sustainability project strategies to buildings used for such purposes.

The transparent facade that sets off the Genzyme Center Headquarters from other buildings in this area was conceived to deal with local climatic conditions. It consists of high-performance glass – with windows on each floor – and around one-third of its surface has a double-glazed, ventilated curtain wall. The operable window system is regulated automatically by a centralized system to optimize the temperature of the indoor environment, and also has an operable shading system for light regulation. The ventilated curtain wall, on the other hand, protects the building from summer glare, while retaining solar gain in the winter, in order to limit heat exchange.

The transparent facade and its irregular shape both evoke and reveal an articulated structure consisting of full and empty spaces, and spaces with different heights used mainly as offices or to house gardens situated outside and inside the Genzyme Center.

The complexity of the structure, which one perceives when approaching it from its urban surroundings, is by no means any less obvious once inside.

The central atrium extends to the entire height of the building and is defined by volumes that are protruding or recessed for the 12 stories in which the structure is articulated. This empty space is the fulcrum of the project. The main public and private functions of the building revolve around it: the enclosed workplaces, the large open spaces, the more informal areas for relaxation and recreation, and the spaces for vertical circulation and connection. The uppermost part of the building is delimited by a skylight, near which there are air outflow ducts which penetrate the structure through the facade. The atrium therefore functions as both a ventilation tack and source of daylight.

The ascending air currents created in the atrium help to regulate the temperature of the building and insure a constant flow of fresh air, whose quality is improved by the presence of green areas that provide oxygen and purify it.

The sunlight that filters down from the skylight is improved in its intensity and thoroughly diffused by a system of heliostats and mirrors. The atrium also has suspended elements that hang down its entire length. Like small sculptures whose components seem to be fluttering in empty space, these devices consist of smaller elements that reflect the light and spin around thanks to the ascending airflow that animates the atrium.

Furthermore, the reflection and diffusion of sunlight is enhanced by the use of reflecting surfaces placed in the parapets and walls that surround the atrium, as well as by the pools in the interior.

Another noteworthy aspect of the bioclimatic strategies employed is the collection of rainwater which is reused in the building. Its evaporation helps to decrease the need for cooling towers and irrigation of the green areas. The result is a saving of about one-third of the water consumed compared to a building used for similar activities.

The Genzyme Center Headquarters was awarded the USGBC Leed Platinum Rating (the highest level of the classification of Leadership in Energy and Environmental Design of the US Green Building Council) for the project's application of excellent sustainability strategies. Other such measures include: integrated systems for the reduction and regulation of water consumption, the use of low-emission building material, recycled contents, local production and the use of FSC (Forest Stewardship Council) certified wood.   S.L.

BEHNISCH ARCHITEKTEN

179

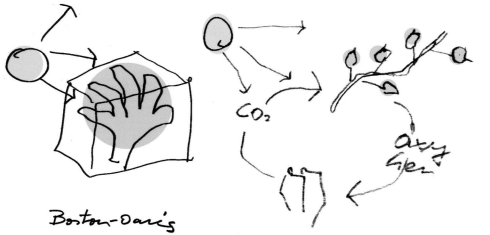

Boston-Davis

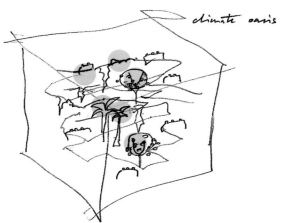

climate oasis

CO₂

181 *The two axonometric diagrams, respectively empty and solid areas, describe the volumetric complexity of the project characterizing it both internally and externally.*

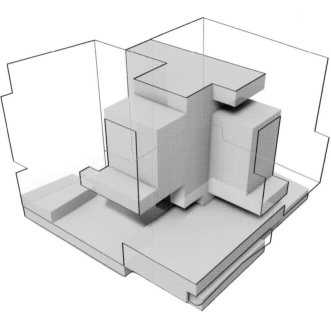

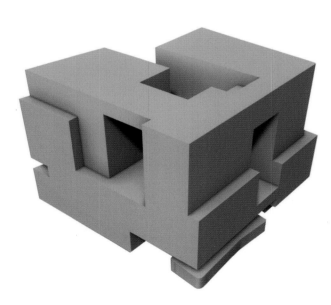

180-181 *The shell is faced with different, alternating panels – mainly glass – and has an irregular shape. This structure is characterized for its empty and solid areas and overhangs and recesses.*

180 bottom *The diagram explains the main reasons for added green areas to the project in an effort to contribute to improving the quality of the indoor air.*

182 top The central atrium and its high ceiling are defined by masses and flat areas that jut out or withdraw along the structure's 12 levels.

182 bottom The cutaway view describes the building's bioclimatic function and the role of the central atrium, a hollow area whose peak is outlined by a skylight operating as a ventilation stack and light well. Specific reflective surfaces have been placed in the parapets, walls and expanses of water to improve the diffusion and intensity of the natural lighting.

182-183 The project focused on the atrium, which is surrounded by the main functions: closed working areas, open spaces, informal meeting areas, distribution areas and vertical connection. Elements have been hung inside such as lightweight, floating sculptures composed of smaller elements free to rotate and reflect light.

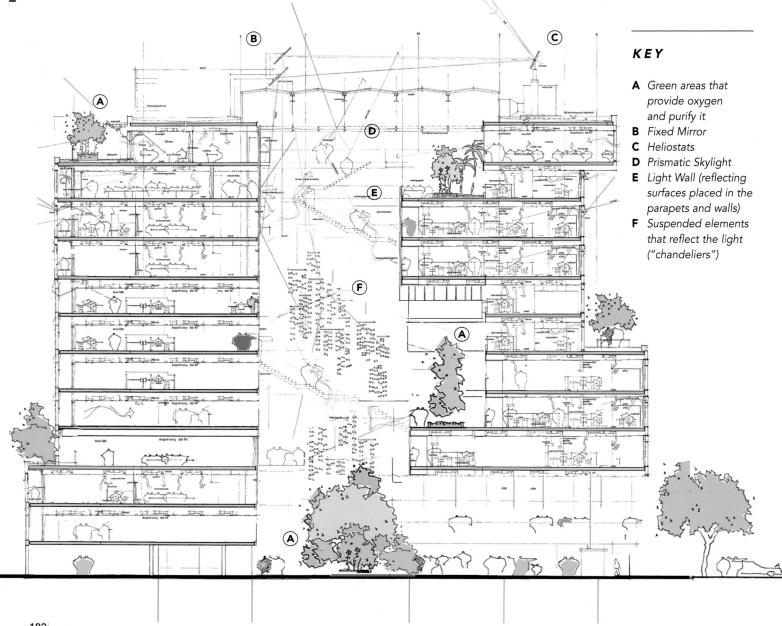

KEY

A *Green areas that provide oxygen and purify it*
B *Fixed Mirror*
C *Heliostats*
D *Prismatic Skylight*
E *Light Wall (reflecting surfaces placed in the parapets and walls)*
F *Suspended elements that reflect the light ("chandeliers")*

Federal Agency for the Environment

DESSAU, GERMANY

Given its objectives, the main office of the Federal Environmental Agency is an architectural complex whose basic construction principles had to be sustainability, a decrease in energy consumption, the use of ecological building material, whilst ensuring comfort and safety to the 800 employees who work there. However, this project also set out to be a model for the conversion of a former industrial site into part of a public park.

This is why the new offices in Dessau are located in an area that was once occupied by the so-called Gas Quarter – whose production of industrial gas had seriously polluted the surrounding territory – and by the city's main railway station, whose abandoned tracks covered most of the area. The contaminated land was reclaimed, the railway tracks were removed and a park laid out in their place, and the railway station and an old gas heater plant were converted.

In 1998 the architects Sauerbruch Hutton won the competition promoted the previous year by the German Federal Republic, and proposed a four-story irregularly curved building which measures 1,500 feet long and 37 feet wide. It looks somewhat like a ribbon and is inserted in the surroundings, enclosing both a courtyard that the architects call the Atrium, and the Forum, a crescent-shaped space facing the countryside. Therefore, the park not only defines and characterizes the outside environment, but also penetrates the building, creating continuity between architecture and nature. It becomes the element that links the various public functions of the complex centered in the isolated buildings scattered in the area. These include the canteen, which is a border element, a sort of screen that shields the complex from the neighboring bypass, while toward the park it becomes a transparent cylinder; the old railroad station, which now houses the information center; the other converted building that was enlarged and connected to the main body by means of a one-story block housing the library; and other small structures the architects call "stones" which are inserted at the base of the main building. The auditorium is the largest of these and is situated inside the Forum, intersecting with the glass wall that delimits this space. In fact, although the Forum is an enclosed and roofed area, it was conceived as a large foyer open to the public and affording access to all the Federal Environmental Agency's public activities and can also be the venue for various events, exhibitions, etc. From here one enters the Atrium, the enclosed courtyard that also has a steel and glass roof.

184-185 top The complex of the headquarters of the Federal Agency for the Environment was obtained by reconverting a former industrial site in a public park. To do this, the main building was given the shape of an irregular crescent open towards the park but closed in and delimited by a roof and glass facade.

184-185 bottom The longitudinal cutaway view cuts across the central courtyard and shows the passageways connecting the two sides of the main building, elevations of the indoor areas and the new library building that creates continuity between the agency main structure and the old factory that was re-utilized.

185 center The cross-sections show the relationship between the building and the cafeteria which delimits the peripheral area, the main building home to the low auditorium and the park connecting the various parts.

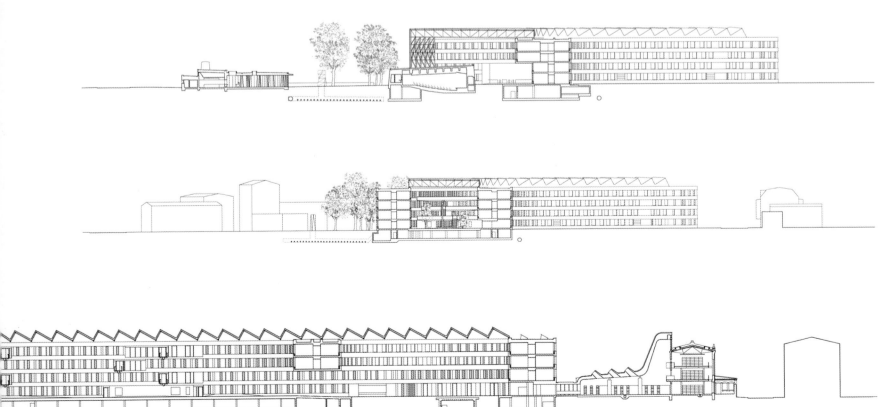

186-187 and 187 bottom The vivacity of the elevations is the result of the curvilinear direction and alternating horizontal and vertical wood strips between the colored windows. All materials implemented are recycled and biodegradable.

186 bottom The picture shows the new building in the foreground, which connects pre-existing Building 109 with the main one. This one-story building rises 49 feet toward the old construction, as if to wrap around it.

This is the area where Agency employees can mingle, and where all the circulation of the entire complex is concentrated. It is traversed by a series of bridges that connect the various departments located on either side of the Atrium, and most of the offices overlook this space.

This large roofed court contains many plants, together with a geothermal energy exchange system to regulate the climate of the rooms. The Atrium absorbs the sunlight, and thanks to a system of high-level thermal insulation creates an area with a mild temperature that is overlooked by the offices, which can thus take advantage of the natural ventilation produced by this large cavity. Even the offices facing the outside can eliminate unhealthy air without consuming energy.

The configuration of a narrow building with a central corridor containing offices on either side makes it possible for these rooms to enjoy a great amount of natural light for most of the day. Moreover, the pools inside the Atrium and along the facades of this court (60% of which is made of glass) make these areas brighter, since the reflecting water of the pools attracts more light. Other apparatuses make use of passive solar energy possible: solar panels and collectors; mobile protection on the facade that allows the sunlight to penetrate the building in the winter while protecting it from the heat in the summer; and the use of three layers of protective glazing and a system of shading on the roof also shield the edifice from the sun.

Besides all these bioclimatic, environmentally friendly devices, the architects also came up with other ecological solutions, such as the use of natural biomasses and recycled and biodegradable materials, including the local wood used on the facades and the green roof. G.S.

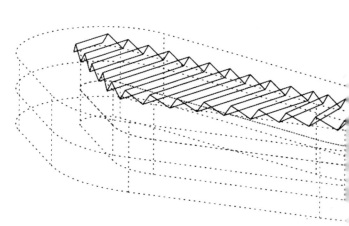

188 top The glass facade outlining the public area (atrium), intersects with the building home to the auditorium, which is the largest of a series of small, one-story buildings (called stones by architects) at the bottom of the main building.

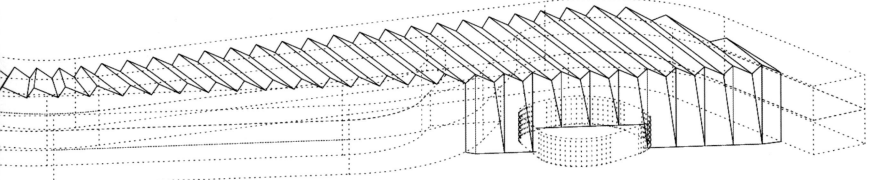

188 center The area in the indoor courtyard connects the elements and is crossed by a series of bridges uniting the departments on two sides and the various levels through a system of stairways.

188 bottom The axonometric diagram shows the

main building, the cafeteria and library located on the edge of the area and the park in between.

188-189 top This view of the atrium shows the auditorium (in the foreground), defined by a wall wrapped around itself and opening

up to allow access to the area inside.

188-189 bottom The shed roof is faced with glass panels and continues along the entrance wall. Both of these two glass surfaces make the courtyard and office area overlooking it extremely bright.

KEY

A Chlorophyl Garden
B Turbulent Lawn
C Wave Meadow
D Bubbling Marsh
E Filter Court
F Wetlands Pond

Whitney Water Purification Facility and Park

HAMDEN, USA

Recycling an old water purification plant, converting it into a water treatment plant, and creating a public park extending over 140,000 square feet, were the proposals for the Whitney Waterworks Park in Connecticut, made by architect Steven Holl, winner of the AIA Top Ten Green Projects in 2007. His project combines a series of strategies to improve the environment, the scenery, and even the lives of the citizens of Hamden. The waterworks is situated in an area flanked on one side by part of a suburban residential neighborhood and on the other by the Eli Whitney Museum across the street; neither of which is at all affected by the plant since it is hidden by a roof carpeted with greenery. The park hosts a mixture of traditional activities – such as dog walking, areas with benches for sitting and reading, picnicking, or skateboarding – with educational activities aimed at teaching the importance of water as a resource. It even has areas with many pools that form a natural habitat for migratory birds and other animal species.

The new landscape, which is suspended over the stainless steel reservoir (most of which is underground), thus creates continuous links with this subterraneous world, represented metaphorically by Holl's concept of the project "from micro to macro": from the infinitesimal dimension of water to the scale of the landscape as represented by a park dotted with pools. Both levels consist of six sectors, which are arranged in hierarchical order based on the proportions and the dimension of the old sand-filtration plant.

190-191 top and center The two pictures show the north facade of the drop-shaped building emerging from the ground. The picture above shows the view from the east in all its height (42 feet), given that the surface area of the park on this side progressively descends. The photograph below shows the same facade seen from the west side, where the building emerges only 16 feet from the ground.

190 bottom The park includes six different sectors differentiated by character, use and materials selected in relation to the activities of the underlying water purification facility.

191 top The only mass emerging from the surface of the park is the access building in the shape of an upturned teardrop.

This creates underground spaces and landscapes on ground level that take on characters, materials and atmospheres that are always different. In the part of the plant that serves as the ozonization zone, that is to say, where oxygen O_2 becomes O_3 through boiling, the surface area of the park is dotted with a series of "bubbles" in a field of moss that are skylights affording natural light to the underground areas. On a level with the flocculation zone, marked by agitation caused by waves, the grass is continuously traversed by small brooks that lend movement to the overall configuration, and above the underground area with turbulent movement there are hills. Again, in that part of the plant with a GAF sedimentation bed, the park becomes a garden of shadows. The green roof provides insulation to the waterworks plant and also maintains a constant temperature inside, thus saving a considerable amount of energy.

This underground world is "announced" on ground level by the entrance structure, which is made of steel and has the shape of an inverted drop of water. Cased by stainless steel that reflects the light, the elements and colors of the landscape, this structure changes continuously, as do the surroundings, according to the season and time of day. The casing is made up of thin and very luminous steel plates that have been bent to conform to the shape of a drop of water and which absorb the sun's energy to heat the interior. The casing also has many tiny windows that afford natural ventilation. The upper level contains the laboratories and offices, while the lower level has an exhibition atrium and a small auditorium for video screenings on water treatment and purification. All the materials used, from those for the casing to those for the doors, windows, etc. were chosen for their low chemical emission and because they can be recycled and are rapidly renewable. Even the cement, which comprises 40% of the building material, came from local plants and was partly prefabricated so as to reduce construction time and expenses.   G.S.

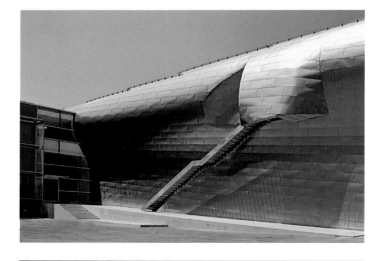

192 The entrance to the building is through a glass wall (visible on the left) which connects the outdoor landscape with the internal areas, making them extremely bright. The outdoor stairs lead to the areas on the upper level used for offices and laboratories.

192-193 The entrance area is finished with stainless-steel shingles, a material that absorbs solar rays to heat the interior rooms and that reflects light and the colors of the landscape so its image constantly mutates based on the changes in the weather and the seasons.

Tour Signal

PARIS, FRANCE

The new landmark of the Défense district of Paris will be the Tour Signal, or Signal Tower. Its 71 stories will rise up near the West Gate, to the left of the Grande Arche de la Défénse and will cover a surface area of 1.5 million square feet. It will be 987 feet high, which will make it the second tallest structure in Paris after the Eiffel Tower (1,063 ft). In short, it will be the icon of the renovation of this district, which calls for changing it from a services industry and office center into a comprehensive urban neighborhood with residences, shops and public spaces. To this end, in July 2007 EPAD, the public body responsible for supervising the development and renewal of the Defénse district, announced an international competition that was won by French architect Jean Nouvel, the 2007 Pritzker Prize winner. Nouvel proposes a monolithic building involving four overlapping cubes, each of which is defined on one side by a large cavity opening up towards the landscape. The other three steel and glass facades are differentiated by thicker or looser weave. Each cube or section of the building will have a different function.

Nouvel's project is extremely innovative, both as a new type of structure and also from an urban-town planning standpoint. The Tour Signal will be the first poly-functional skyscraper in France, and it aims at becoming a hub of orderly development compared to the chaotic configuration of the Défense district, which now consists of an assemblage of disparate and bizarre structures whose only connecting link is the Grande Arche.

Thus, the second goal is to make the tower an example of calm, a basic structure of connection and relation with the heart of Paris by continuing the historic axis of the Champs Elysées. And it is precisely thanks to the link with the latter and the reinterpretation of its basic features that Nouvel's project will succeed in becoming truly urban, in direct dialog with its setting. Much like the Grande Arche – which reinterprets the theme of the triumphal arch as a cube that is hollow so that one of the main structural arteries of the French capital can penetrate it and continue into the district – the four cubes of the new tower will be hollowed by large loggias, an extraordinary element of urban architecture inspired by historic cities, in particular Italian urban culture.

194-195 and 195 top The Tour Signal is close to the West Gate on the left side of the great boulevard connecting La Défense with the center of Paris and ending at the Grande Arche. It communicates with the latter through an analogous figure: a hollow cube – the reinterpretation of the Arc de Triomphe – repeated four times by Nouvel, who stacks the various blocks to create a vertical object exceeding 987 feet (301 meters) in height.

195 bottom The plan demonstrates the wealth of the figures defining the heterogeneous landscape of La Défense, to whom however a multitude of uses doesn't correspond. The new work by Jean Nouvel aims precisely at introducing this variety with the mixed-use tower.

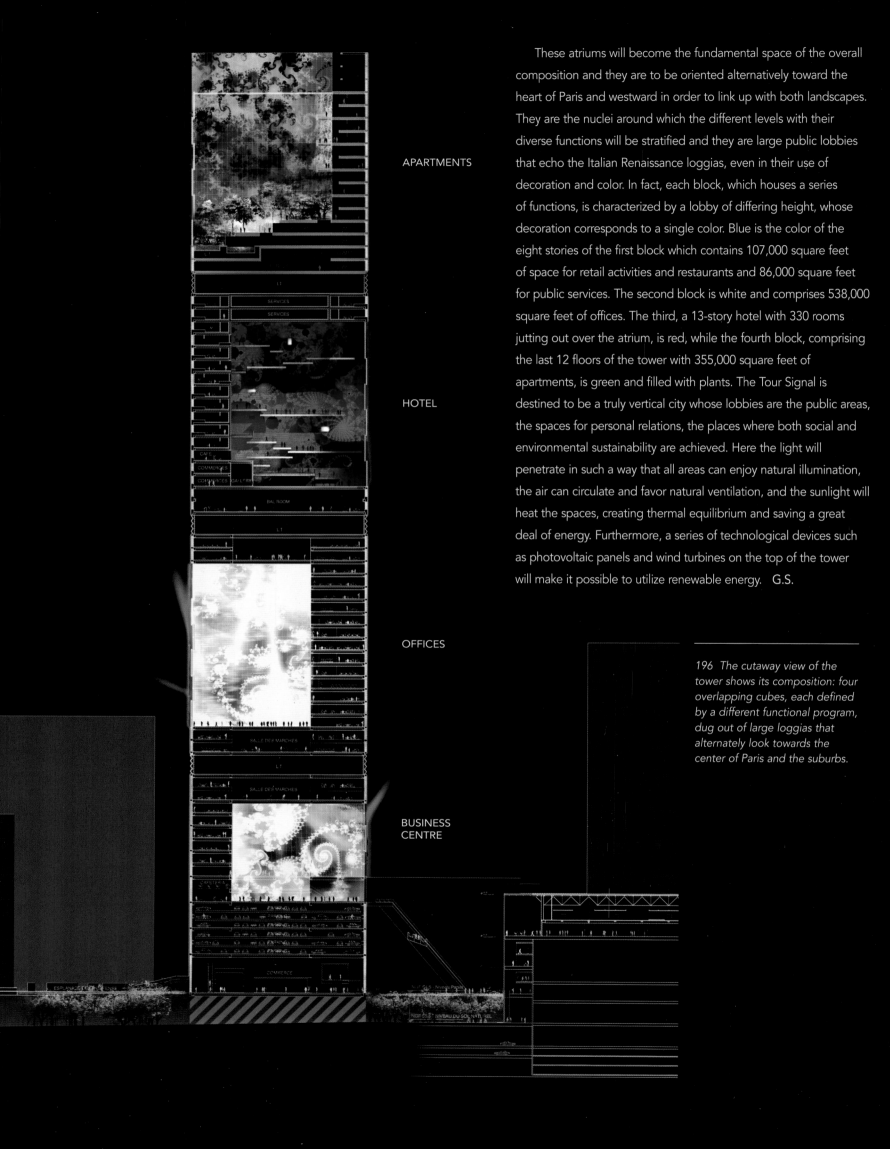

APARTMENTS

HOTEL

OFFICES

BUSINESS
CENTRE

These atriums will become the fundamental space of the overall composition and they are to be oriented alternatively toward the heart of Paris and westward in order to link up with both landscapes. They are the nuclei around which the different levels with their diverse functions will be stratified and they are large public lobbies that echo the Italian Renaissance loggias, even in their use of decoration and color. In fact, each block, which houses a series of functions, is characterized by a lobby of differing height, whose decoration corresponds to a single color. Blue is the color of the eight stories of the first block which contains 107,000 square feet of space for retail activities and restaurants and 86,000 square feet for public services. The second block is white and comprises 538,000 square feet of offices. The third, a 13-story hotel with 330 rooms jutting out over the atrium, is red, while the fourth block, comprising the last 12 floors of the tower with 355,000 square feet of apartments, is green and filled with plants. The Tour Signal is destined to be a truly vertical city whose lobbies are the public areas, the spaces for personal relations, the places where both social and environmental sustainability are achieved. Here the light will penetrate in such a way that all areas can enjoy natural illumination, the air can circulate and favor natural ventilation, and the sunlight will heat the spaces, creating thermal equilibrium and saving a great deal of energy. Furthermore, a series of technological devices such as photovoltaic panels and wind turbines on the top of the tower will make it possible to utilize renewable energy.   G.S.

196 The cutaway view of the tower shows its composition: four overlapping cubes, each defined by a different functional program, dug out of large loggias that alternately look towards the center of Paris and the suburbs.

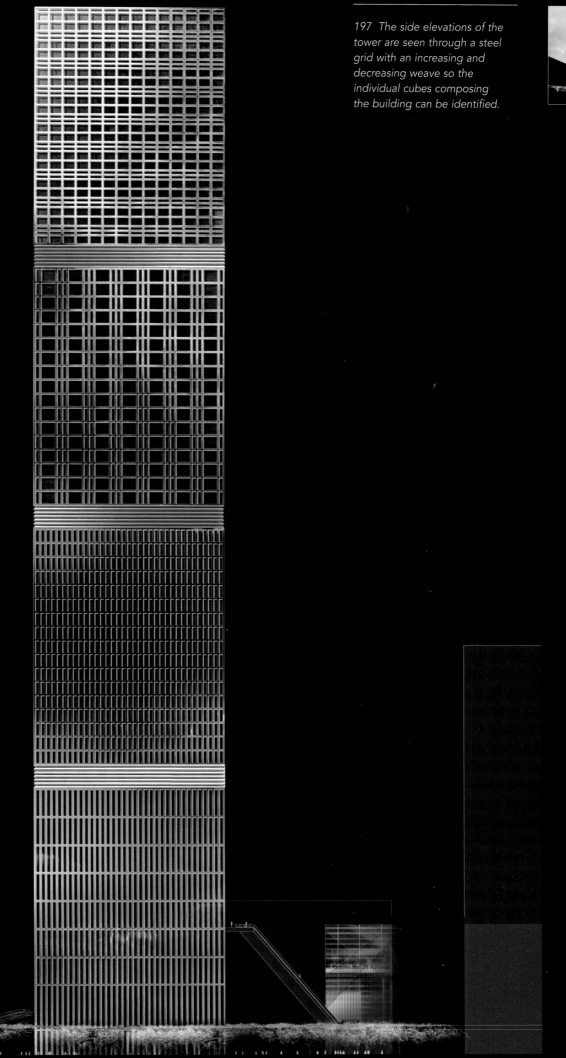

197 The side elevations of the tower are seen through a steel grid with an increasing and decreasing weave so the individual cubes composing the building can be identified.

ATELIERS JEAN NOUVEL

198 A blue lobby is on the
bottom level, which is home
to shops. The picture shows
shop windows opposite
a public area.

198-199 An escalator from the
square in front of the tower directly
leads inside the first cube. Another
escalator brings individuals to an
atrium surrounded by offices.

200-201 *The atrium in the first cube (whose interior is shown here) is characterized by blue filigree drawings and a marvelous view over La Défense.*

The pictures respectively show the elevation of the tower from the east and a cutaway view of its base, which houses commercial areas in the lower levels and the offices in the first cube.

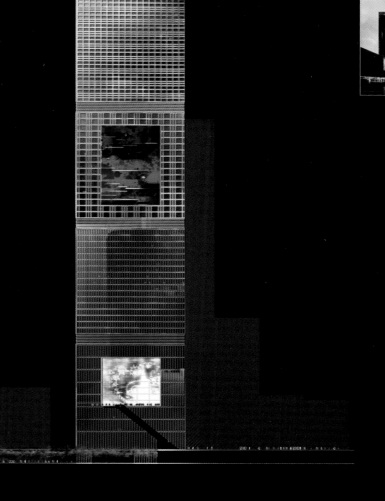

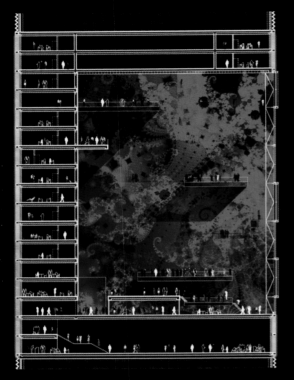

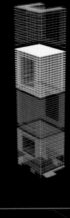

202, 202-203 and 203 top The third cube is home to a hotel and is in the direction of the center of Paris. The large loggia dug out inside is embellished with shades of red and elegant filigree drawings and provides a pleasant view of La Défense, including the Tour EDF by Henry N. Cobb in the foreground and the skyline of the French capital and the Eiffel Tower in the background.

204 top The loggia in the second cube contains offices and stands out for its white color, which makes the surrounding areas even brighter.

204-205 The charming picture depicts the atrium surrounded by the apartments in the last cube. It hosts semi-public functions and green areas.

205 The elevation from the west of the Tour Signal can be identified by the loggias dug out of the office and apartment cubes.

Energy Plus Building
PARIS, FRANCE

The American architectural studio Skidmore, Owings & Merrill LLP has designed what will become the largest zero emission office complex in the world. Situated in the Hauts-de-Seine *département* in the suburbs of Paris, the Energy Plus Building will be totally self-sufficient: the heating, light and air conditioning for the offices will be produced by the building itself, which may even create a surplus: "carbon credits" that can be transformed into currency.

The project is conceived as follows. A continuous wall winds like a sinuous tape around the perimeter of the area and becomes the foundation of the building itself. These diaphanous and silk-screened curves provide the inner gardens with the necessary isolation from the city and the very busy road that runs beside the premises.

The glass surfaces on the facades facing the road are protected by thin *brise-soleils* made of smooth metal panels and tall vertical screens that almost create a huge architectural order. As we can see from the computer-rendered images, the edifice seems to emerge from empty spaces left by the garden filled with vegetation and pools. The plants that start off from the open courtyards become partitions of ivy that climb up to the top of the architectural volumes, creating green bands, and then continue their "journey" in the interior, enveloping the columns in the atrium.

The decision to arrange the complex not as a rigid body but rather to develop it into a ramified configuration offers more opportunities for contact with the greenery and water that penetrate this office complex.

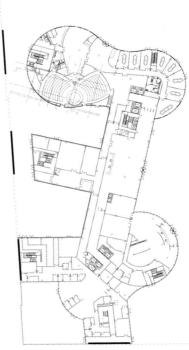

206 and 206-207 top The Energy Plus Building located in Paris' Hauts-de-Seine département occupies a lot next to the Seine and runs along a freeway. Solar panels will be installed on the roof and water from the Seine pumped into the building will be used for cooling.

206-207 bottom A winding foundation contrasts with broken lines of the bodies of the buildings that capture the lot's green areas.

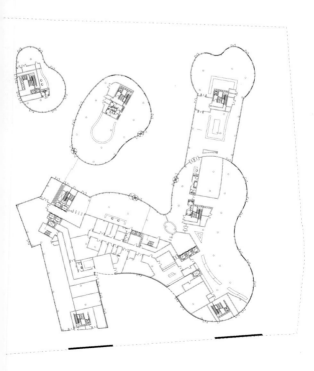

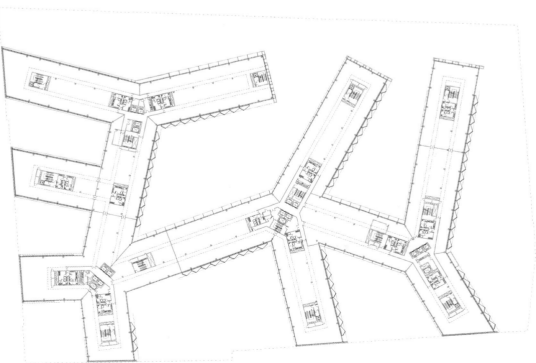

208 top The vegetation develops around the glass strips of the top surface areas of the structures.

208 center An image of the hall shows the designers' desire to also cover indoor areas with ivy plants.

208 bottom The brise-soleils made with stretched sheet-metal panels contribute to reducing insolation and thermal insulation.

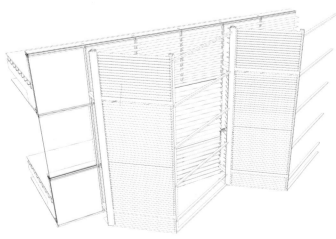

208-209 The glass facades are the most extended surface area of the shell and therefore play an important connotative role. The articular volume of the complex aims to provide the offices with better exposure and increased contact with the green areas and the expanses of water.

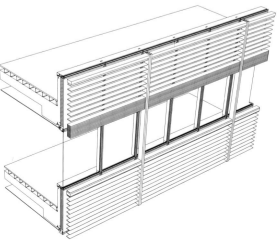

It also increases the surface of the roof, on which solar panels will be installed. As far as the air conditioning is concerned, instead of the usual conditioners there will be a system that uses water from the Seine, which will be pumped into the interior of the edifice.

The 753,000 square feet of the Energy Plus Building will also include innovative systems for the reduction of insolation and for thermal insulation, which will decrease energy consumption to 16 kilowatts per meter every year. It will be the lowest consumption in the world for an office building of this size, as opposed to the 80-250 kilowatts usually consumed in "traditional" buildings. A group of experts from The Rocky Mountain Institute, a nonprofit organization based in Colorado, that fosters the efficient and restorative use of resources, collaborated with the American architects' studio in this project.

The Energy Plus Building should be able to house approximately 5,000 people and the initial cost will be about 25-30% higher than a traditional office building. But if we stop to consider that in France construction is responsible for 47% of pollution, compared to 33% caused by industry and 22% by automobiles, this structure may trigger a "virtuous cycle" of construction of zero emission buildings.   L.S.

Elephant & Castle Eco Tower

LONDON, UK

The Elephant & Castle Eco Tower project is a great endeavor aimed at the urban renewal and upgrading of a zone in South Central London. This will be achieved by transforming about 72 hectares of land into an area that will eventually have a new public transport line, more than 11 million square feet of commercial enterprises, 5 million square feet of offices, 3,500 new homes, 1,100 council houses, a hotel and three public parks. In this urban development area, the project for the Elephant & Castle Eco Tower, designed by T.R. Hamzah & Yeang Sdn Bhd together with HTA Architects, calls for the systems, infrastructures and zoning typical of London to be placed in three skyscrapers.

The tower and the base on which it rests (which houses the commercial areas) look like an urban microcosm, with parks, shops, entertainment and leisure areas, community services, and houses.

The "City-in-the-Sky" project is aimed at finding other systems of urban configuration and mechanisms to manage and control the forms of the city, the consumption of the land and the use of the sites. For the homes the idea is to find a form of social mixture: the types of residence are grouped according to housing needs, which range from homes for one person to those for a family, and up to luxury apartments. The alternation and proximity of the services, such as gardens and shops, make for shared areas. Nature is a dominant factor in the three towers, as there will be a series of outdoor public spaces (the gardens/parks), semi-public areas (the entrance courtyards), and private outdoor areas (the terraces).

The three high-rises will be articulated as two blocks around a central area of greenery. During the winter months, when the sun is lower on the horizon, the central circulation area and the southeast units will receive the most sunlight.

The southern orientation of the towers will make the most of the winter sunshine, which will enter the empty spaces and pedestrian passageways, thus providing sufficient lighting to the service areas of the housing units.

As mentioned, the project aims at reproducing – on the various levels of the towers – the conditions that normally prevail in a "horizontal" city. Vegetation, open-air courtyards, balconies and a winter garden will lie against the surfaces of the tower and even penetrate them. Indeed, the Elephant & Castle towers are nothing more or less than landscape architecture, which is a characteristic feature of all of Ken Yeang's projects, a line of research typical of his vision and aesthetic.

Tower 3

Tower 2

Tower 1

210 top The Elephant & Castle Eco Tower is a large urban project that will radically modify London's skyline by introducing buildings of an unusual height, considering the architectural panorama of the English capital.

210 bottom The picture depicts a standard floor (23rd floor) in the three complex towers.

211 The plan consists in realizing a "green structure" including housing, restaurants, parks, playing fields, shops and sports facilities. A protected garden in the middle of the towers will allow individuals to surround themselves with nature.

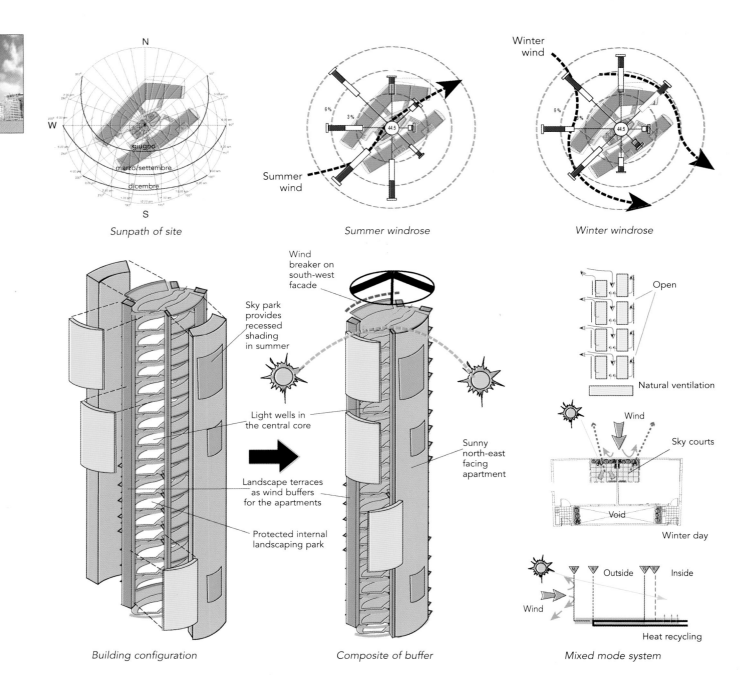

Sunpath of site

Summer windrose

Winter windrose

Winter wind

Summer wind

Building configuration

Wind breaker on south-west facade

Sky park provides recessed shading in summer

Light wells in the central core

Landscape terraces as wind buffers for the apartments

Protected internal landscaping park

Composite of buffer

Sunny north-east facing apartment

Mixed mode system

Open

Natural ventilation

Wind

Sky courts

Void

Winter day

Outside   Inside

Wind

Heat recycling

The vegetation, which from the ground proceeds upwards on the buildings, has a two-fold objective: it imparts a human dimension to the huge spaces and also filters the action of the sun and wind. In the winter it acts as a sort of barrier against the cold wind, while during the summer it blocks, absorbs and reflects most of the sun's radiation, thus lowering the temperature in the interior.

The porous outer surface of the towers will consist of a multi-strata system that allows for the passage of light but by means of windbreak screens will become a barrier against cold currents. Specially built doors, windows and shutters will retain the heat during the cold winter nights.

The roof connecting the two separate bodies of the tower will make what is really a divided edifice full of holes and separate parts look like a single architectural volume. And it is precisely this complex articulation that makes this work an extraordinary instrument that registers the movement of both the sun and the wind.   L.S.

212 top and center This analysis and study diagram to optimize the characteristics of the shell and passive systems relating to climate and intended use highlight the following passive methods: configuration and direction of the building, drawing of the facade, landscape and vegetation.

212 bottom The sketches highlight how the area outside the tower was thought of as a porous surface to house vegetation.

212-213 The north-south section (through the park) of towers 1 and 2 shows how nature progressively enters the buildings.

One Gallions
LONDON, UK

The One Gallions housing development project lies somewhere between pure architecture and town planning, affording the concrete possibility to construct a zero carbon emission complex in an area that presents many critical problems. One Gallions will be a complex of high-density structures – consisting of prevalently horizontally-oriented residential blocks and only one high rise – laid out in a perimeter around landscaped courtyards. The overall rationale of the project takes into consideration the highest environmental standards and the use of renewable energy sources.

The site of the project is mostly bordered by roads with fast flowing traffic and is near London City Airport; consequently the layout of the development has been conceived to solve one of the most important problems this project faces: acoustic pollution. The large inner courtyard is a sheltered space surrounded by the residential buildings and will act as the community area of the various structures, at once a private and open, urban-like space. Virtually all the homes will have two aspects, one overlooking the streets and the other with a view of the courtyard, thus ensuring a good level of acoustical comfort for each home that compensates as much as possible for the inconvenience of being located near busy roads.

The facades overlooking the streets will be protected from traffic noise by cutting-edge technological devices such as panels specially designed to facilitate noise dispersion. The inner courtyard has been conceived as a sort of "green lung", which will be complemented by a series of other garden plots located on the roofs or on the terraces and balconies. These green spaces will help to improve the air quality of the entire complex whilst particular attention will be paid to ensure adequate natural light for each home. The orientation of the buildings has been studied precisely

214 One Gallions is a zero emissions building complex based on the highest environmental standards and strategies to exploit renewable energy sources.

214-215 The inner courtyard is the heart of the project and is a protected area where relations can be developed among the alternating private areas surrounded by other, larger, mainly green public areas, which contribute to increasing the quality of the One Gallions residences both in terms of noise pollution and atmospheric pollution.

with this in mind and also takes into account the need to avoid unfavorable exposure, such as north and south, in order to minimize dispersion or excessive accumulation of heat. Should there be unavoidable cases of non-optimal exposure, the project proposes the use of materials and colors which can help reduce its effects. The courtyard pavement will be of a light color, and the surface will be irregular rather than smooth in order to improve the reflection and diffusion of sunlight. Furthermore, the collection of rainwater and the presence of fountains or pools in the courtyard will help increase the humidity level of this community area.

The ambitious aim of the One Gallions project is not limited to the use of optimal architectural and technical means and solutions and sustainability strategies, but also seeks to create the prerequisites for a community in which respect for the environment is coupled with a lifestyle in sync with this principle, which entails social interaction and exchange, careful use of resources, and receptiveness to new approaches to community life to discover the advantages and satisfaction it affords. Furthermore, the various green spaces, especially those on the roofs and balconies, will encourage tenants to make the most of them and grow their own fruit and vegetables. It will also enhance biodiversity as different flora and fauna will be able to colonize the complex, thus increasing its ecological value.

The communal facilities and amenities of One Gallions will include "green transportation" (car and bicycle pools) which will be managed by the community itself. There will also be low energy consumption facilities that utilize renewable on-site energy. The use of natural and recycled materials is another aspect of this project, which is also manifested in the ecological and integrated management of refuse as well as the collecting and recycling of rainwater. S.L.

carlos ferrater *(fitness center)* - ate

evolution) - 24h-architecture *(dragsp*

ito & associates *(grin grin park)* - st

museum of art) - renzo piano buildin

the california academy of sciences) - eisen

land arch:
architecture takes on the shapes of nature

jean nouvel *(museum of human*

- hans hollein *(vulcania)* - toyo

holl architects *(the nelson-atkins*

kshop *(renovation and expansion of*

rchitects *(city of culture of galicia)*

land arch:
architecture takes on the shapes of nature

"Are emerging [new] positions, made up of strange slippages between old semantic categories - architecture, nature and landscape - the meaning of which are tending to mix and, therefore, become unnatural. New dynamics conform to an incipient vocabulary of a hybrid contract: Land and Arch, never a brutal grafting, but rather an imbrication between two heretofore alien categories. Constructions that would artificially integrate movements – or moments – of nature, in some case 'architecturalising' the landscape (modelling, cutting, folding…), proposing new topological shapes (relief, waves, folds, sheared trays); in others, landscaping (lining, enveloping, covering) an architecture in ambiguous synergy with the strange nature that surrounds it." [Manuel Gausa, Land Arch, in The Metapolis Dictionary of Advanced Architecture, Actar, Barcelona, p. 379].

The term "land arch" was coined by Manuel Gausa – to whom an issue of his periodical Quaderns was dedicated in 1997 –

to define certain types of architecture that take on the form of the landscape. This type of architecture establishes a new way of relating with nature and the environment, different from the one exemplified in the three preceding sections. The first is "eco tech", which is characterized by highly technological systems that make for a reduction in energy consumption. "Low tech" utilizes natural material that is connected to the context and which also results in saving energy. And finally "green arch", which uses plants as a construction material, in some cases in order to "camouflage" the architecture, and in others to allow for the bioclimatic functioning of the building. Land arch, on the other hand, establishes a relationship with nature that is above all formal, in which architecture seeks new figures in the imagery of nature.

There are two different approaches in this type of architecture. On the one hand, underground constructions which enjoy a special relationship with the land, and that sacrifice their own identity, so to speak,

in order to become one with the landscape. On the other hand there is the figurative approach, which sets out to establish the metaphor of nature, and in particular of geology and topography, taking on the shape of landforms, in some cases even the archetypal form of the cave.

By almost totally eliminating its presence in the landscape, underground architecture sets itself against the spectacular nature of contemporary trends – such as high tech, which exalts technology and artificial building material, and the architectural current characterized by bizarre creations – since the volumes and facades no longer appear, and the only signs one can see on the land surface are folds, cuts and tracks on the soil that illuminate the spaces below them or give access to them while highlighting the artifice of architecture through the use of recognizable geometrical shapes. Examples of this are Carlos Ferrater's Fitness Center in Barcelona, in which a star, formed by seven large partitions embedded in the ground, marks out the central court; the Contemporary Art Museum on the island of Naoshima designed by Tadao Ando as a series of regular geometric figures such as triangles, squares, and rectangles; and Hans Hollein's Vulcania – the Parc Européen du Volcanisme – with two cones, one of which emerges from the earth while the other is carved into the ground. The choice of such decidedly architectural and artificial forms – which, however, barely emerge from the earth – demonstrates that this type of structure, rather than being camouflaged, meets the ecological need to conserve one of the depletable environmental resources: the soil. By constructing such structures under ground level, the land above is free to be utilized for other purposes, thus providing the densely built-up cities with more public space.

Then there is the type of construction that is like a metaphor of nature and its infinite shapes, with the aim of defining small architectural works. Amongst these are Elisabeth Diller and Ricardo Scofidio's project for the Blur Building, a pavilion consisting of a perpetual cloud of artificially produced mist; or the "butterfly" in the small house in Sweden that was enlarged by 24H-architecture and which changes from a sort of cocoon or shell in winter into a butterfly shape in the summer. Add to this such mega-structures as the "bird's nest" which becomes both a formal and structural metaphor in the Beijing Olympic (or National) Stadium designed by Herzog & de Meuron, and the various geological and topographical metaphors that seem to have prevailed in recent years. The City of Culture of Galicia, designed by Eisenman in Santiago de Compostela, takes on the shape of a hill "carved" by a series of irregular paths produced by a long historical process that is anything but natural through which the building relates to the site, consisting of three superposed layers: one that represents a shell, the symbol of the pilgrims, the structure of the historic center of Santiago, and a gridiron plan. A landform is Jean Nouvel's proposal for the Museum of Human Evolution in Burgos; a sequence of variously articulated hills create the Grin Grin Park designed by Toyo Ito; and the volcano is the metaphor used by Renzo Piano for the recently completed huge shopping center near Nola, in Campania (Italy). These are artificially created configurations in which the soil, excavated to make room for the underground architecture, is once more placed over the edifice and covered with vegetation: an ephemeral operation that is perhaps analogous to the plant camouflage previously mentioned. But in any case, besides representing the contemporary situation defined by a third nature and a third landscape that transcend the traditional opposition between natural and artificial, these configurations also function as bioclimatic agents that make for a decrease in energy consumption.

The numerous green surfaces covering artificial hills isolate the spaces beneath them, which therefore remain cool in the summer and retain rainwater. As is only natural, the underground spaces do not need any artificial air conditioning.   G.S.

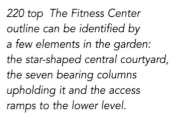

Fitness Center
BARCELONA, SPAIN

An annex of a 14-story hotel situated in an area along the Avenida Diagonal in Barcelona, where town planning and zoning regulations prohibit any construction above street level, this Fitness Center had to be hidden underground and built in an excavated plot. This choice was two-fold. On the one hand it was formal, that is, it expressed the desire to create "camouflaged architecture" whose form is annulled by the natural context in which it is built (hence the term "land architecture" or "land arch"); and on the other, it was based on sustainability, that is, connected to the conservation of a depletable resource, which in this case is the land. Thus, the area not occupied by the Fitness Center was left free to be used for other purposes. Ferrater decided to lay out a garden, under which he placed the building, making it virtually invisible from the outside with the exception of some partitions arranged in the form of a star that emerge from the land. These elements seem to be fundamental components of the composition on which the Spanish architect works and they crop up in many of his projects: from the hotel next to the Fitness Center to the entrance structures of the botanical garden, also in Barcelona. In the Fitness Center they constitute the very structure and framework of the underground area: more than partitions, they are reinforced concrete cantilevers of a certain height that support the weight

220 top The Fitness Center outline can be identified by a few elements in the garden: the star-shaped central courtyard, the seven bearing columns upholding it and the access ramps to the lower level.

220 bottom The upper level (whose plan is seen here) is home to the center's main areas: swimming-pool, areas to relax in, wellbeing center, gyms, changing rooms and bathrooms.

220-221 The underground location of the center (as seen here from the hotel next door) leaves ground zero free (in compliance with construction legislation), which becomes a garden for hotel guests and the wellbeing center.

221 bottom The Fitness Center is totally underground and entirely dug out of the ground. The only elements visible from the outside are the tops of the cement pillars emerging from the lawn.

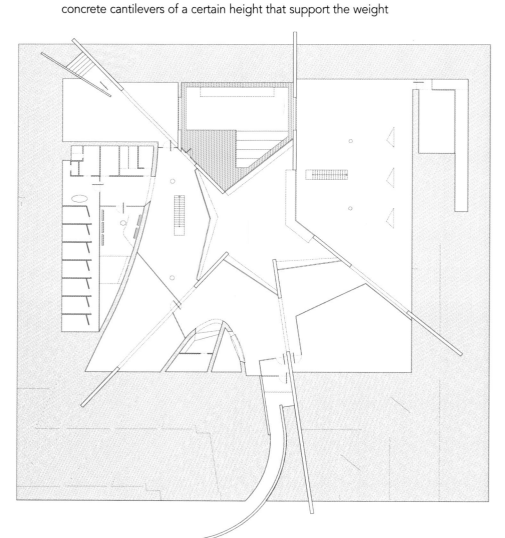

of the roof (which is the garden) and make it possible to create a continuous open space in the interior, without need of any other supports. These elements differentiate the spaces and are arranged radially around a small central courtyard measuring 1,000 square feet. The courtyard thus takes on the shape of a star, so that despite its relatively small size it receives ample sunlight. Furthermore, the very shape prevents it from being seen in its entirety, so that its small scale passes unnoticed. The cobblestone pavement is covered with water, and as a result the reflections produced increase the luminosity of the inner spaces, which, although underground, benefit from natural lighting. The Fitness Center is a two-story building, the lower level of which is occupied by areas and rooms that need less light, such as dressing rooms, saunas, the Turkish bath and more private activities. The upper level, on the other hand – which

connects directly with the garden both visually by means of the courtyard and physically by means of ramps and access stairways to the center – houses the swimming pool, the relaxation area, the beauty and medical centers and the gymnasium for aerobics, dancing, and yoga, as well as shops and auxiliary services. Since they were hewn out of the earth and are not affected by the heat of the sun, all the rooms are extremely cool in the summer, which means much less energy consumption. What is more, the green roof insulates the areas underneath, thus reducing heat dispersion in the winter and keeping them cool in the summer. The necessary equipment is placed in a double wall along the perimeter of the buildings which is connected to the main technical room: this leaves the ceilings and floors free, which means that they need carry out only their static function and therefore can be thinner. G.S.

222 top All indoor areas overlook the central courtyard, which provides light. This is freely diffused throughout the rooms, which are only partitioned by thin sheets of glass so areas intertwine with each other and people inside are unable to perceive their true dimensions.

222 bottom The swimming-pool, like the gyms, can be identified by just a few materials: the wooden floor and the glass and clear cement used in the roof. This way, the rooms are both warm and welcoming in addition to being extremely airy and bright.

223 The central courtyard is surrounded by glass walls supported by a very thin frame. This provides maximum transparency and allows the indoor areas to be naturally lit, constantly providing them with a perceptive relationship with the outside world.

Museum of Human Evolution

BURGOS, SPAIN

Ateliers Jean Nouvel participated in the competition for the Museum of Human Evolution in Burgos, which was won by Juan Navarro Baldeweg, with a project proposing to place an artificial hill in the middle of the Spanish city to house the museum.

The area proposed is not underground as the result of digging in the ground, rather the soil is placed on the building to create, according to Jean Nouvel "a resurrection in the city of the geography and landscape surrounding Burgos." In this way the French architect aims at reinserting inside the city and its historic center an architectural structure that belongs to the natural world and that does not relate to or compete with the textiles museum or the nearby cathedral. The use of such structures is becoming more and more widespread in contemporary architecture, so much so that an actual category called "land architecture" has been created. This is characterized by a series of projects by Jean Nouvel ranging from the Burgos Museum of Human Evolution to the Learning Resource Center of the University of Cyprus (2003) and the Guggenheim Museum in Tokyo (2001). Here the topographical surfaces intermingle with regular volumes such as parallelepipeds and spheres, creating disorientating spaces in which the confine between the natural and artificial becomes more and more indistinguishable. At Burgos the very theme of the museum led to the choice of archetypal spatial configuration, something that symbolizes the origins: a cavern, a natural cavity that precedes all human construction. The Burgos museum therefore looks like a green hill in the middle of the city that echoes the surrounding natural landscape. The rich vegetation covering the roof of the structure will reduce its impact on the environment and insulate the spaces below, thereby cutting down on energy consumption.

The interior is defined by a very large enclosed area that has no relation whatsoever with the outside except for the entrance, which is placed in such a way that it frames the urban landscape and focuses on Burgos Cathedral. This large public atrium is illuminated from above by several skylights that provide natural lighting, and enclosed within an earthen wall that in effect conceals the museum proper.

Furthermore, it is articulated into a series of metal and glass partitions and volumes that form a sort of interior urban landscape. These structures – the largest of which houses a large hall, a hotel, shops and cafés, while the smaller ones contain a restaurant and cafeteria – are situated inside the hill itself, thus creating an ambiguous, rather indefinable relationship between urban and natural space, whose simultaneous presence in the same space cannot fail to produce a sense of bewilderment in those who visit or work there. G.S.

224-225 top The large entrance hall to the museum has the spatiality of a cavern defined by an earth-like wall and large holes through which light penetrates. The presence of steel lattices and steel and glass masses reveals its artificiality.

224-225 bottom The museum is located in the center of the Spanish city and from the outside, looks like a green hill with a large opening that attracts individuals inside.

226-227 and 226 bottom
The Dragspelhuset is located in a nature reserve in Sweden and represents the extension made to a small fisherman's hut. For this reason, the architects chose an organic shape similar to a butterfly cocoon able to be camouflaged by this landscape.

Dragspelhuset

ÖVRE GLA LAKE, SWEDEN

In the Glaskgen nature reserve on the banks of Övre Gla Lake in Sweden, Maartije Lammerrs and Boris Zeisser – two Dutch architects who founded the 24H-architecture studio in 2001 – bought a fishermen's hut in which to spend their vacation, far from the congestion so common in many parts of The Netherlands. The house is rather small, about 320 square feet, and since it lies in a reserve the zoning regulations are very severe. Only existing structures can be enlarged, and only by twice their original size, and they must be a certain distance from the property line. In this case the property was right in the middle of a stream.

This very special natural setting, the severe prescriptions and limitations, as well as the strong influence Frank Lloyd Wright's Fallingwater had on Zeisser, who has visited this house several times, coupled with his desire to reproduce that type of relation between architecture and nature, led the Dutch architect to use a butterfly as a symbol for the project.

The house is an organic form that blends in with the landscape, so much so that it is partly camouflaged, but it can also be transformed and change its self-contained cocoon-like aspect into the shape of a butterfly spreading its wings. The renovation of the shack was conceived in such a way as to consist of two rooms, one of which fits into the other and is moveable. In the summer, this extension rolls outward on steel rails toward the stream, thus increasing the space of the interior from 580 to 800 square feet, while in the winter it fits back into the other room, forming a double "shell" that prevents heat dispersion. This type of organic structure was realized by utilizing a building procedure calling for a steel frame comprised of a succession of irregular arches. These were clad on the inside with birch laths sourced from around the lake, and reindeer hides, thus reviving an old tradition of the Scandinavian Laplanders, who use them for their excellent thermal insulation. The exterior of the home is clad in red cedar shingles. This wood was chosen for two reasons: it is a very resistant material which is also suitable for roofing and does not require frequent maintenance.

227 top and center Building regulations in the reserve have restricted the size of the house and therefore architects had to come up with a changeable organism able to modify its shape and dimensions. The pictures show the smallest and largest configurations.

227 bottom The cutaway views show the transformation of the building: (left) the look of the house in the winter when the two shells overlap and (right) the configuration it takes on in the summer, when the interior one slides outwards to form a new room.

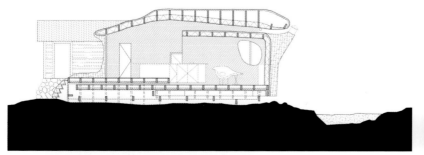

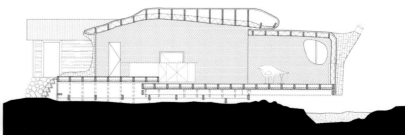

Secondly, it can be mounted in small pieces, which adhere so well to the irregular shape of the old shack that it takes on the appearance of the skin of a reptile, tree bark, or layers of rock. This analogy is made even more apparent by the color of the wood, which in time turns gray, like the stone upon which the house stands. Thus, the structure blends in perfectly with the surrounding pine and birch forest and also adheres to the local zoning regulations.

However, total respect for a place with such extraordinary natural and environmental features cannot be achieved merely through the form and materials of the structure, and must also include all those elements that make it function. In fact, the house has no running water or electricity.

The water is taken from the adjoining stream, while the electricity, used mostly for lighting the interior, is produced by photovoltaic panels. The house is heated by two wood fireplaces, while the kitchen has a propane gas stove – all of which minimizes energy and water consumption.

Sustainability understood as integration with the site and surroundings of the architectural work, respect for the environment, and minimum use of exhaustible natural resources in this house seem to take on an archaic lifestyle.   G.S.

228 and 228-229 The detailed picture shows the
red cedar shingles defining the home's shell and
making its outer skin appear as though it were that
of a reptile, especially when they lose their reddish
hues and become gray.

Dragspelhuset

230 and 231 top left Inside, the home's shell is composed of birch-strip covered beams and buckskin, which isolates the rooms and gives them a warm, welcoming aspect. The shell stops next to an irregular-shaped window providing a pleasant view of the surrounding landscape.

230-231 The picture shows the house in its largest form, that is when the smaller area juts out towards the stream and the large window connects the indoor and outdoor areas.

231 top right Thanks to the use of natural, very light materials such as birch and buckskin, the large window within the indoor area of the extendible portion makes the area very bright.

Vulcania

SAINT-OURS LES ROCHES, FRANCE

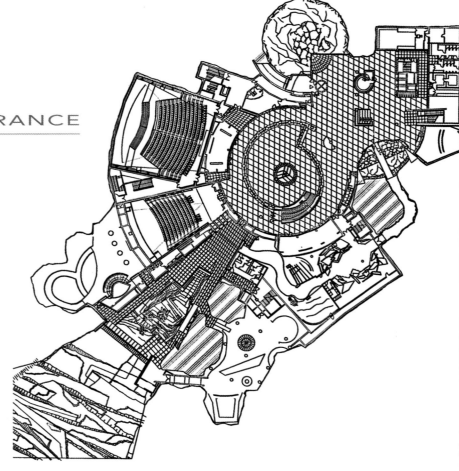

The Parc Européen du Volcanisme is an evocative work whose configuration, materials and contents blend into the surroundings, with the aim of introducing visitors to the park's theme. This volcanism center is based on education and entertainment. It lies on the Puys range, a group of volcanic hills in the Auvergne region, and was designed by Austrian architect Hans Hollein, with the collaboration of Atelier 4 architects, landscape architect Gilles Clément and scenographer Rainer Verbizh.

The common objective of this team was to create an attractive structure lying in the terrain among layers of basaltic lava that would blend in well with the surrounding landscape.

This is underground architecture whose presence is manifested in only a few, but strong, essential signs that crop up from the entrance. Therefore the work is to be interpreted as an ecological rather than mimetic operation. In fact, the work does not reject volume and form, which are respectively both the symbol – and sign – of the park and the recognizable geometric visitors' path that runs through the high points of the project.

The decision to excavate the site was a concrete way of pursuing the conservation of resources, with the aim of achieving sustainable development. In this specific case this means not continuing to occupy the available space, creating an advantage in terms of reducing energy consumption, as well as reutilizing the material that is excavated for the project or that merely lies in the area by adapting it anew. This strategy

is particularly in sync with the theme of the park. It entails getting visitors acquainted with volcanism and earth sciences by taking them inside the layers of basaltic lava.

The plan of the park develops mainly around two circular forms or traces, that generate two truncated cones: one that emerges from the land, tapering upwards, and the other that on the contrary penetrates the earth and tapers downwards. The first one, simply called Le Cone, is an independent structure clad in dark basalt which evokes the image of the volcano. It has a vertical cut that allows one to catch a glimpse of an inner cladding in gilded metal – partly made of three-dimensional elements – that creates effects with the natural and artificial light. The characteristic feature of the cone is a footbridge that links it with a nearby structure, one of the many circulation areas facing the complex that encourage visitors to look downward.

Around Le Cone, below ground, there is an exhibition hall for temporary shows, a 3-D hall, an IMAX cinema, and a large and fascinating hothouse, the so-called volcanic garden.

232 top The project consists of underground architecture around two circumferences, the outline of Le Cone and La Caldèra. From a volumetric perspective, they are the outlines of the entrance quotas of two truncated cones developed in opposite directions: the first upwards and the second downwards.

232 bottom The cone plays a central role in the project. Its form is clearly an allusion to a volcano. In the foreground, the transparent roof of the volcanic garden.

233 The interior of the cone is finished with golden metal. This finishing was partially realized with three-dimensional elements to create effects with the natural daylight and artificial light at night.

234 top The outer finish of the cone is basaltic and its hollow area can be accessed by an elevated walkway. It provides one of many charming views over the void, characterizing the center of volcanology.

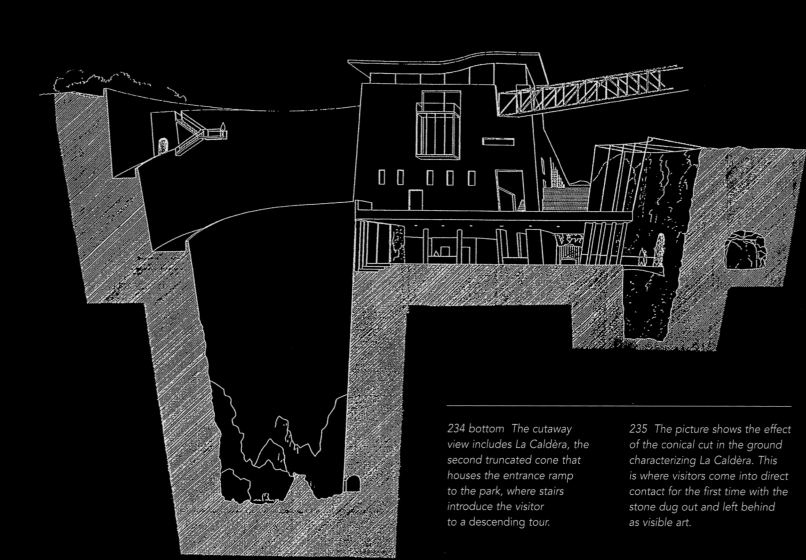

234 bottom The cutaway view includes La Caldèra, the second truncated cone that houses the entrance ramp to the park, where stairs introduce the visitor to a descending tour.

235 The picture shows the effect of the conical cut in the ground characterizing La Caldèra. This is where visitors come into direct contact for the first time with the stone dug out and left behind as visible art.

The hollow space of this geometric element plays a two-fold role, channeling natural light into the entrance atrium and contributing to its ventilation.

The second truncated cone, La Caldèra, houses the entrance ramp to the Parc Européen du Volcanisme, where the most direct contact with the stone on the site begins to manifest itself. This relationship is further developed in various spaces in the park in two ways: by leaving some excavated parts open to view, and through the use of the local volcanic stone – including the excavated stone or the red Jura variety – and of an aggregate of basalt known as *béton Vulcania*, which is specially prepared for this purpose.

All the components of this project confirm the continuity and respect between the architectural work and the landscape on which it was built, that ideal and concrete integration that allows the separate parts to live in symbiosis. S.L.

236 top A view from above shows the Parc Européen du Volcanisme project in detail. It tends to insert itself in and above the ground, with only a few – but strong – essential signs drawing attention to it.

236 center The drawing isolates the geometrical elements used to configure the project: a rectangle and a smaller cube, in addition to two cones, whose circumferences dominate the composition as the outlines of the intersection with the ground.

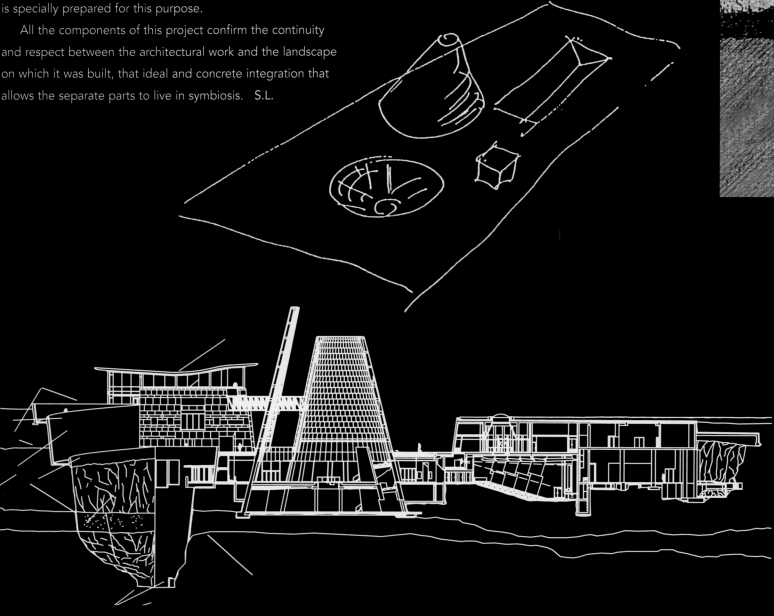

236-237 The colored drawing highlights the poetic relationship that exists between the project and its main shapes, and the natural surroundings of the Puys mountain range on which a group of Alvernia volcanic hills rises.

236 bottom and 237 bottom The two cutaway views show the complexity with which the structures make room for themselves in the ground, and especially, the relationship they establish with the surface willingly left visible. This relationship with matter is strengthened by the use in the construction of local volcanic stone and the use of a basaltic aggregate realized specifically for this project.

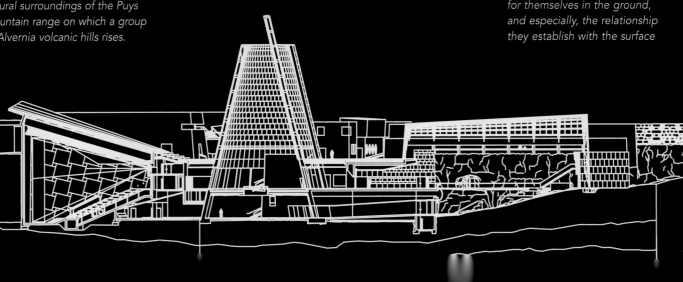

Vulcania

238 The pictures respectively show the inside and outside of the greenhouse, the so-called volcanic garden. Its glass structure opens towards the dug-out ground to create the strongest relationship with the larger, natural surface area made available to visitors.

This area – more than any other – clearly expresses the continuity between architecture and the landscape, which tend to penetrate each other in the ideal and concrete integration between parties that generally crosses the center's entire project.

238-239 and 239 bottom
At night, the complex comes to life through enchanting lighting allowing one's look to penetrate individual buildings through large glass walls. Soft lighting also gives the indoor areas a unique atmosphere.

TOYO ITO & ASSOCIATES

Grin Grin Park

FUKUOKA, JAPAN

sland City is an artificial island with a surface area of 400 hectares that lies in Hakata Bay, in the city of Fukuoka, Japan. Built with national and local funds as well as private contributions, the island has a container port, a business hub and a residential area. In the middle of the island, the Japanese architect Toyo Ito, who won the competition for the work, created a sustainable 15-hectare park on a green ring approximately one mile long.

Grin Grin Park is a strip of land that unfolds for 623 feet, creating a series of rolling hills. A thin layer of cement winds its way, reproducing the rippling of the sea's waves. The irregular geometric configuration of the volumes covers and encloses green areas, hothouses, places offering views of the landscape and rest areas.

The three greenhouses of 9,000-10,000 square feet are not only places where visitors can learn about the local flora, but are also used for studying, reading and simply relaxing.

Credit for the realization of these structures is due to the close collaboration between Ito and Mutsuro Sasaki, one of Japan's foremost engineers, who designed, among other things, the steel tube spiral framework for the Mediatheque in Sendai.

By means of the Sensitivity Analysis method and the 3D Extended Evolutionary Structural Optimization method – which utilize the principles of evolution of the self-organization of living beings to generate rational structures with the computer – it was possible to transcend rigid geometric configurations and create biomorphic shapes.

A thin layer of reinforced concrete (16 inches) creates seamless curved surfaces. Covered with vegetation, these surfaces are perfectly integrated in the topography of the site and, by accompanying the subtle movements and nuances of the landscape they become pedestrian walkways that link the interior with the exterior, the cavities and embankments. The "shell" thus becomes a route for visitors offering a changing, undulating configuration of dunes and humps, greenery, and wooden gangways supported by thin columns that dot the carpet of greenery and FRP (Fiberglass Reinforced Plastic) surfaces. These are large glazed "eyes" that illuminate the winding spaces under the roof and that afford light and air to the plants to enable their growth.

Ito possesses the extraordinary gift of being able to design an intermediate space that is no longer natural yet not totally artificial, and he skillfully and discreetly succeeds in assimilating the apparent irregular features of a manifestation of nature that is in constant flux and never the same. The carpet of plants in the Grin Grin Park at Fukuoka, which is reflected on the artificial lake opposite, generates hybrid configurations halfway between architecture and nature.   L.S.

240 top The structural shells of the roof (one is seen here in detail) were made with fiberglass reinforced plastic.

240 bottom The Grin Grin Park is a strip of land along a path 623 feet long including hills and valleys. The architectural body overcomes rigid geometric configurations to delicately rest on the outdoor vegetation.

241 The Grin Grin Park is located in Island City on Hakata Bay in the city of Fukuoka. The 15-hectare park also includes the artificial lake in front of it. The park was built on a green ring one-mile long.

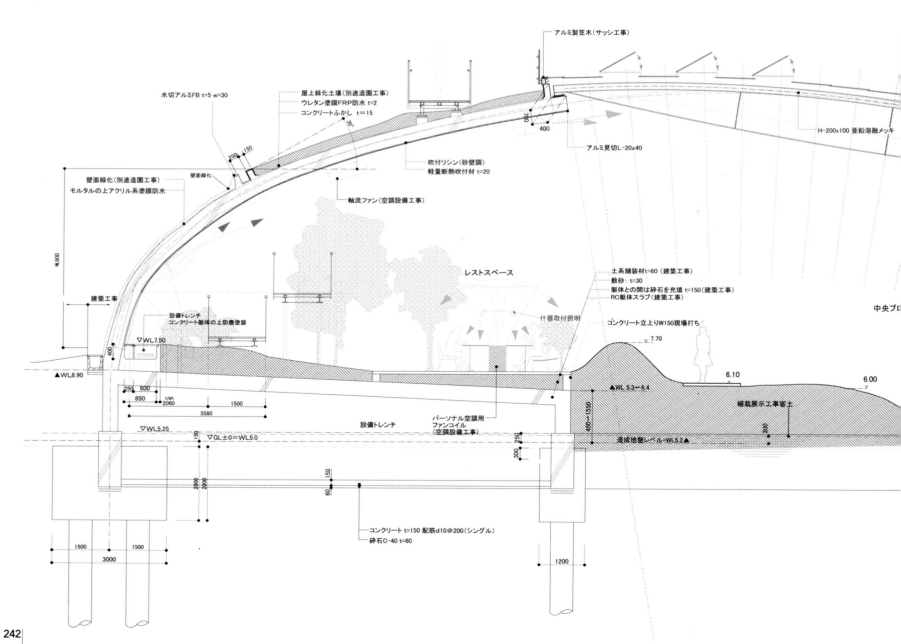

アルミ製笠木（サッシ工事）

水切アルミFB t=5 w=30

屋上緑化土壌（別途造園工事）
ウレタン塗膜FRP防水 t=2
コンクリートふかし t=15

H-200x100 亜鉛溶融メッキ

アルミ見切L-20x40

壁面緑化（別途造園工事）
壁面緑化
モルタルの上アクリル系塗膜防水

吹付リシン（砂壁調）
軽量断熱吹付材 t=20

軸流ファン（空調設備工事）

レストスペース

土系舗装材t=60（建築工事）
敷砂：t=30
躯体との間は砕石を充填 t=150（建築工事）
RC躯体スラブ（建築工事）

什器取付照明

建築工事

コンクリート立上りW150現場打ち

中央プロ

設備トレンチ
コンクリート躯体の上防塵塗装

▽WL7.50

7.70

6.10

6.00

▲WL6.90

▲WL 5.3～6.4

植栽展示工事客土

250　600

850　　　　100
　　　　　　2060

3560　　　　1500

パーソナル空調用
ファンコイル
（空調設備工事）

設備トレンチ

450～1550

▽WL5.25

造成地盤レベル＝WL5.2▲

▽GL±0＝WL50

150

300

250

300

60
150

2000
2000

コンクリート t=150 配筋d10@200（シングル）
砕石C-40 t=60

1500　　1500

3000

1200

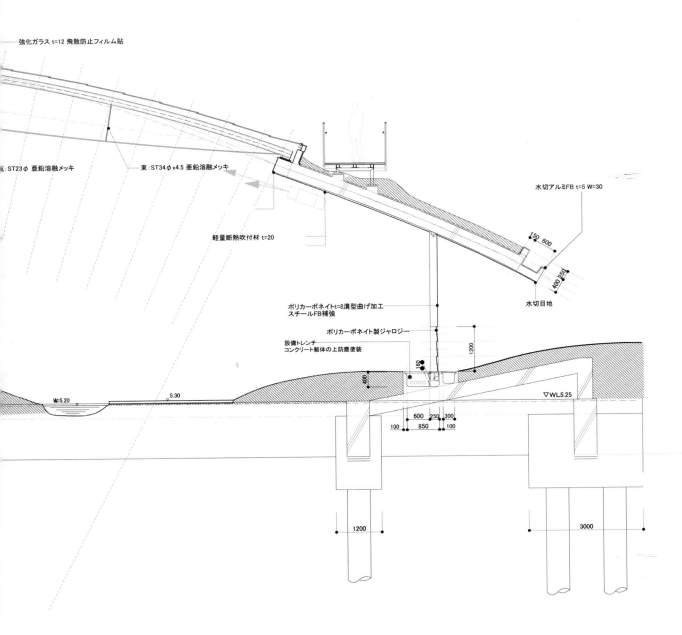

強化ガラス t=12 飛散防止フィルム貼

東:ST23φ 亜鉛溶融メッキ

東:ST34φ×4.5 亜鉛溶融メッキ

水切アルミFB t=5 W=30

軽量断熱吹付材 t=20

150 600

400 250

水切目地

ポリカーボネイト t=8溝型曲げ加工
スチールFB補強

ポリカーボネイト製ジャロジー

設備トレンチ
コンクリート躯体の上防塵塗装

1200

400

▽WL5.25

WL5.20

5.30

600 250 300

100 850 100

1200

3000

242 and 243 The irregular geometry of the bodies built encompasses green areas and places to observe nature. The greenhouses built under the grassy surface serve to educate visitors on the local flora while at the same time provide an area to relax in. The large glass eyes of the greenhouses illuminate the winding areas under the roof and allow the plants to grow.

242-243 A thin layer of reinforced cement just 16in. thick and covered by a grassy surface forms the curved surfaces of the roof on which visitors can move about in a continuous effect of dunes and small hills, and of the elevated walkways rising up out of the ground with their slender supports (original design).

244-245 The picture shows
the large entrance plaza to
the museum in the middle of
which is the sculpture of Walter
De Maria entitled One sun/34
Moons: a pool with large
skylights (the moons) which
illuminate the parking lot below.

The Nelson-Atkins Museum of Art

KANSAS CITY, USA

Architecture and landscape merge in the new addition to the Nelson-Atkins Museum of Art. Five translucent volumes become part of a topographical green surface that covers the gallery spaces. Thus, a variety of different spaces and atmospheres are offered to visitors, who experience them first-hand by moving in and around them. The basis of the architectural composition is the contrast with the original museum building. Steven Holl counters its weight, opaque quality, exterior and directed visitors' circulation with transparency, lightness, permeability and free circulation among the museum areas.

The sculpture garden that once occupied this site, on the eastern edge of the campus, now unfolds among the glass "lenses" and continues inside, creating a dynamic relationship among art, architecture and landscape. This course or path can be taken from many different points and heights. For example, from the wide entrance plaza in front of the north facade of the original museum – which features artist Walter De Maria's work *One Sun/34 Moons*: a large pool dotted along the bottom with 34 "moons" which are round skylights that afford natural light to the garage area underneath – direct access is gained to the large lobby inside the first "lens". This in turn is directly connected both to the older building and, at a higher level, the sculpture garden. This large and very tall atrium is traversed by ramps and stairways and houses a host of activities situated on different levels: a café, an art library, and a bookstore. This is the starting point for the museum exhibition galleries. Although for the most part underground, the new galleries open out several times to the surrounding environment, and are extremely bright thanks to the "lenses", the large skylights that surmount them.

244 bottom The five lenses composing the Nelson-Atkins Museum of Art are illuminated at night and their outlines can be seen, even from a distance.

245 bottom The axonometric exploded diagram shows the elements in the project: the T-shaped columns, green surface and the lenses.

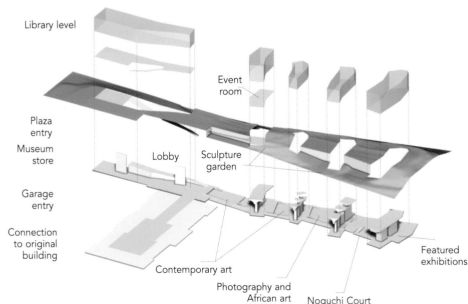

These large glazed prisms are supported by T-shaped columns that Holl himself calls "Breathing Ts", since they cast light and channel air in their interior. Their curved shape refracts and diffuses the light, mixing the cold light from the north with the warm southern light. What is more, they house the heating, ventilation and cooling ducts and serve as vents to eliminate stale air. The double shell of the lenses also contributes to the bioclimatic efficiency of the building. The outer layer consists of two rows of transparent glass slabs, while the inner one has a double layer of translucent glass, so that the light can be diffused and the spaces illuminated in a natural fashion. The glass cavities of the lenses absorb sunlight in the winter, channeling the warm air into the galleries, and discharge it in the summer. Again, these cavities contain computer-regulated screens facing south that protect the building from glare and light; insulating material that prevents thermal dispersion; and artificial lighting that transforms them into luminous prisms providing light for the park and making it possible to present exhibitions and other events all day long.

Another ecological, bioclimatic element is the green roof, which insulates the rooms below and keeps them cool in the summer, while also controlling rainwater.

Since the rooms in the building are not entirely below ground level, they can open out to the landscape by means of large windows that also afford natural ventilation.

All the elements in this project, the topographical surface of the park, and the glass prisms inside, together with the material used – including the greenery, light and water – create an experiential and sensual atmosphere in which the visitors who circulate in the interior are always the principal elements, the protagonists. G.S.

246-247 The contrast between old and new also characterizes the shapes of the buildings. The rigid composition of the neoclassical building is contrasted by a more fluid one including a topographic surface and a series of irregular prisms.

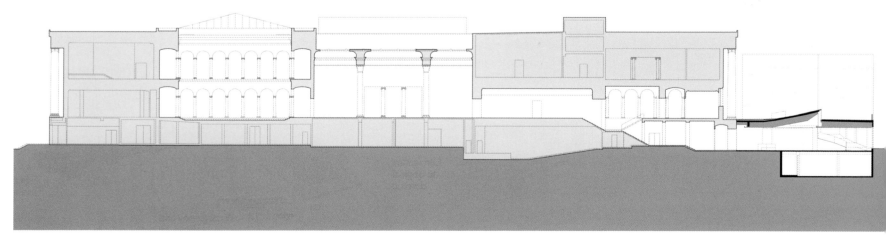

246 bottom The cross-section shows the continuity of the exhibit. It occupies various levels in the pre-existing building and connects with the lower part of the entrance lobby for the new museum located in the first lens.

247 bottom The galleries are entirely covered by a green surface along the eastern side, which borders with the campus. The western side stands out for its glass walls between the lenses connecting the gallery areas and the sculpture park.

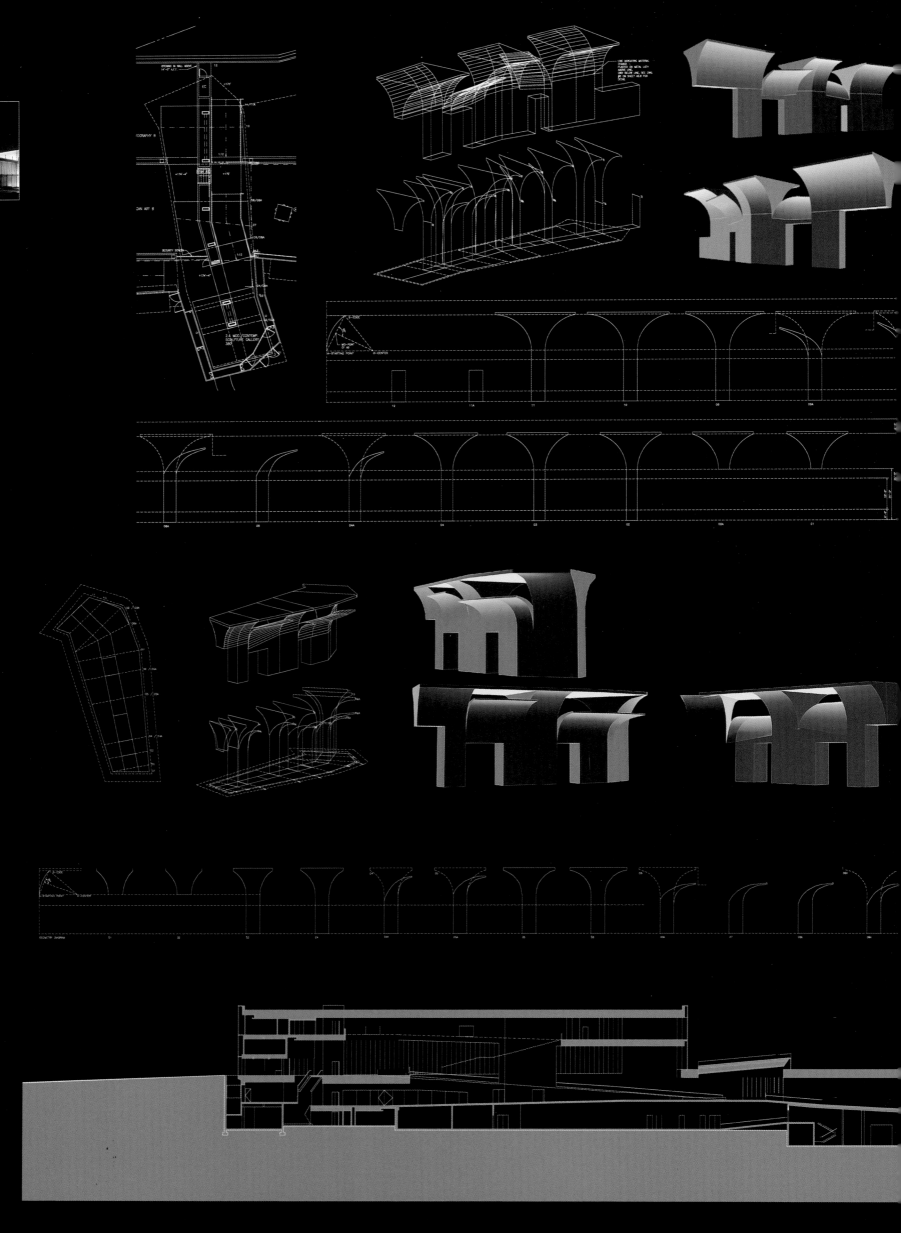

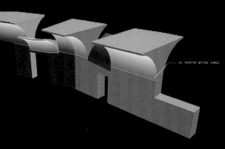

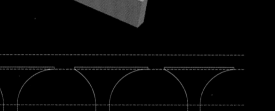

248-249 top The details show the axonometric and cutaway views of the T-shaped column system defining both the structural system of the lenses and the illumination and ventilation systems defined by Steven Holl as "Breathing Ts".

248-249 bottom The longitudinal section of the entire complex shows the different levels organizing the main lobby lens, the areas and the galleries and a cross-section of the other lenses.

249 The picture shows the base of the T-shaped column seen from below in the point of intersection with the topographic surface area covering the galleries.

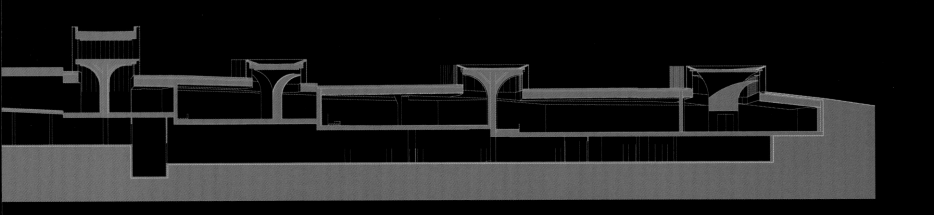

250 top The detail of the cutaway view of the "Breathing Ts" shows the different angles of light throughout the day: the cold light from the north and the warm light from the south are mixed, reflected and diffused by the round surface.

250 bottom The picture shows the lobby as seen from the upper level. It can be directly accessed from outside. Entry to the cafeteria, library and multipurpose area located on different levels is provided by the ramp and stairway.

251 The lobby areas are extremely bright, thanks to the double glass shell that is translucent in some parts and transparent in others. It connects the interior with the exterior.

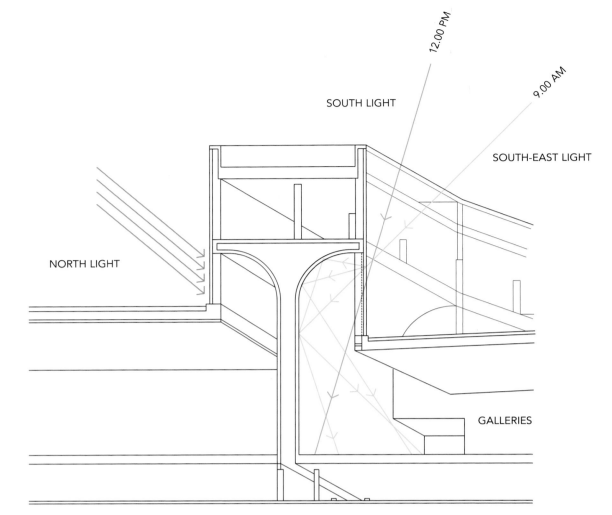

12.00 PM

9.00 AM

SOUTH LIGHT

SOUTH-EAST LIGHT

NORTH LIGHT

GALLERIES

Renovation and Expansion of the California Academy of Sciences

SAN FRANCISCO, USA

The California Academy of Sciences in San Francisco is one of the few natural science institutes in which the public experience of the visitors is combined with the more private, reserved experience of scientific research. Renzo Piano's new project is located on the same site of the institute it replaced – in the city's Golden Gate Park – and has maintained the same size and multifarious vocation. Exhibitions, educational activities, research and conservation, with offices, refreshment zones and spaces for cultural events are the principal functions carried out in the new structure, under a single, huge green roof. The available space provided by the site has been organized so as to house a more complex system of activities – which coexist and interact – and state-of-the-art equipment and facilities that make the Academy one of the most prestigious and innovative cultural institutions in the world. The fluid distribution of these functions and an amply glazed exterior denote the permeability of the structure and its relational capabilities. Thus, the spaces in the interior mingle with those of the outside, that is, the construction with the natural element of the park itself. This hybrid aspect of the project is strongly highlighted by the roof, all of which is green, like an elevated rolling hill that wishes to indemnify Golden Gate Park for the land it has removed.

The most important sections of the Academy of Sciences tend to emerge from this green roof, deforming it while manifesting themselves and imparting a new, undulating topography similar to that of the city itself. These are the Planetarium Dome, the Rainforest Biosphere and the 'Piazza'. The latter is an empty courtyard with a glass roof that marks the center of the composition, while two spherical volumes, one opaque and the other glazed, house the Planetarium and Rainforest respectively. The porthole-like skylights that characterize the green roof tend to become denser on a level with the above-mentioned domes.

252-253 The foreground depicts the visible part of the roof-garden next to the Rainforest Biosphere. The circular skylights characterizing the roof can be opened and tend to increase in number, especially above this area, providing adequate illumination and ventilation inside.

253 top The complex is located in the Golden Gate Park, as is the structure it replaces. The Planetarium Dome and Rainforest Biosphere – among the most significant indoor areas – appear to emerge from the roof and deform it. The roof characterizes the project and appears as raised, wavy ground.

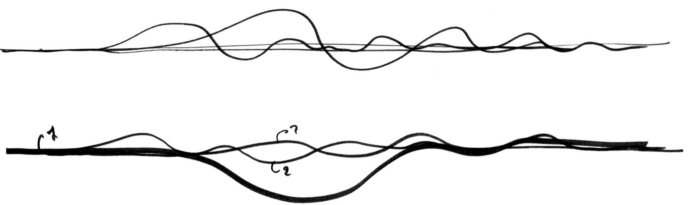

Since they can be opened, they provide natural ventilation as well as adequate lighting for the exhibition areas.

The Piazza is an extremely flexible area that can be utilized for various purposes depending on the time of day. During the day it serves as an area for social gatherings and lunch, while in the evening it is the venue for concerts, dinners and parties.

Its glass roof, which is supported by a web-like steel structure, is flanked by a screening system that ensures high-level comfort, as well as good illumination, acoustic insulation and bioclimatic control performance. The Piazza is the only place in the complex where one notes the presence of the underground Steinhart Aquarium.

The large green roof distinguishing the project is outlined by an external horizontal band – partially made of a glass surface and in part by photovoltaic panels – outlining an outdoor and indoor area. It is resting on a steel structure and makes the complex autonomous in terms of energy. The tangentially placed glass windows are operable in the highest section in order to allow fresh air to pass through the entire building.

The new Academy is living proof of the great attention now paid to sustainability and ecology in general, as is demonstrated by the choice of new building material and the recycling of the material recovered from the demolition of the old Academy, the only remaining part of which is the African Hall.   S.L.

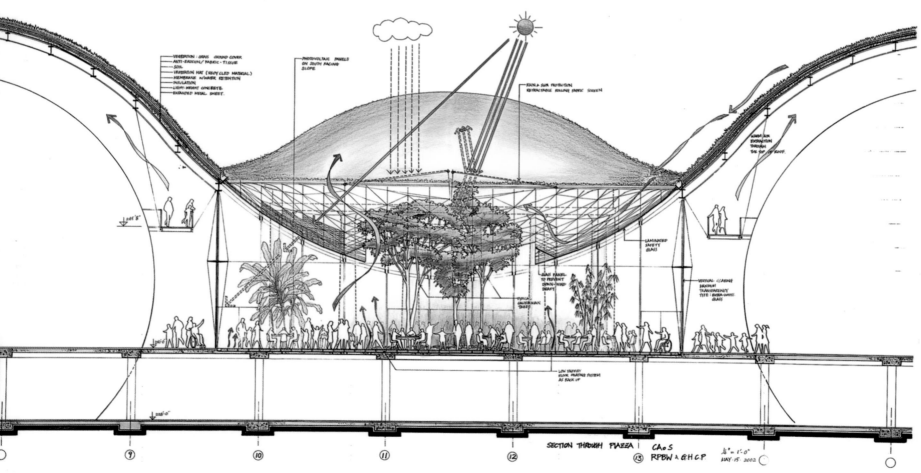

254-255 The central portion of the roof-garden has a glass roof that closes the plaza area, a free area inside that can be used as needed in the daytime as a meeting place and for lunch, and in the evening to host concerts, dinners and parties.

254 center The project's concept is a distorted line with a wavy appearance.

254 bottom The cutaway view depicts the most significant areas open to the public: (from left) the sphere of the Planetarium Dome, the central area and plaza with its high ceiling, the sphere to the right of the Rainforest Biosphere and the Steinhard Aquarium in the central, underground part.

255 bottom The detail describes the function of the plaza from a bioclimatic perspective. The glass roof upheld by a light steel structure is integrated with a shielding system that ensures adequate indoor comfort.

256 top The picture shows one of the areas close to the plaza and the Planetarium Dome from which the Steinhart Aquarium at the underground level can be perceived.

256 bottom The perspective is the same as the previous picture, but positioned in the diametrically opposite location close to the Rainforest Biosphere.

257 Parts of the roof-garden covering the Planetarium Dome and Rainforest Biosphere spheres can be seen from the plaza and its sophisticated roof.

258 and 259 The two pictures (respectively inside and outside
the Rainforest Biosphere) highlight how the skylights in the roof
characterize this area, especially during the hours when the artificial

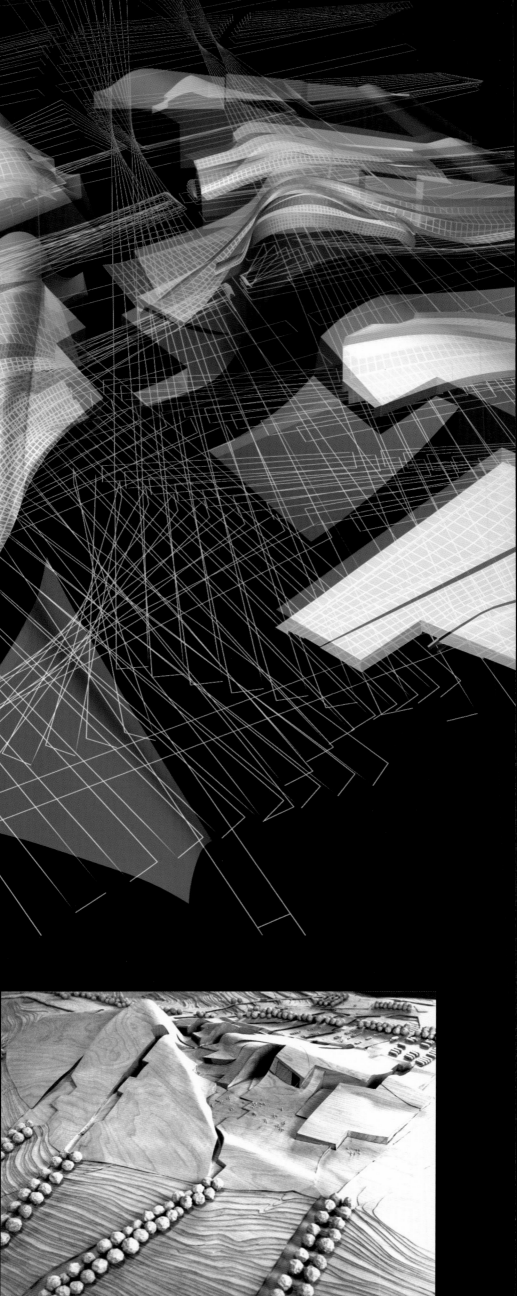

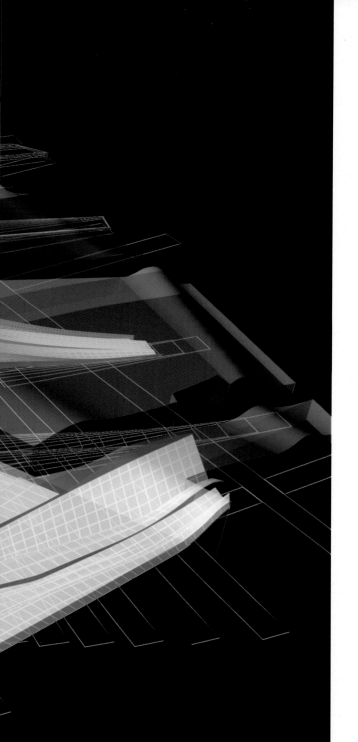

City of Culture of Galicia

SANTIAGO DE COMPOSTELA, SPAIN

260 bottom The plastic model describes the desire to overcome this figure-background approach in favor of the figure-figure approach in which architecture and topography merge to become figures.

261 top The City of Culture is within the project area and carves out the ground with its structure.

261 bottom The diagram shows the details of the project based on three pairs of buildings so the layout can be organized in smaller sections that are better integrated with the urban reality of Santiago de Compostela. Each pair respectively houses: the New Technologies Center and the Museum of Galician History, the Central Services Building and the Music Theater and the Periodical Archive and the Galician Library.

The City of Culture project is unexpectedly complex compared to other works of this kind which tend to become related to or blend into the natural environment and whose objective is on the one hand not to harm the image of the environment and on the other not to occupy available green areas, in keeping with common ecological awareness and sensibility. On the contrary, the cultural complex in Santiago de Compostela starts from the principle of breaking free from artificial naturalism. For example, an underground project, or one that takes shape as a derivation of the topography of the site or as a superposition of nature onto the construction, in the ambitious hypothesis that architecture does not take away the space, potential or supposed integrity of the landscape, but on the contrary adds to it by creating more under the ground. Thus, Eisenman aims at discovering the capacity and potential of the site by inserting his structures into its heart and enhancing it. The work is an addition of space that through removal of earth below ground level creates new possibilities that the site in its natural state could not provide. In other words, the project informs the site. One of the guidelines of the project is precisely meditation on our contemporary nature and how it conceptually tends to implode in the age of informatics. The tendency of architecture to occupy spaces and sites and to impose itself upon the land, in keeping with a concept of expansion, now seems to have been transcended by an orientation that is often the opposite, considering instead the possibility of utilizing and occupying space as an opportunity and not a limitation.

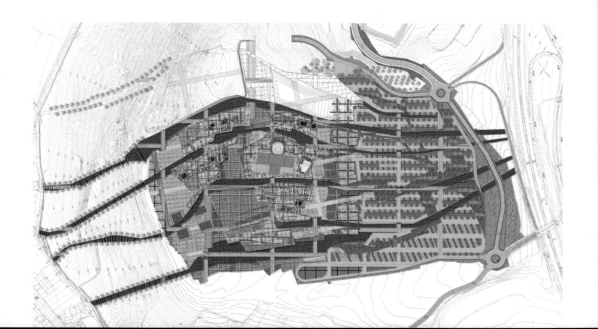

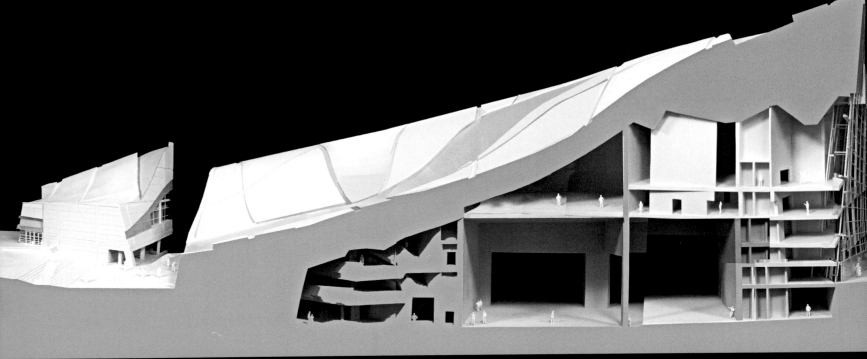

*262-263 top and center
The cutaway view describes the
effects of conceptual deformation
– described as one of the basic
project operations of the project's
concept – giving rise to this
urban layout, which is a new
figure that simultaneously
contains architecture and
topography.*

*262 bottom The photograph
shows a detail of one of the first
buildings to be completed in
the complex.*

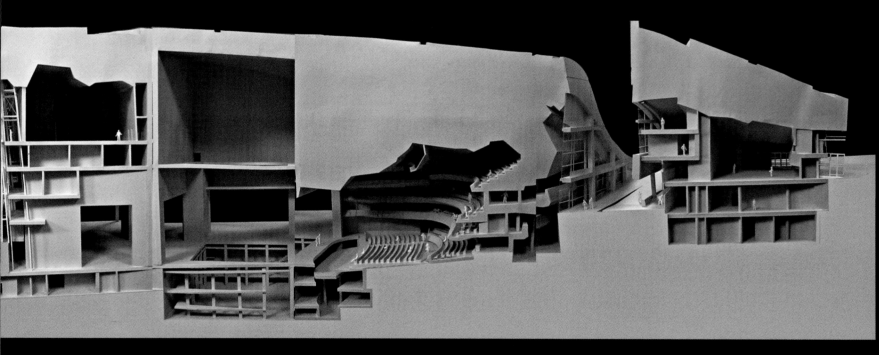

Thus, architecture that penetrates the landscape, informs it and provides it with new possibilities and new meanings. It relates directly with it, utilizing every aspect entailed in this operation and every advantage it may offer.

The above considerations are to be flanked by a more pragmatic datum, which enters into play to define its concept; the idea – which is also poetic, if you will – of relating the City of Culture to the historic part of Santiago de Compostela and at the same time to the symbol of the shell that history has associated with the city.

These references take shape like a trace of genetic code, delineating the features of the new structure. The forms of the consolidated, historic part of the city, of the shell, and of the site, literally produce the traces and volumes of the architectural configuration.

Clearly, this strategy of insertion in the soil means that a large portion of land is not dotted with the new constructions

– which necessarily form an impressive complex such as the City of Culture – thus giving rise to a project that is only relatively invasive in this sense. And it is equally clear that this strategy offers the possibility of profiting from this displacement to achieve, in an easier and more economic way, excellent levels of comfort, and amenities that also in this sense constitute a considerable advantage in such a huge complex as this one.

In fact, like every project aiming at inserting architecture in the land or covering it with artificial soil, the structure is naturally facilitated in maintaining a constant inner microclimate, regardless of the season, thanks to the compact mass that surrounds and envelops it. Therefore, less energy is needed to heat and cool the interior compared to a less favorable configuration on the land.

Memory and research constitute the matrix of the City of Culture, a major and yet discreet part of the development in time of Santiago de Compostela.   S.L.

lucien kroll *(hellersdorf)* - foster + p
partners *(trinity buoy wharf container c*
erskine-tovatt *(greenwich millennium*
(caixaforum madrid)

recycle arch:
the sustainable transformation of existing structures

rtners *(reichstag)* - nicholas lacey &

v) - unstudio *(tea house on bunker)* -

village) - herzog & de meuron

recycle arch:
the sustainable transformation of existing structures

The subject of transforming our existing architectural heritage has always been a major feature of European cities, the basis of potential programmatic action understood as urban ecology. This originated with the modality of "stratification", which is part and parcel of European culture and embraces cities and urban areas in general, as well as individual buildings or parts of buildings. In fact, history provides us with instances of the recycling of materials or architectural elements, at times in an uncritical fashion, which produced splendid architecture created with cast-off materials.

The procedure of the architectural project based on existing structures, in its various forms and scales, regained a central role in the 1980s, when it initiated a course of action still in progress that includes Recycle Architecture.

In the last century, a period in which new projects basically conformed to the prevailing spirit of the time – Modernism – was followed in the years immediately after the Second World War by an approach that restored existing architecture simply in order to be able to use it again. This phase was in turn followed by a period around the 1980s – when the cities had stopped expanding – in which people began to favor the strategy of a project that begins from and consists of existing structures. This stance also transcended the simple and prevalently conservative transformation of any existing structure, in addition to those instances in which protection or restoration would be considered reasonable solutions.

This was therefore an approach that entails upgrading existing architecture, when possible, by recycling it; that once again considers it as the material and basis of a project, as history has taught us; that regards it as indispensable for the realization of a work of a unified nature – on a par with those excellent works constructed in available areas; and that continues the above-mentioned stratification as the extension of the life cycle of our cities.

Generally speaking, and this time referring to an urban scale, a period in which the growth of cities took place through expansion was followed by a phase – around the 1980s – in which the opposite occurred, that is, a period that witnessed the growth of cities through reconversion. This consisted in the transformation of areas and complexes, some of which were quite large, in a strategic position in cities or their immediate surroundings. These were former barracks, abandoned port and industrial complexes, ex-productive areas (once occupied by firms that later moved to locations outside the urban centers), and former railroad or mining areas.

From that time on, this trend became increasingly unrestrained with respect to existing architecture – a new field of architectural and urban experimentation which in the following decades became more sophisticated and came up with techniques of manipulation that were more and more complex and/or poetic. Indeed, what is known as Recycle Architecture may be understood as one of the latest important variations on the theme, which includes the aspect of sustainability as state-of-the-art evolution.

Therefore, while in the postwar period transformation aimed at renovating structures in order to use them again, in the period immediately afterward emphasis was placed on modernizing obsolete structures solely from a technological standpoint and only as much as necessary, without any pretense of imparting "meaning" or "overtones" of an architectural project. In the last few decades this transformation took on the nuances of new words that identified it, such as "reconfiguration", "resignification", "requalification", and "regeneration". In these cases we have a procedure that allows us to conceive the operation in terms of a project and everything it entails, including aesthetics, formal research and experimentation. In short, long-term transformation in time addressed first of all what was necessary, it then turned to quality, project research and aesthetics, and now it also encompasses ethical values.

Recycle Architecture as a new development of the process of transformation includes both strategies of sustainability and everything that in the past meant working with existing structures, understood as an initial genetic code.

Indeed, the theme of transformation is now deeply rooted, with a host of nuances, each of which has a series of names or virtual synonyms (some of which are mentioned above) that would be difficult to explain to someone who has not grown up in a "culture of stratification" that has always been mindful of its heritage and the changes it has undergone.

Recycle Architecture is basically so deeply rooted that it cannot be simply dismissed as yet another approach that follows one of the latest tendencies in architecture, but must be understood as the expression of sensibility and respect – or of new awareness – regarding the environment that is applied to an already consolidated practice: transformation, and the consequent reuse, already constitute an ecological act.

In a context in which the possibilities offered by new materials and technologies allow for a wide range of expressive – and operational – license and where action regarding sustainability and ecology can no longer be postponed, Recycle Architecture is a policy of project orientation made possible by a new cultural and technological context applied to the theme of transformation.

It is also the step subsequent to the tendency in which architecture and town planning had already learned directly from nature – besides having emulated its incessant process of rebirth and its elements, that is, its already metabolized processes of stratification – also in keeping with a trend that was often manifested in architectural works that transfer to architecture forms and/or functions drawn freely from nature.

Therefore, Recycle Architecture involves compromised areas, abandoned urban areas,

single buildings or medium-sized urban complexes, and even encompasses the dimension of building elements. But it also means both addressing the problem of recycling of used materials after the possible demolition of planned structures, and the possible use – quite similar to a Dada approach – of structures and elements that are difficult to dispose of, some of which have already been utilized in new creative constructions such as Nicholas Lacey & Partners' Container City (2002) in London.

To recycle literally means introducing a new life cycle, a procedure already widely adopted in the field of design. This can be seen in the projects for the Tea House on Bunker at Vreeland in The Netherlands (2006) designed by the UNStudio, as well as the Reichstag, the new home of the German Parliament (1999) designed by Foster + Partners, and Lucien Kroll's Hellersdorf (1994), both of which are located in Berlin.

Even the mere restyling of a structure – another variation on the theme of transformation connected more to aesthetics and to the image, and limited to the "shell" – might be an instance of recycling according to the criterion proposed in the projects that begin as objects to be recycled and create new frames and shells. This is the case of the recycled synthetic PET bottles utilized in the construction of the Miniwiz POLLI-Brick curtain walls, which were chosen as the casing for the Far Eastern Group Fashion Pavilion in Taipei for the 2010 Expo. But in this context one

must also consider the many green surfaces that colonize walls, playing a role similar to that of winter gardens or greenhouses in improving the quality of the air in a structure. The CaixaForum Madrid (2008) designed by Herzog & De Meuron, or Jean Nouvel's Musée du Quai Branly (2006) in Paris, projects that called upon Patrick Blanc to lay out the vertical gardens, are exemplary demonstrations of this.

On the other hand, there are instances to the contrary, such as that proposed by the Graft firm, the designers of the Pink Project – the temporary "tent town" created to house the homeless of New Orleans after the devastation wreaked by Hurricane Katrina in 2005 – whose pink material will be transformed into useful containers by the local Institute for the Blind – the recycling of architecture into an object of design.

The change in the meanings, as well as in the scales of the project (from the city, or territory, to design) and in the exercise of Recycle Architecture, gives us an idea of the breadth of this theme.

Transforming existing architecture in a sustainable, eco-friendly manner is what is proposed in this section of our book. Thus the reader will find transformation projects that sum up different variations on this theme, but that also pay particular attention to the strategies of sustainability and more generally speaking to ecology, precisely by starting from the awareness that transforming existing structures and reusing them is nothing more or less than recycling. S.L.

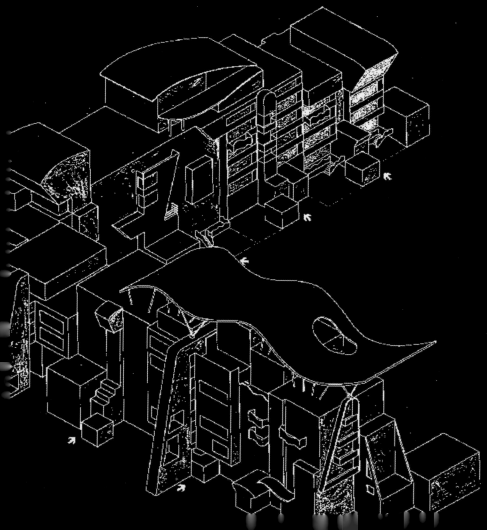

268-269 top The plastic model shows how the rigid and homogeneous mass characterizing the Hellersdorf district was modified by adding detailed shapes to the base and roof and loggias on the facades.

268 bottom and 268-269 center The axonometric section and elevation show the final results of the process to demolish the sticks and later add small masses with layered and wavy roofs and gardens.

268-269 bottom The elevation shows the different-shaped loggias and balconies with their colored panels chosen by the residents in order to make each dwelling recognizable and which replaced the identical prefabricated panels.

Hellersdorf

BERLIN, GERMANY

L ucien Kroll is more interested in the relationships his works establish among those who live or work in them, than the final shape they may take. This is the reason why he has fought against the dehumanizing effect brought about by certain principles of the modern concept that have determined the construction of large, beehive-like, homogeneous and monotonous housing unit districts. His works are fragmentary, complex, irregular, never definitive, flexible, and unfinished so that they can evolve with time by leaving ample margin for those who live in them to mold and change them.

According to Kroll, architects must not design eternal, complete structures, but rather open systems such as those called CASCO in The Netherlands, which call for the separation of tasks and costs between those who realize the "supports" – the long-lasting and stable parts of the structure such as foundation, frame, circulation and distribution elements and communal areas – and the "accessories" such as partitions, internal stairways and cladding, which can be chosen and built by the residents themselves. In this way, architecture respects and meets the needs of ecological principles: since they are long-lasting, the "supports" can be made with material and energy that is neither renewable nor recyclable, while the "accessories", which have an average life span of about 25 years, must be made of renewable material that can be dismantled and replaced according to the needs of the residents. These principles can also be applied to existing structures, and to the "bedroom suburbs" that were laid out in the 1960s and 1970s. Hellersdorf is an example of this type of architectural complex, widespread in East Berlin and throughout East Germany.

The Belgian architect was asked to step in after a column of loggias collapsed. He replaced it with a supporting structure inside which each tenant was allowed to choose the shape of his/her loggia and parapet, in order to create a diversified facade. This was only one of the solutions Kroll proposed to modify the monotonous layout of this rationalist district. Other changes made were the demolition of parts through which the rows of structures were divided, and the superposition of other elements and volumes.

All the communal spaces were occupied by the tenants, who transformed them into living spaces using components selected from a list of 50 options supplied by Kroll's studio. This allowed them to renew green and public areas, and change the appearance of the facades through recessing, balconies, additions, roofing, etc. Thus, Hellersdorf was transformed into an urban landscape based on the relation between the natural and artificial, man-made elements, between the residents and the environment, which transforms the desolate image so typical of working-class block unit quarters. G.S.

270-271 *The dome is the central element. Its shape is analogous to the previous one, but it was made with glass and mainly symbolizes the transparency of the German democracy it represents.*

Reichstag

BERLIN, GERMANY

After the unification of West and East Germany, the old Reichstag in Berlin was chosen as the seat of the new German Parliament. Foster + Partners were commissioned to draw up the project for the reconstruction of this historic building, which had already been rebuilt several times. The project aimed at providing the symbolic expression of the new democratic Germany and its political power, while at the same time offering the opportunity to revamp a structure dating back to 1894 to make it fit for its new and prestigious role.

In fact, from both a formal and functional standpoint, the Reichstag is now one of the most interesting and technologically innovative buildings in Berlin. Answering the new needs of the structure, Foster's project was the subject of long debate before it was definitively approved.

From an architectural-compositional standpoint the most important initiatives were the insertion of a new parliamentary hall; the glass partition at the main entrance that allows passersby to see the legislative chamber, including the President's and Chancellor's seats; and the construction of a transparent dome crowning the building, which has restored the original shape of the destroyed building and has become a striking landmark in the urban landscape.

This was a symbolic operation, wholly in line with the principles and aesthetic of Foster + Partners, which aim at combining high tech with sustainability. In fact the operation of the Reichstag is based on the utilization of the features of the original massive structure – which by its very nature is able to maintain a constant inside microclimate – and the integration of different systems. The accomplished objective is to provide a high level of comfort in terms of natural heating, ventilation and illumination, as well as energy efficiency. This is achieved thanks to the production of energy through systems of solar absorption and cogenerators, which greatly reduce the annual emission of carbon dioxide.

The cupola, made of glass, is the central element of Foster's project and basically symbolizes the transparency of the German democracy that it represents. Visitors can go up and down this dome by means of two helical ramps in the interior, which allow them a bird's-eye view of the parliamentary activities below, thus placing the citizen – once again symbolically as well as physically – above political power.

The cupola is oval and is supported by a steel structure made of arches and horizontal rings which is linked to the crown by means of a circular beam, and discharges its weight on columns that mark the rhythm of the hall below. The helical ramps also contribute to the stability of the overall structural system. The shell consists of stratified slabs of safety glass that characterize its singular fragmentary form.

Inside the cupola is an overturned cone that plays a role in the eco-friendly management of the structure. Clad with inclined mirror panels, in the daytime it casts natural light into the assembly chamber, while at night it radiates artificial light toward the city. Furthermore, the cone favors the exchange of fresh air, which is channeled inside and then flows out in the uppermost part of the dome, which is open and has a special system that facilitates upward movement.

A large and moveable sun shield is also situated in the cupola. It runs automatically, following the movement of the sun and screening only what is necessary with each move. Its operation, like that of the ventilation system, is charged by the photovoltaic system placed on the roof of the Reichstag. S.L.

272-273 and 273 top The two cutaway views show the most consistent interventions by the project to reuse the Reichstag: the new plenary chamber, the completely transparent cupola above it and (in the cross-section) the glass wall closing the chamber overlooking the city.

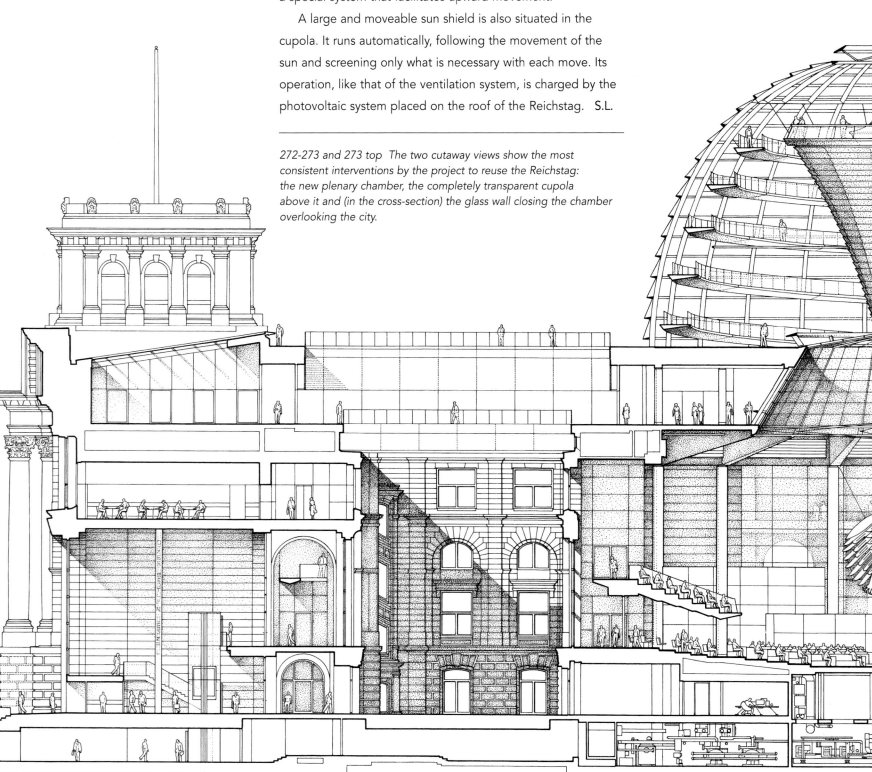

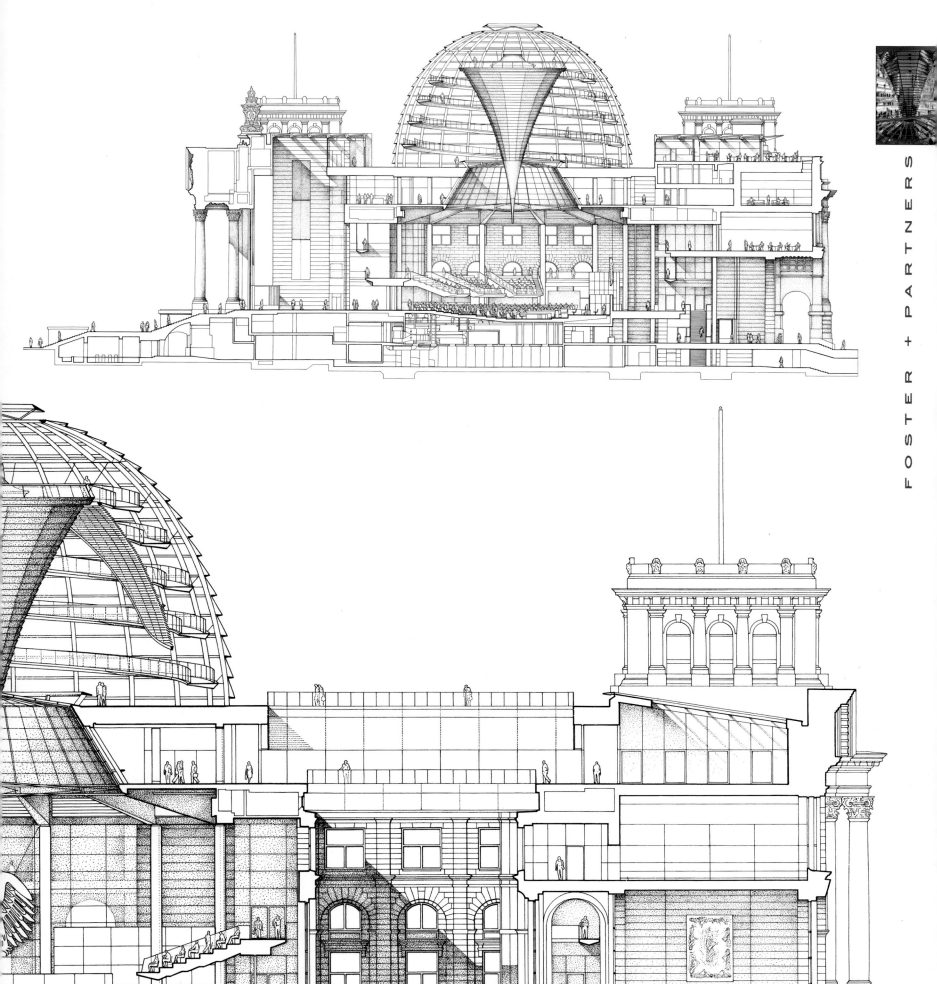

274 top *The purpose of the upside-down cone is to expel the air it channels through the opening at the top of the dome.*

274-275 The transparent cupola is made of tilted glass sheets to form the recognizable jagged outline.

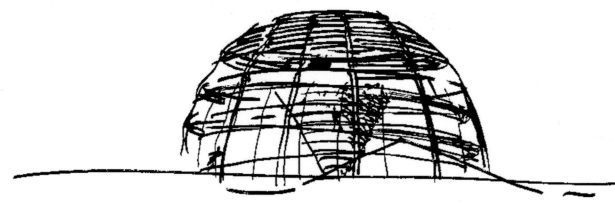

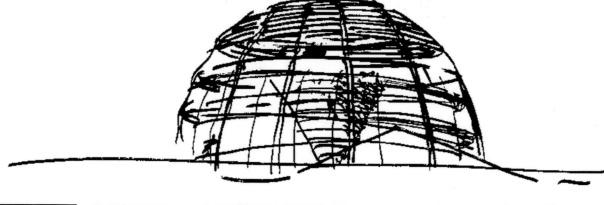

275 top The dome is oval-shaped and its sketch is like a logo that identifies and summarizes the Reichstag project by Foster + Partners architectural firm.

275 bottom The bearing structure of the cupola is in steel and includes arches and horizontal rings. The internal helicoidal stairs contribute to the static nature of the system.

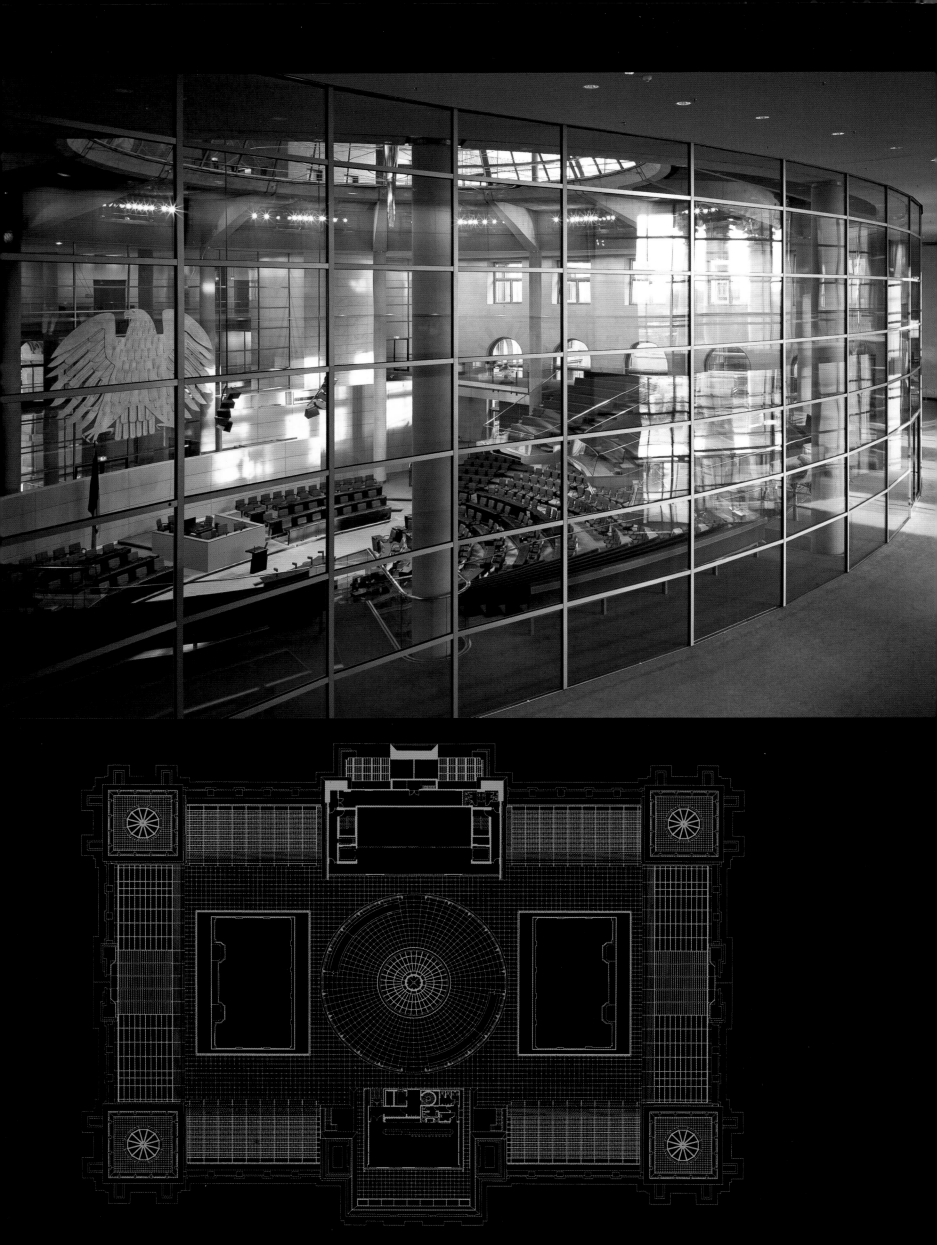

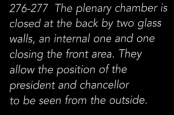

276-277 The plenary chamber is closed at the back by two glass walls, an internal one and one closing the front area. They allow the position of the president and chancellor to be seen from the outside.

276 bottom The roof (a diagram of which is seen here) is one of the floors with free access by the public and offers a charming look over reunited Berlin. A portion of it houses photovoltaic panels, which contribute to making the structure self-sufficient in terms of power.

277 top The plenary chamber is outlined by a series of columns supporting the new, transparent dome above.

277 bottom The upside-down cone in the cupola is finished with mirrored panels to favor the natural lighting in the Reichstag. This structure also has the job of exchanging the air in the plenary chamber.

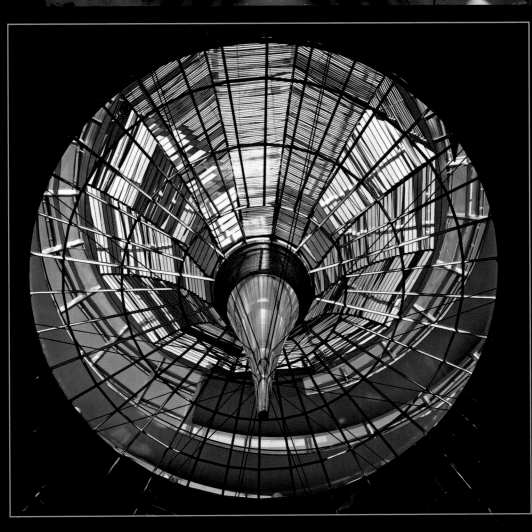

278-279 The dome is an area open to the public and can be completely crossed on two helicoidal stairways. Work by the parliament in session can be seen from this privileged position.

278 bottom As shown in the sketch, the stairways animate the cupola due to the movement of the people on them.

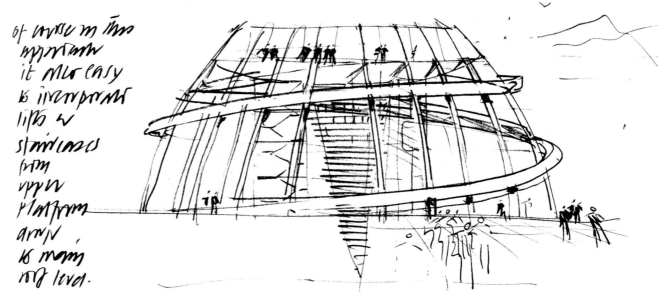

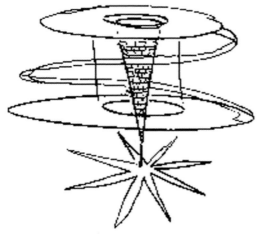

279 bottom left The sketch is an example of a stairway around the upside-down cone in the center of the dome.

279 bottom right The center of the intervention on the Reichstag is precisely the central part of the existing structure, and home to the plenary chamber and dome, but it is also one of the areas in which both aspects characterizing the project and tied to high-tech and sustainability are most visible.

Trinity Buoy Wharf
Container City

LONDON, UK

Container City is an extremely innovative project based on the sustainable principle of recycling; as in the conversion and reuse of a former industrial area such as Trinity Buoy Wharf, and of a group of metal shipping containers that could not comply with the standards of new and rigorous safety regulations and were therefore abandoned and replaced by new ones. Many of these discarded containers are scattered all over the world, but since recycling steel containers is a complicated and costly affair, architects Nicholas Lacey & Partners proposed using the ones

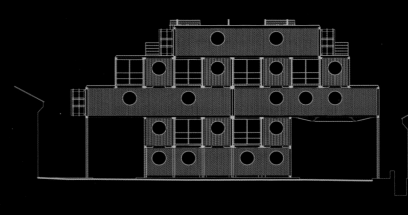

280-281 The picture shows Container City 2, a complex built by placing old containers on top of each other and bolting and soldering them together. The containers no longer serve their purpose and were recycled as boxes to be used for various uses, such as dwellings, offices, studios and ateliers.

281 The elevations of Container City 2 are different. The containers were placed on the east side parallel to each other and perpendicular on some levels, resulting in windows and balconies. The west side has a large entranceway and the north section is more enclosed and almost defined solely by the windows cut out of the walls.

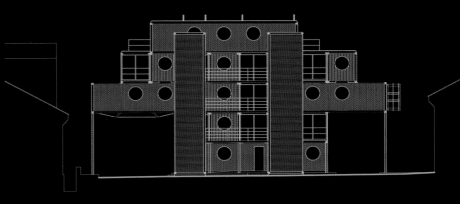

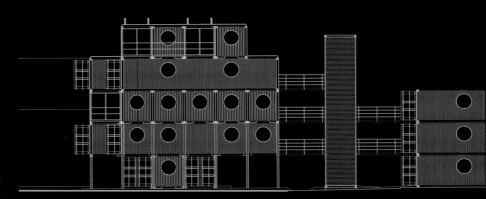

in London as habitable spaces. In fact, containers are solid steel structures that can easily be adapted as construction blocks and converted into laboratories, artists' studios, offices and houses.

The innovative nature of the architects' proposal does not lie so much in recycling containers, since this was done in other projects, but rather in grouping and stacking them together into more complex and larger structures to form multi-units, in order to use them for activities requiring much more space.

The first example of a Container City is at Trinity Buoy Wharf, an area in the eastern part of London's Docklands.

It was ideal for this type of operation because it housed long-abandoned and deteriorated manufacturing industries, shipyards and wharves that were in urgent need of an urban renewal program. Thus, in 1997 the Dockland Development held a competition for the renewal of the area. The winning project proposed its conversion into a cultural-arts center and envisaged both the reuse of the brick warehouses and the construction of new buildings by recycling abandoned containers which could serve as workstations, laboratories and studios.

282-283 Container City 2
is the second complex of its
kind realized in London and is
connected to the first complex
by a series of walkways placed
at different levels and accessible
through two towers (one housing
the elevators and the other the
stairs). The towers form a sort
of entranceway to the complex.

Two complexes were laid out. Container City 1 utilizes 40 containers stacked on three levels and arranged in four parallel rows that house 12 studios. Container City 2 comprises 30 containers, five stories high, stacked so as to create some overhanging areas at 90 degrees and running access balconies. The overall effect of this second group is much more vibrant, not only due to the different configuration, but also because of the different color schemes adopted to differentiate the architectural volumes, as opposed to the uniform red that characterizes Container City 1. Between the two groups are two towers, one containing the elevators and the other the stairway, which create an entrance lobby and circulation area for the various levels.

To make them habitable, the containers were stacked, bolted or welded together, and walls were removed in order to create larger spaces. Their original structure had to be modified somewhat by creating windows to admit air and light. Entrance doors were replaced with sliding glass, and the inner walls and roof were covered with thermal and acoustic insulating material. However, it was found that these changes weakened the original structure of the containers, which therefore needed to be reinforced, with pillars replacing the walls that had been removed in order to expand the spaces. By using containers, buildings can be constructed very quickly and at a very low cost. Lacey purchased them for £1,000 each ($1,400), took them to the factory for the necessary changes, then to the construction yard, where they were assembled easily and quickly, just like prefabricated structures. This is part of the reason why the system conceived by this architect is spreading more and more throughout the world.   G.S.

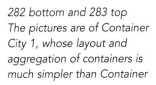

*282 bottom and 283 top
The pictures are of Container
City 1, whose layout and
aggregation of containers is
much simpler than Container*

*City 2. In fact, they all face the
same direction and are placed
in parallel rows, painted a single
color and have windows of the
same shape and size.*

Tea House on Bunker

VREELAND, THE NETHERLANDS

The Tea House is a work lying halfway between architecture and design, or even sculpture, that emerges from the typical landscape of the dike-protected polder in The Netherlands, among polo fields and stables.

This project grew out of the desire to change and renew an existing structure – even on a formal architectural plane – by means of adding a new part, thus discreetly increasing its rather small size while radically modifying its exterior appearance.

The old structure was a bunker built in 1936 as part of a complex defensive system laid out to thwart enemy attacks which called for a series of sluices, that could be opened to flood the land if need be, and a group of military bunkers dotting the area.

The renewal project aimed at regenerating one of bunkers, providing it with new functions and meaning, while wholly respecting the original construction and preserving its memory. In fact, except for a portion of the roof that is in contact with the new structure, the addition – which is an autonomous, superposed construction – was planned so that it could perhaps be moved to another site, in order to avoid causing any permanent damage to the historic bunker. Thus, the concrete bunker was almost totally covered by the addition, whose supporting structure and cladding are made of steel sheets, except for a small part of the original facade, which was left visible from the outside.

The entrance to the tea house is afforded by a stairway situated between the newly constructed facade and a short side of the rectangular bunker. The new construction is virtually a deformation of a basic form conceived as a place to receive and entertain guests, and the entire complex was to be visible together with the polo fields. In fact it is both a special viewing area overlooking the natural landscape and sports fields, and at the same time an enclosed, private and comfortable space.

284 The Tea House combines the pre-existing structure – in this case a bunker – and the new structure, in an ambitious project aimed at recycling and giving a new purpose and image to a small protected building.

284-285 The Tea House project reveals part of the historic, pre-existing structure. In fact, the strategy of the intervention is to clearly stratify and recycle the existing structure.

285 bottom The volumetric configuration of the project starts with the re-elaboration of the initial bunker. Computer modeling deforms and twists the structure to define architecture whose small sizes have a great expressive ability.

286-287 top The drawing
of the shell of the Tea House,
partially composed of the
new structure and the original
construction (an old bunker
built in 1936), is schematically
opened to describe each
surface area involved.

286-287 bottom The pictures
of the plastic model shown
in sequence result in the final
volumetric configuration, which
cannot be simply described by
4 elevations given the complexity
of its geometry, which is the result
of computer modeling.

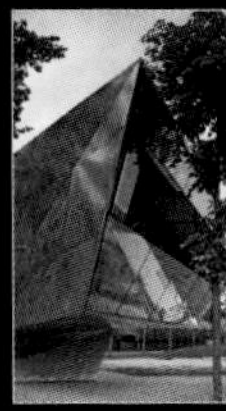

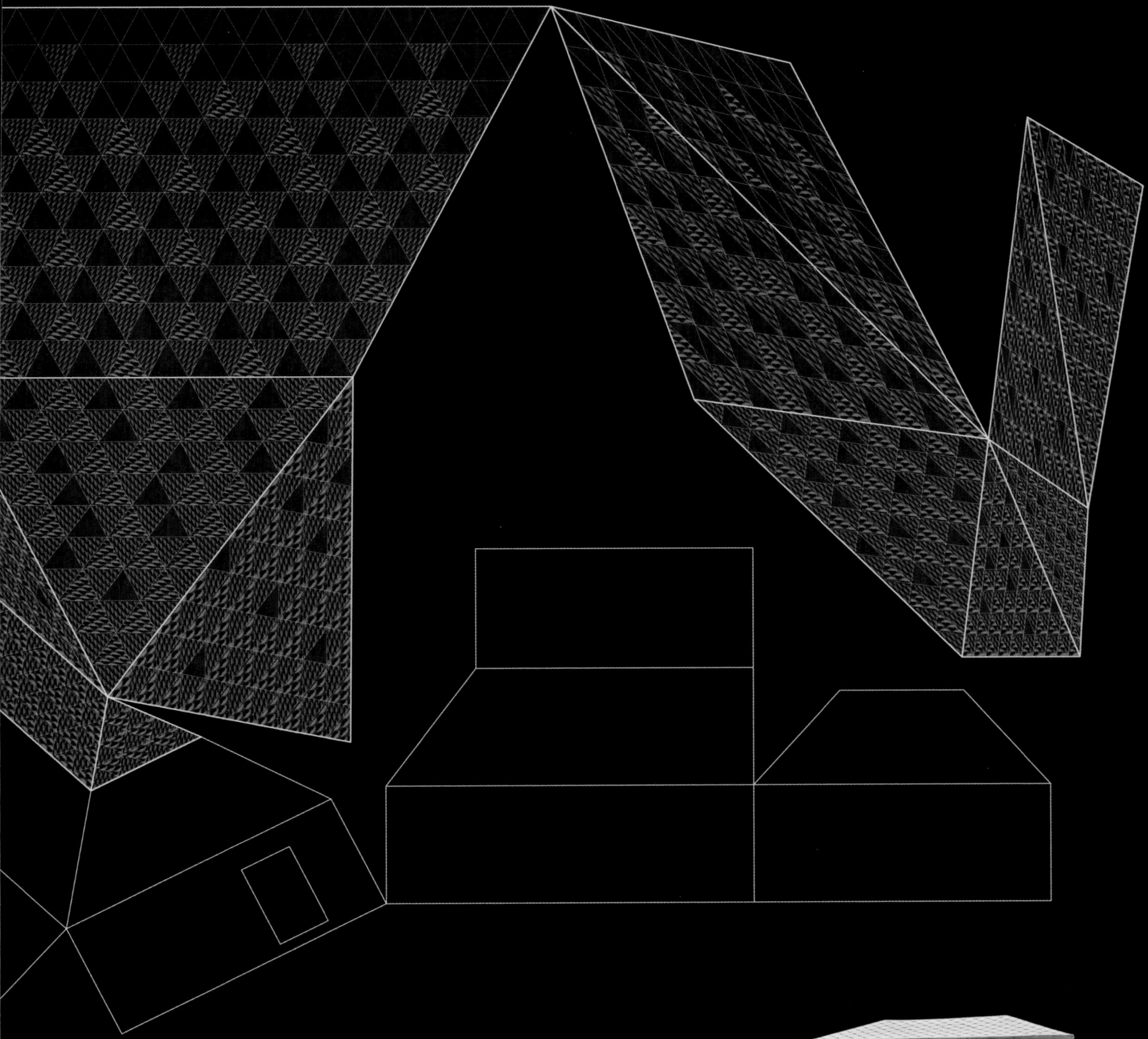

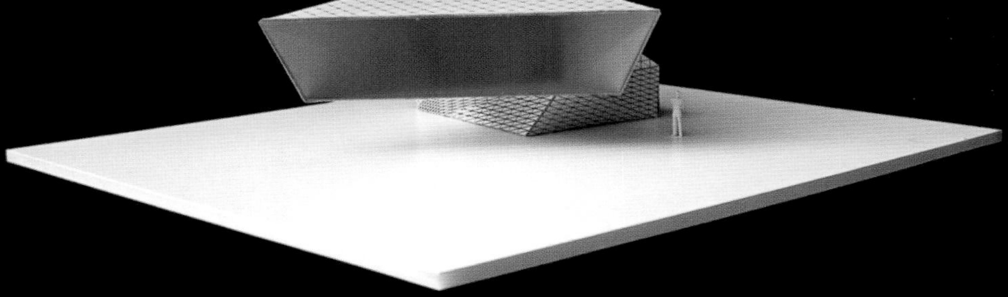

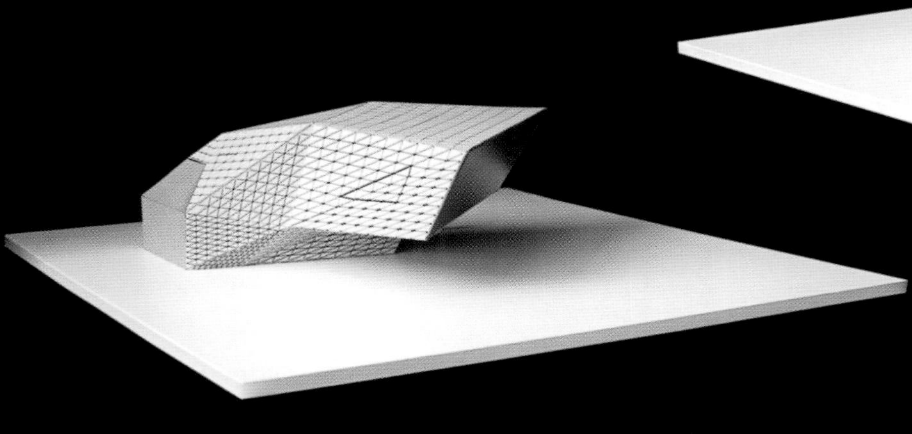

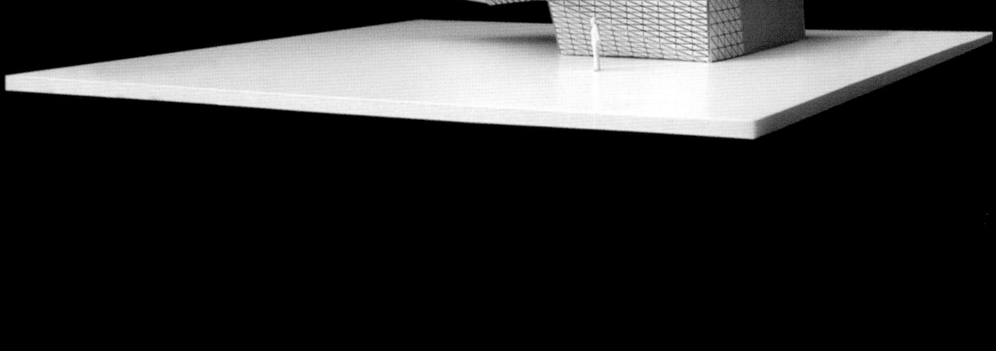

In the interior the steel beams are open to view, and the main cladding, made of wood, greatly contributes to making the interior cozy and is ideal for the new purpose of the Tea House.

The tea room, which represents the principal function of the new addition, occupies the protruding section of the structure. The entire side facing the polo fields is a window that frames and overlooks the typical Dutch countryside, giving the viewer the impression of being a privileged spectator.

The Tea House project promotes the concept of stratification as a means of architectural renewal or modification that is synchronized with natural processes. This is something that has always characterized European architecture and which guarantees the vital cycle of the edifices – and urban settlements in general – in keeping with the custom and practice according to which pre-existing structures are considered the springboard and very material of any project, hence of recycling. On the other hand, this building expresses state-of-the-art architectural design, which makes use of the possibilities offered by the latest technology, which is an integral part of UNStudio's theory and practice. The configuration of this work, which lies somewhere between architecture and sculpture, reveals the two-fold vocation – or two-fold soul – of this Dutch architecture studio in relation to the type of education and experience of its chief architects, Ben van Berkel and Caroline Bos.   S.L.

288-289 The tea room overlooks the polo fields through a large window that can be opened. Inside, the steel bearing structure is visible. The floors, walls and ceiling were finished in wood.

289 top The window of the cantilevered mass is a privileged observation point overlooking the polo fields.

289 bottom left The detailed cutaway view describes the division and components of the terminal part of the cantilevered mass.

289 bottom right The cutaway view clarifies how the added portion of the project is an autonomous steel structure (with respect to the bunker) and for the most part, is cantilevered.

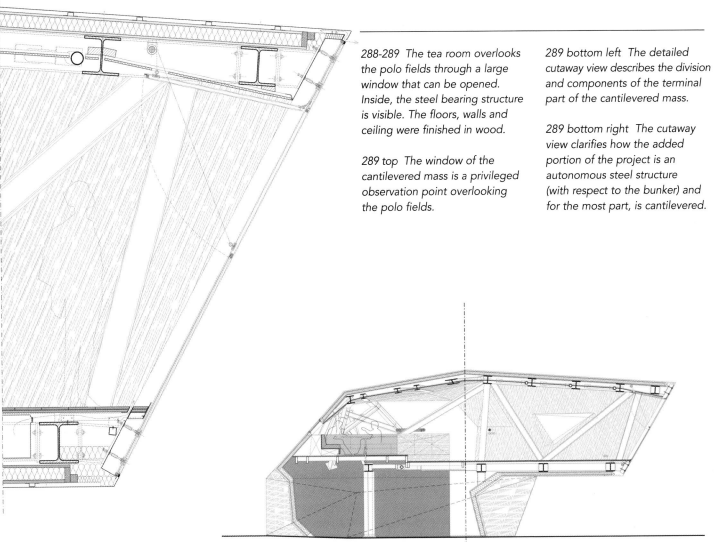

Greenwich Millennium Village

LONDON, UK

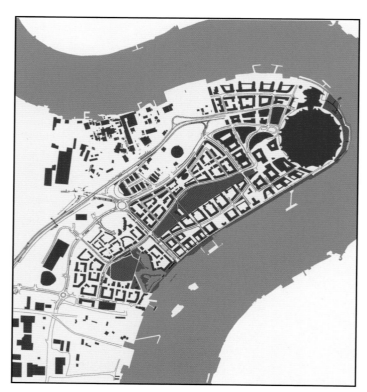

290-291 *A view of the front of the Greenwich Millennium Village from the Thames, with the Millennium Dome in the background, shows how the profile of the complex designed by Erskine has different heights, preventing cold currents from entering. The variety of materials used to finish the buildings makes them lively and bright.*

There are several aspects to sustainability: the recovery of an abandoned area to be renewed as a vital part of a city; the creation of a natural ecological habitat; the recycling of resources that are not unlimited; the absorption of garbage; the quality of urban life improved by an efficient public transport system; the presence of various activities, services and social areas in a neighborhood; and the spatial quality of the living quarters, together with the technology and material used during construction which, if prefabricated, means a decrease in time, cost, waste and the subsequent emission of CO_2. All these elements were applied jointly to the Greenwich Millennium Village project.

Ralph Erskine won the competition for the construction of 1,080 residences called for in the master plan drawn up by Richard Rogers, which involves the entire Greenwich Peninsula, an area that includes a fine village green that up to the 1990s was quite degraded from an environmental standpoint. This was due to the presence of the South Metropolitan Gas Works which, besides the abandoned plants and machines, had left 27,000 tons of tar in the subsoil. Therefore the first necessary ecologically sustainable act was

ERSKINE-TOVATT

reclamation of the area. The subsoil was removed and transported to special dumps, after which a network of geo-grilles was placed on the site to isolate the layers of earth underneath that were still polluted, while the subsoil was replaced. At this stage, 121 hectares of the site were slated to become a park, designed by landscape architects Desvigne & Dalnoky, who proposed using local plants and a network of artificial lakes and canals which, besides constituting the landscape, would make it possible to collect and recycle rainwater to be used for irrigation. The residential spaces were also planned in keeping with various bioclimatic strategies in order to reduce energy consumption and the production of carbon dioxide, and to increase living comfort. Erskine created a new type by combining the traditional London square and the single family house with a private garden. The buildings form large open courtyards with a garden that serves as the roof of two-story underground parking areas.

The three-dimensional composition decreases from north to south in order to create a barrier that prevents the cold northeasterly wind from penetrating the courtyards but which also lets in sunlight through the glazed walls to the south. These walls are protected by heavy louvers, that reduce nocturnal heat dispersion, and by a system of mobile shading for the summer. The numerous holes on both facades provide natural light for the interiors, and the use of glass with a low thermal dispersion coefficient retains the heat inside the

homes. The facades are covered with prefabricated panels, (the building elements are also prefabricated), consisting of two layers: the inner one made of plywood and the outer one made of various recycled materials. This reduces the consumption of raw materials as well as the energy needed for their transformation and transport.

Indeed, recycling was a strategy that was applied in various sectors of the construction. The prefabricated modular panels on the facades may in the future be selectively demolished, the collection of domestic garbage is differentiated, and waste disposal is carried out on the spot. Thanks to a cogeneration plant, the CO_2 produces electricity and the heat thereby derived is in turn recycled to heat the apartments and the water. Gray water from the wash basins, showers, sinks and washing machines is purified and used for toilet flushing.   G.S.

290 bottom The intervention by Ralph Erskine to realize 1080 dwellings that reinterpret a standard London plaza is part of the master plan for the entire Greenwich Village area designed by Richard Rogers, involving the entire peninsula (a rather degraded district from an environmental perspective).

291 The view shows the two main facades at the Greenwich Millennium Village. Their volumetric layout, position and size of the holes and balconies and the variety of the facing panels and facades are all devices that allow the bioclimatic operation of the complex and the reduction of energy consumption.

CaixaForum Madrid

MADRID, SPAIN

If one thinks of a building as an organism with its own life cycle that ranges from its design to construction, from its use to abandonment, and then from its demolition to renewal; and if one conceives sustainability as a policy aimed at improving the environment, including the urban environment, and decreasing waste and refuse – including that produced by the demolition of a building – then the CaixaForum Madrid designed by Herzog & de Meuron is truly an act of urban regeneration, the renewal of a central area and part of the abandoned equipment inside. In other words, it is a sustainable project.

The area is situated near the Paseo del Prado in Madrid, facing the Botanical Garden, but it is isolated and enclosed by dense urban construction. It once had two abandoned buildings: a power station, classified and restricted as an example of industrial archaeology, and a gas station. The latter structure was demolished and replaced by a square that connects the CaixaForum Madrid with the Paseo del Prado, along which there is a concentration of cultural institutions, including the Thyssen-Bornemisza Museum, the Prado Museum with its recent addition designed by Rafael Moneo, and the Reina Sofia Museum designed by Jean Nouvel. This small public area therefore plays a fundamental urban role as a link between the Paseo, the building and the Botanical Garden, which is evoked by the "vertical garden" designed by Patrick Blanc that covers one of its walls. Here Blanc (who is known for his collaboration with Jean Nouvel in the realization of the Musée du Quai Branly in Paris) aimed at inserting nature into the city, and not only for aesthetic reasons, since the vertical garden also serves as thermal and acoustic insulation as well as a means of purifying the air. It consists of two layers of felt wrapped in PVC and connected to a metal structure mounted on the old original wall. The felt preserves the water that nourishes the plants by means of a drip irrigation system.

This square is slightly inclined in order to connect with the difference in height of the area, and then continues in another open space, created by eliminating the stone base of the power plant, while preserving its brick exterior. Thus, the CaixaForum Madrid seems to float over an urban area that allows people to cross over the entire area and links it with its setting, inserting it in this circuit of great museums, so that the CaixaForum Madrid is like an urban magnet, an area that attracts a large number of people, from the museum visitors to the inhabitants of the Spanish capital. The square under the building, an area for socializing that is cool and shaded in the summer, is a compressed space which despite its different size reminds one of the plaza designed by the same Swiss architects in the Forum in Barcelona. The irregular configuration of the roof, with its triangulations, both compresses and expands the space, which can be entered from the section of the building that touches the ground as well as from the suspended section. The architects were obliged to extend the CaixaForum Madrid two floors under ground level and two floors above the original building in order to meet the needs of the vast functional program envisaged for this institution. The underground area includes an auditorium with a seating capacity of around 300, as well as service and parking spaces. The section above the atrium houses the art galleries, a restaurant and the administrative offices. Thus, the simple original structure becomes an articulated and sculptural volume that seems foreign to its setting but in reality is closely linked to it since its shape resembles that of the surrounding buildings, and the cast iron panels that clad the new part have a texture and color similar to that of the bricks of the old power plant. G.S.

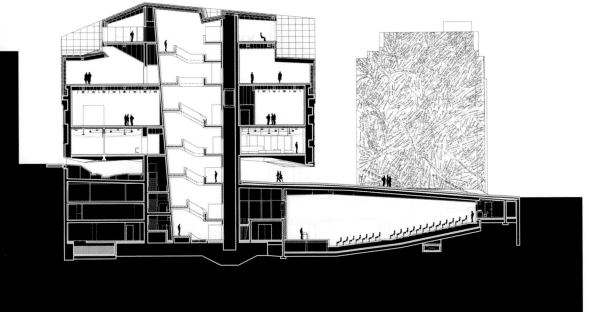

292 and 292-293 The pre-existing building was cut out at the base to create a plaza that extends from the Paseo del Prado, under the building and beyond, to another public area running alongside the northern side of the CaixaForum Madrid.

293 bottom The transversal cutaway view shows the main stairway crossing and connecting all levels of the CaixaForum Madrid: those in the pre-existing building, those in the terminal part and those underground where architects placed the auditorium.

294 The plastic model of the large three-dimensional roof with an irregular shape creates internal voids. The picture shows the central patio overlooked by and providing light to the areas used by the administration offices.

295 The cast iron panels on the facade take on the grain, texture and colors similar to those of the bricks in the pre-existing building, as a kind of tactile complement to them.

296-297 The large stairway leading from the indoor plaza to the underground world (the location of the auditorium and various service rooms) has the same triangulations defining the spatiality of the plaza.

297 top The picture shows the indoor plaza, a meeting area defined by continuous compressions and expansions of the metal panels, giving it the feeling of an artificial atmosphere. The main entrance is in the center.

297 bottom The area inside the underground foyer is defined by metal panels, by the floor and furniture in light-colored wood and by a ceiling with large pipes and a series of spotlights creating a hard spatiality that contrasts the areas above.

298 top and 298-299 The two charming views
of the stairs connecting all upper floors (seen
respectively from above and from below) highlight
this plastic element which is characterized by
a reinforced-steel structure with natural-colored
cement floors and balustrades, making it rather
elegant and bright.

BIBLIOGRAPHY

Carpenzano, Orazio and Toppetti, Fabrizio, *ModernoContemporaneo*, Rome: DiAR/Gangemi editori, 2006.

Gausa, Manuel, *The Metapolis Dictionary of Advanced Architecture: City, Technology and Society in the Information Age*, Barcelona: Actar, 2003

Gauzin-Müller, Dominique, *Sustainable Living.*

25 International Examples, Basel: Birkhäuser, 2006.

Lloyd Jones, David, *Architecture and the Environment Bioclimatic Building Design*, London: Laurence King Publishing Ltd, 1998.

Minguzzi, Gianluca, *L'architettura sostenibile. Una scelta responsabile per uno sviluppo equilibrato*, Milan: Skira, 2008 (bilingual edition, Italian and English).

Pirillo, Claudio, Barahona Pohl, Ethel and Reyes, Cesar, *Architecture Sustainable*, Valencia: Editorial Pencil, 2007.

Sassi, Paola, *Strategies for Sustainable Architecture*, Abingdon-New York: Taylor & Francis, 2006.

Website of the Department of Architecture (DiAR) at the University of Rome "Sapienza:" W3.uniroma1.it/diarambiente

INDEX

PHOTO CREDITS

Fernando Alda: pages 93, 98, 98-99
Archenova/Arcaid.co.uk: pages 124-125, 126 center, 126-127 top
Manuel Armand: pages 232 bottom, 236 top
Atlantide Phototravel/Corbis: page 274
Iwan Baan: pages 294, 296-297, 297 top, 297 bottom, 298 top, 298-299
Marcello Bertinetti/Archivio White Star: pages 270-271
Victor Brigola/Arturimages: page 25
Anthony Browell: pages 130 bottom, 130-131 top and bottom
Richard Bryant/Arcaid.co.uk: pages 66-67 top
Inigo Bujedo Aguirre/View: pages 39, 41
Lluis Casals: pages 220-221, 221, 222 top, 222 bottom, 223
Tom Chance: pages 58-59
Franck Chazot/Explorer/Hoa-Qui/Eyedea/Contrasto: page 238 top
Peter Cook/View: pages 50 top left, 50 bottom right, 51, 52 top, 52 bottom, 52-53, 54-55, 55 bottom, 56-57
Michel Denancé/Artedia: pages 73, 74, 74-75, 126 top
Bilyana Dimitrova: pages 62, 63, 64 top, 64 bottom right, 65
Stefan Falke/laif/Contrasto: page 256 bottom
Fausto Giaccone/Anzenberger/Contrasto: page 125 top
Dennis Gilbert/View: pages 9, 276-277
Philippe Giraud/Corbis Sygma/Corbis: page 122 center
Kirk Gittings: pages 86 top, 86 bottom, 86-87 top, 86-87 bottom, 90, 90-91, 91
John Gollings/Arcaid.co.uk: pages 122-123
John Gollings/Arcaid/Corbis: pages 16-17
Reinhard Görner/Arturimages/View: pages 188-189 top
Tim Griffith: pages 252-253, 253, 256 top, 259
Roland Halbe/Arturimages: pages 14-15, 40 top, 40 bottom, 76-77, 77 top, 84 top, 84 bottom, 99, 138, 138-139, 179, 182 top, 244-245, 246-247 top, 247, 292, 292-293

Jochen Helle/Arturimages/View: pages 186-187, 188 top
Karin Hessmann/Arturimages/View: page 161
Hiroyuki Hirai: pages 140, 140-141
Eduard Hueber/archphoto.com: pages 34, 34-35, 35
Nicholas Kane/Arcaid.co.uk: pages 282-283
Tony Korody/Sygma/Corbis: pages 112-113 bottom
Ian Lambot/Arcaid.co.uk: pages 162 top left, 163
Dieter Leistner/Arturimages: pages 22, 22-23, 24-25
Benedict Luxmoore/Arcaid.co.uk: pages 280-281
Raf Makda/View: pages 59, 60 top, 60 bottom, 60-61
Duccio Malagamba: pages 295, 298 bottom
Rudi Meisel, Berlin: pages 278-279
Christian Michel/View: pages 233, 238 bottom
Monika Nikolic/Arturimages/View: pages 184-185 top, 186, 187
Pedro Pegenaute: pages 4-5, 92 bottom, 95, 96, 97, 100-101
PhotoserviceElecta/Artur: pages 80 center, 81, 82
Paul Raftery/View: page 188 center
Christian Richters/Arturimages: pages 226, 226-227, 227 top, 227 center, 228, 228-229, 230, 230-231, 231 left, 231 right
Christian Richters/Arturimages/View: pages 284, 284-285, 285, 288-289, 289 top
Chie Rokutanda/Scarletgreen: pages 240 top, 243
Philippe Ruault: pages 38-39
Andy Ryan: pages 192-193, 244 bottom, 249, 250 bottom, 251
Ulrich Schwarz: pages 170-171, 171
Svenja-Foto/Zefa/Corbis: pages 274-275
Torino/Mauritius Images: page 36
Paul Warchol: pages 190-191 top, 190-191 center, 191
Jens Willebrand: pages 162-163
Nathan Willock/View: pages 82-83, 85
Charlotte Wood/Arcaid.co.uk: page 291

Nigel Young/Foster + Partners: pages 275 bottom, 277 top, 277 bottom

Courtesy of:
24H-Architecture: page 227 bottom
Architect - Emilio Ambasz, Hon. FAIA: pages 156-157, 158 top, 158 bottom
Satoshi Asakawa: pages 142, 142-143, 144-145, 145 top, 145 bottom
Atelier Hollein: pages 232 top, 234 bottom, 236 center, 236 bottom, 236-237, 237
Atelier Hollein/Sina Baniahmad: pages 234 top, 235, 238-239, 239
Atelier Kempe Thill Architects: page 170
Ateliers Jean Nouvel: pages 37, 194-195, 195 top, 195 bottom, 196, 197, 198, 198-199, 200-201, 201 top, 201 bottom, 202, 202-203, 203, 204, 204-205, 205, 224-225 top, 224-225 bottom
Atkins/Golden Horizon: pages 103 bottom, 104 top, 104 bottom, 106 top
Shigeru Ban: page 139
Behnisch Architekten: pages 42, 43 top, 44-45 bottom, 165, 166 top, 167 top, 168 bottom, 180, 181, 182 bottom
Behnisch Architekten/Photographer Anton Grassl: pages 178-179, 180-181, 183
Behnisch Architekten/Photographer Robert Hösle: page 43 bottom
Behnisch Architekten/Photographer Christian Kandzia: pages 164, 166 bottom, 167 bottom, 168 top, 169
Behnisch Architekten/Photographers Adam Mørk and Torben Eskerod: pages 42-43, 44, 44-45 top, 46, 46-47, 47 top, 47 bottom
Behnisch Architekten/Photographer Martin Schodder: pages 6-7, 164-165
Michael E. Brown: pages 118-119
Bruce Colbert: page 113
Cosanti Foundation: pages 112-113 top, 115 top, 115 bottom, 116 bottom, 117 in basso right, 118-119, 120-121
Jean De Calan, courtesy of Archivio Fotografico iGuzzini: pages 26 top, 27

Geoff Denton: pages 290-291
Eisemann Architects: pages 260, 260-261, 261 top, 261 bottom, 262-263
ELEMENTAL-Alejandro Aravena: pages 146-147 basso
Erskine-Tovatt: page 290
Feilden Clegg Bradley Studios/BioRegional Quintain: pages 214, 214-215
Carlos Ferrater: pages 220 top, 220 bottom
Foster + Partners: pages 160 top, 160 bottom, 162 bottom, 272-273, 275 top, 276, 278, 279
Hayley Franklin/Sean Godsell Architects: pages 132-133 top, 134, 135 top, 135 bottom
Sean Godsell Architects: pages 1, 132, 132-133 center, 133
Golden Horizon: pages 102, 103 top, 105, 106 bottom, 107
John Gollings: pages 128-129 top
Grimshaw Architects: pages 48, 50 right, 55 top
TR Hamzah & Yeang Sdn Bhd: pages 152 top, 152 bottom, 210 top, 210 bottom, 211, 212, 212-213
TR Hamzah & Yeang Sdn Bhd/K.L. Ng: page 153

Hemeroteca: page 262 bottom
Herzog & de Meuron: page 293
Herzog + Partner: page 23 bottom
Steven Holl Architects: pages 64 bottom a sinista, 190 bottom, 192, 245, 246-247 bottom, 248-249, 250 top
Toyo Ito & Associates, Architects: pages 240 bottom, 242 top, 242-243
Lucien Kroll: pages 268-269
Kengo Kuma and Associates: page 143
Nicholas Lacey & Partners: page 281
Nic Lehoux: page 258
Teresa Lundquist: pages 282, 283
Francisco José Mangado Beloqui: pages 92 top, 94
MCA/Architects: page 26 bottom
John McNeal/RPBW: pages 254-255, 257
Glenn Murcutt: page 130 top
Nagano Consultant: page 241
Cristóbal Palma: pages 146-147
Renzo Piano Building Workshop: pages 72, 122 top, 123, 125 bottom , 126-127 bottom, 128-129 bottom, 254 center, 254 bottom, 255
Antoine Predock Architect PC: pages 88, 89 top, 89 center, 89 bottom

Rogers Stirk Harbour + Partners: pages 2-3, 28, 28-29, 29, 30-31, 31, 32, 33, 66-67 bottom, 68-69
Rogers Stirk Harbour + Partners/Manuel Renau: pages 68, 70, 71
Sauerbruch Hutton: pages 184-185 bottom, 188 bottom, 188-189 bottom
Sealand Aerial Photography Chichester: page 49
SITE: pages 11, 172 top, 172 bottom, 173, 174-175, 176-177
SOM (Skidmore, Owings & Merrill LLP): pages 206, 206-207 top, 206-207 bottom, 208 top, 208 center, 208 bottom left, 208 bottom right, 208-209
UNStudio: pages 77 center, 77 bottom, 78 top, 78 bottom, 79 top, 79 bottom, 80 top, 80 bottom right, 84-85, 286-287, 289 bottom
Simon Vélez-Deboer Architects: pages 136 top, 136-137, 137 bottom
Hiromi Watanabe/Architect - Emilio Ambasz, Hon. FAIA: pages 154, 155, 156 top, 156 bottom, 159
Yuki Yanagimoto: pages 114-115, 116 top, 117 top, 117 bottom
www.zedfactory.com: pages 58, 61

ACKNOWLEDGMENTS

The Publisher would like to thank:

24H-Architecture, Rotterdam: Anja Verdonk
ADCK - Centre Culturel Tjibaou, Noumea: Jean Pipite
Emilio Ambasz & Associates, New York: Brad Whitermore
Architecture Foundation Australia, Brooklyn, Australia: Lindsay Johnston
Atelier Hollein, Vienna: Elisabeth Rahbari
Atelier Kempe Thill Architects, Rotterdam: Oliver Thill
Ateliers Jean Nouvel, Paris: Charlotte Huisman
Atkins, Manama: Helen Dixon
Australian Institute of Architects, Barton: Laura Di Pauli
Shigeru Ban Architects, Tokyo: Mayu Inoue
Baumschlager & Eberle, Lochau: Bettina Tipotsch
Behnisch Architekten, Stuttgart: Renate Blauth and Ingrid Weger
Centro Studi e Ricerca iGuzzini, Recanati: Cristiana Matassini
Mario Cucinella Architects, Bologna: Alessandro Bini
Bill Dunster Architects - ZEDfactory Ltd, Wallington, Surrey: John Shakespeare
Eisenman Architects, New York: Cynthia Davidson
ELEMENTAL - Alejandro Aravena, Santiago: Alejandro Aravena, Victor Oddó and Cristóbal Palma
Feilden Clegg Bradley Studios, Bath: Fliss Childs, Stephanie Laslett and Alex May
Carlos Ferrater Partnership (OAB), Barcelona: Birgit Eschenlor
Foster + Partners, London: Kathryn Tollervey
Sean Godsell Architects, Melbourne: Hayley Franklin
Golden Horizon Real Estate S.P.C., Manama: Bashar Rashdan
Grimshaw Architects, London: Sophie Baettig and Carly Vandenberg

TR Hamzah & Yeang Sdn Bhd, Ampang: Ken Yeang and Anderson Lee
Herzog & de Meuron, Basel: Susanna Rusterholz and Simon Kneubühl
Herzog + Partner, München: Sybille Fries and Annette Hecht
Hill & Knowlton, Manama: Mark Lawlor
Steven Holl Architects, New York: Julia van den Hout
Toyo Ito & Associates, Architects, Tokyo: Eriko Kinoshita
Lucien Kroll, Bruxelles
Kengo Kuma and Associates, Tokyo: Balazs Bognar and Mariko Inaba
Nicholas Lacey & Partners, London
Teresa Lundquist, London
Mangado & Associates, Pamplona: Olaia Caicoya
Glenn Murcutt, Mosman
National Geographic, London and Washington: Dan Pierce, Michael Garrity, Jesse Gordon, French Horwitz, Paul Johnson, Mara Mellin, Melissa Molyneux, Catherine Yelloz and Amel Ziad
Renzo Piano Building Workshop, Genoa: Stefania Canta and Chiara Casazza
Antoine Predock Architect PC, Albuquerque and Los Angeles: Rebecca Davila and Mira Woodson
Rogers Stirk Harbour + Partners, London: Aba Amihyia and Jenny Stephens
Sauerbruch Hutton, Berlin: Karine Stigt
SITE, New York: James Wines and Sara Stracey
Soleri Archives, Arcosanti: Hanne Sue Anaya
SOM (Skidmore, Owings & Merrill LLP), New York: Lauren Bebry and Elizabeth Kubany
Studio Noris Morano, Milano: Noris Morano and Stefania Dessolis
Tovatt Architects & Planners, Drottningholm: Geoff Denton
UNStudio, Amsterdam: Karen Murphy and Sandra Duijser
Simón Vélez-DeBoer Architects, Alameda, CA: Simón Vélez, Darrel DeBoer and Sara Franco
Vulcania, Saint Ours Les Roches: Françoise Perret

WHITE STAR PUBLISHERS

WS White Star Publishers® is a registered trademark property of Edizioni White Star s.r.l.

© 2009 Edizioni White Star s.r.l.
Via Candido Sassone, 24
13100 Vercelli, Italy
www.whitestar.it

Translation: Richard Pierce (text)
Donna St. John (captions)
Editing: Jane Pamenter

ISBN 978-88-544-0497-7
1 2 3 4 5 6   13 12 11 10 09

Printed in Italy

304 The sketches are of the Elephant & Castle
Eco Tower complex, the project for the urban
improvement of an area in South Central London
fine-tuned by studio TR Hamzah & Yeang Sdn Bhd.

← – – – TO THE WEST SIDE (MIRROR IMAGE)

ELEVATORS

15 UNITS × 8 FL. = 120 = ~ 150 BEDS